Working Hard for the American Dream

The American History Series

Abbott, Carl *Urban America in the Modern Age: 1920 to the Present*, 2d ed.

Aldridge, Daniel W. *Becoming American: The African American Quest for Civil Rights, 1861–1976*

Barkan, Elliott Robert *And Still They Come: Immigrants and American Society, 1920 to the 1990s*

Bartlett, Irving H. *The American Mind in the Mid-Nineteenth Century*, 2d ed.

Beisner, Robert L. *From the Old Diplomacy to the New, 1865–1900*, 2d ed.

Blaszczyk, Regina Lee *American Consumer Society, 1865–2005: From Hearth to HDTV*

Borden, Morton *Parties and Politics in the Early Republic, 1789–1815*

Carter, Paul A. *The Twenties in America*, 2d ed.

Cherny, Robert W. *American Politics in the Gilded Age, 1868–1900*

Conkin, Paul K. *The New Deal*, 3d ed.

Doenecke, Justus D., and John E. Wilz *From Isolation to War, 1931–1941*, 3d ed.

Dubofsky, Melvyn *Industrialism and the American Worker, 1865–1920*, 3d ed.

Ferling, John *Struggle for a Continent: The Wars of Early America*

Ginzberg, Lori D. *Women in Antebellum Reform*

Griffin, C. S. *The Ferment of Reform, 1830–1860*

Hess, Gary R. *The United States at War, 1941–1945*, 3d ed.

Iverson, Peter *"We Are Still Here": American Indians in the Twentieth Century*

James, D. Clayton, and Anne Sharp Wells *America and the Great War, 1914–1920*

Kraut, Alan M. *The Huddled Masses: The Immigrant in American Society, 1880–1921*, 2d ed.

Levering, Ralph B. *The Cold War: A Post–Cold War History*, 2d ed.

Link, Arthur S., and Richard L. McCormick *Progressivism*

Martin, James Kirby, and Mark Edward Lender *A Respectable Army: The Military Origins of the Republic, 1763–1789*, 2d ed.

McCraw, Thomas K. *American Business Since 1920: How It Worked*, 2d ed.

Neu, Charles E. *America's Lost War: Vietnam, 1945–1975*

Newmyer, R. Kent *The Supreme Court under Marshall and Taney*, 2d ed.

Niven, John *The Coming of the Civil War, 1837–1861*

O'Neill, William L. *The New Left: A History*

Perman, Michael *Emancipation and Reconstruction*, 2d ed.

Porter, Glenn *The Rise of Big Business, 1860–1920*, 3d ed.

Rabinowitz, Howard N. *The First New South, 1865–1920*

Reichard, Gary W. *Politics as Usual: The Age of Truman and Eisenhower*, 2d ed.

Remini, Robert V. *The Jacksonian Era*, 2d ed.

Riess, Steven A. *Sport in Industrial America, 1850–1920*, 2d ed.

Schaller, Michael, and George Rising *The Republican Ascendancy: American Politics, 1968–2001*

Simpson, Brooks D. *America's Civil War*

Southern, David W. *The Progressive Era and Race: Reaction and Reform, 1900–1917*

Storch, Randi *Working Hard for the American Dream: Workers and Their Unions, World War I to the Present*

Turner, Elizabeth Hayes *Women and Gender in the New South, 1865–1945*

Ubbelohde, Carl *The American Colonies and the British Empire, 1607–1763*, 2d ed.

Weeks, Philip *Farewell My Nation: The American Indian and the United States in the Nineteenth Century*, 2d ed.

Wellock, Thomas R. *Preserving the Nation: The Conservation and Environmental Movements, 1870–2000*

Winkler, Allan M. *Home Front U.S.A.: America during World War II*, 3d ed.

Wright, Donald R. *African Americans in the Colonial Era: From African Origins through the American Revolution*, 3d ed.

Wright, Donald R. *African Americans in the Early Republic, 1789–1831*

Working Hard for the American Dream

Workers and Their Unions, World War I to the Present

Randi Storch

WILEY-BLACKWELL

A John Wiley & Sons, Ltd., Publication

This edition first published 2013
© John Wiley & Sons, Ltd.

Harlan Davidson, Inc. was acquired by John Wiley & Sons in May 2012.

Registered Office
John Wiley & Sons Ltd, The Atrium, Southern Gate, Chichester, West Sussex, PO19 8SQ, UK

Editorial Offices
350 Main Street, Malden, MA 02148-5020, USA
9600 Garsington Road, Oxford, OX4 2DQ, UK
The Atrium, Southern Gate, Chichester, West Sussex, PO19 8SQ, UK

For details of our global editorial offices, for customer services, and for information about how to apply for permission to reuse the copyright material in this book please see our website at www.wiley.com/wiley-blackwell.

Library of Congress Cataloging-in-Publication Data
Storch, Randi, 1970–
 Working hard for the American dream : workers and their unions, World War I to the present / Randi Storch.
    pages cm
  Includes bibliographical references and index.
  ISBN 978-1-118-54140-1 (cloth : alk. paper) – ISBN 978-1-118-54149-4 (pbk. : alk. paper) – ISBN 978-1-118-54147-0 (cs) – ISBN 978-1-118-54141-8 (epdf) – ISBN 978-1-118-54157-9 (epub) – ISBN 978-1-118-54163-0 (mb) – ISBN 978-1-118-54148-7 (vb) 1. Labor unions–United States–History.
2. Working class–United States–History. 3. Labor movement–United States–History. 4. Labor–United States–History. I. Title.
  HD6508.S697 2013
  331.880973–dc23
                                      2012050381

A catalogue record for this book is available from the British Library.

Cover image: More than 10,000 people from across Wisconsin marched on the state capitol to protest Governor Walker's proposed budget repair bill that would eliminate collective bargaining rights for public employees, among other things. Courtesy, Emily Mills.
Cover design by Simon Levy

Set in Meridian 10/13 pt by Toppan Best-set Premedia Limited
Printed in Malaysia by Ho Printing (M) Sdn Bhd

1 2013

Contents

Contents

List of Illustrations

List of Illustrations

Acknowledgments

I first came across Harlan Davidson's American History series as a student, browsing library shelves and eager to immerse myself into the field of US history. Each book in the series gave me exactly what I needed, an accessible introduction to the topic's central questions, sources, and scholars. When my colleague Don Wright suggested I contact Andrew Davidson to propose this volume, I embraced the endeavor as a chance to give back to future students. I owe a great debt to Don and Andrew for supporting this project, helping to make the move to Wiley seamless, and their wit and vision. This book is better because they are brilliant editors. Jim Barrett, Steve Rosswurm, Brett Troyan, Sandy Gutman, Kathy Mapes, and Dan Katz provided invaluable encouragement at its earliest stages, and both Kathy and Dan, along with Karen Pastorello and Judith VanBuskirk, combed the chapters and offered helpful revisions. Howard Botwinick suggested excellent readings. I also benefited from the generous and talented research assistance of Ashley Bertrand while she completed her graduate studies. Linda Gaio worked magic gaining permissions and helping to find photos. Thanks are also due to SUNY Cortland's Office of Sponsored programs, which provided summer research support to help kick-start this project.

Of course, none of this would have been possible without the support of my family. My parents, Hyman and Adrienne, and my sister, Jenelle, have encouraged me at every turn and helped give their insight into the later part of this book. My in-laws, Merrill and Irene, shuttled me to and from San Diego State so that I could make progress on the book. My husband, Merrill, is the backbone of our family unit, and I am eternally grateful for his unyielding support. My kids, Merrill Anne and Henry, inspire me every day to do my part to make the world they will inherit a better place. This book is dedicated to them.

Introduction
Back to the Future

When I think back on my undergraduate courses, I cannot recall one instance when a professor uttered the words "class conflict," "labor movement," or "union struggle." Growing up in a working-class neighborhood as a daughter of a union electrician and housewife, I took it for granted that history in general and US history in particular were not about me, my family, or my neighbors, but instead, about people with power who somehow controlled national events.

What a surprise, upon entering graduate school, to find that United States Labor and Working-Class History was an actual course being offered. It seemed as though I had entered some parallel universe where one's reality is turned upside down. In this case, working-class people, replete with their own ideology, politics, and movements, determined the historical narrative. Students discussed how different American history looked when examined from the perspective of people who lacked family wealth or access to higher education and instead had to rely on their own hands and labor to put food on the table and pay the bills. From the first day of class, I was hooked.

Working Hard for the American Dream: Workers and Their Unions, World War I to the Present, First Edition. Randi Storch.
© 2013 John Wiley & Sons, Ltd. Published 2013 by John Wiley & Sons, Ltd.

1

Over the course of my graduate training I learned about new subdisciplines, including social history and the new political history. They showed that labor historians were not alone but part of a generation of historians trained in the 1960s and 1970s who conceptualized an entirely different way of doing history. Labor history pioneers of the 1920s penned an institutionally driven picture of the past with a heavy emphasis on major labor unions and leaders: this new generation struggled to understand how ordinary people experienced work and how class shaped their lives, their interactions with others, and their relationship to the state. Yet despite all the time passed, books written, songs sung, websites created, and films produced, the predominantly working-class students who enter my classes still do not have an inkling that labor and working-class history is a dynamic field of interest and, study, and, even more sadly, these students lack an understanding of the role that working-class people play in American history.

Perhaps these observations are not surprising. Most young people in college today do not identify with the working class or as working class. My students even feel uncomfortable with the term "working class" and reveal their biases when they choose to write and speak the term "low class" instead. It is not that they cannot connect to the history of the working class, but they would rather see themselves as upwardly mobile members of an amorphous, but all-American, middle class. At first glance, they cannot see how steel workers' struggles back in the 1930s have anything to do with their twenty-first century lives. In addition, there are not many working-class groups, such as unions, clubs, musical groups, political parties, or mutual aid societies, clamoring for their attention. Shopping at Wal-Mart, for example, is much closer to their experience than picketing at one. And classes in high school and college, for the most part, do not bother to connect workers' struggles of the past for dignity and power with students' concerns of today.

Because of this situation, this book, and the themes of labor and working-class history upon which it is based, are critical to share with today's student. These themes directly shaped the life of working Americans at the onset of the Great Depression just as they do today. This book will ask the following: How did working people experience the US economy's changing nature? What was the relationship of the state to working people? How did global economic and political forces affect working Americans, and how did they shape these same forces? How has the changing composition of the US working class affected working-class agency and protest, ideologies, and organization? Understanding how these issues developed in the twentieth century encourages us to rethink America's past from a different vantage point. Seeing US history through the lens of class promotes critical thinking and awareness of alternative voices in our history, including those of different races, ethnicities, and sexes. Sharing this perspective creates an opportunity to connect the conflicts and drama of the past with contemporary issues.

The period from 1920 to 2011 is a little longer than the average American lifespan, and yet the average working person of 1920 would find little in their everyday living comparable to their 2011 counterpart. In 1920 the census indicated for the first time that most Americans lived in places defined as "urban," but that still meant that approximately half of them resided on farms or in towns populated with less than 2,500 people-and many did so without access to cars, highways or passenger trains. No one surfed the Internet, ate fast food, hung out at the mall, or owned a credit card.

"Work" took place both inside and outside the home. In 1920 only one third of the homes in the country had electricity. Basic tasks such as cooking, cleaning, and other housework consumed between sixty and seventy hours a week. With few options available to pay the bills, many women earned wages in their homes by doing such "homework," or "piecework," as finishing garments, for which they were paid for each piece completed. Some took boarders, cooked, laundered, and offered lodging for single men or provided domestic service for others. One quarter of women worked in low-paid clerical, service, and sales jobs. Meanwhile, almost half of the male population (45 percent) labored in mines, construction, transportation, or manufacturing industries. Skilled male workers clocked an average of 50.4 hours a week and the unskilled put in 53.7 hours a week. Steelworkers worked on average 63.1 hours per week. Some jobs in the steel mills, however, required workers to work 12 hours a day, seven days a week, including one 24-hour continuous shift. These workers had only one day off every two weeks and had yet to earn an overtime rate.

In 1914 the United States Commission on Immigration conducted a survey of wage earners. In that year, the average annual earning in the country totaled between $550 and $600, but among 10,000 wage-earning men an average annual earning of $413. Half of the men surveyed earned less than $400, and women fared worse. Two thirds of the women made less than $300 a year, most earned half as much as men.

Low wages were exacerbated by dangerous working conditions and job insecurity. Between 1880 and 1900, working people experienced 25,000 workplace deaths per year. They also faced recessions, depressions, and seasonal factory shut downs. Huge waves of immigration from Europe and migration from rural regions meant there was always a fresh supply of people who employers could cajole to work more for less. Workers today face hazardous conditions and insecurity, but before the 1930s job insecurity was a particularly onerous stressor given that the federal government offered no public relief and private charity was provided under demeaning circumstances.

While many of the particulars of making a living in the 1920s may seem different to most working people today, trends in today's economy, politics, and society should sensitize us all to the changes a person living in the early twentieth century faced.

Like the people in this narrative who lived through World War I, World War II, an international economic depression, and the Cold War, today's working people face global challenges. Global forces have shaped the experience of working people throughout the twentieth century, but not always in consistent ways. Global forces have promoted more diverse workplaces and working-class ideologies, increased workers' power at particular moments, and fostered a close identification of working peoples' efforts with America's national cause. They have also increased government repression and undermined working people's civil liberties, increased citizens' fear of foreigners and politics labeled as un-American, and encouraged government and employers to use race and ethnicity as a wedge to divide working people against one another. Toward the end of the twentieth century and into the twenty-first, global economic forces are taking an enormous toll on working people's job prospects, work culture, union activity, and overall sense of security.

Technological change and reorganization transformed the workplace in the 1920s, as it continues to do today. Back then workers watched as managers applied science and technology and asserted their personal control to reshape the work experience. Workers saw older sectors of the economy struggle even as new technology-based ones surged onto the scene. They also witnessed an intense merger movement and the development and use of new technologies that made certain jobs (and the people who did the work) obsolete. Today workers face similar challenges in new ways. Computer technology has changed the nature of how work is done and sometimes where it is done. Rather than contribute to a growing, developing industrial economy, working people today struggle to pay their bills in a de-industrializing one. Retail and service jobs are easier to come by than industrial or extractive ones; and science, technology, and management's strong hand often make for mind-numbing work. Attacks by employers and the state on unions coupled with global competition make these sub-par jobs less than secure.

Throughout the twentieth century, working people have seen the role of the state in their affairs increase, for good and ill. In the 1920s, through its laws and politics, the state worked closely with corporate America. Business leaders reached new levels of national and international power and used it, in part, to turn every American's primary identity into that of a consumer. The state also worked in tandem with corporate America to undermine and silence pockets of dissenters who publicly questioned the morality of capitalism and its government. These radicals-always smaller in numbers than in their impact and "radical" mostly in the sense that they wanted a new economic system rather than superficial fixes-articulated a class politics that valued those who worked with their hands and their central role in the economy and society.

The Great Depression provided the context for a major reshuffling of political partners. In the face of a national discourse about capitalism's shortcomings and the need for a more robust state role, the government moved away from its unilateral, pro-business approach to the economy. Instead it began to create structures to help working people achieve more voice at work and to assist those who fell through capitalism's cracks. Its results were mixed, but even what was considered at one time as successful is today viewed much more critically. In the 1930s and 1940s, the federal government began protecting some workers' civil rights and liberties at work and their general welfare and security in society through the creation of legislation, federal boards, and agencies. Almost as soon as these changes were enacted, however, political forces bent on undermining workers' power, and silencing the working-class dimension of society's issues, usurped them. Today, when real socialist movements are few and powerless, any attempt of the state to pass legislation with such class dimensions as healthcare, is publicly (and incorrectly) attacked as socialist.

Like today, few workers in the 1920s had union representation. In fact, union density is similar today to that at the end of World War I. The difference, however, is that in the 1920s working people were on the verge of growing a major union movement that offered them protection, power, and relevance. Today, unions are on the decline. They and the people they represent are on the defensive and under siege. Big business and capitalist values are in such vogue that in many quarters the word "union" has once again assumed an unfavorable stigma. The pressure for working people to identify primarily as consumers is still strong, but increasingly difficult to realize without lots of credit cards and deep, deep debt.

Given that unions are the only vehicle with the potential to inject democratic principles into our working life and give working people a chance at real staying power and voice while making a living, the low density of unionized workers then and now is troubling. This is not to say that all unions (then and now) are committed to democratic principles, protecting the weak, and working to improve the lives of the most vulnerable, even when those individuals and groups are not in one's bargaining unit. Still, the goal of fighting for the ideal is just as important then as it is now. In the 1920s the main labor organization, the American Federation of Labor (AFL), primarily concerned itself with skilled, craftsmen. This meant that the majority of people who worked for wages (women, minorities, and immigrants) faced their employers as powerless individuals. Labor radicals (working people who questioned capitalism) challenged the AFL to do better and organize more widely, to no avail. Internal attacks of one group against the other plagued the labor movement of the 1920s and leaders of established craft unions were often uninterested in those they did not represent. It was not until the 1930s and World War II when the state created new laws and structures that the union movement expanded into new communities of working people and opened itself to new voices, a broader vision, and a staying, national role for unions and their leaders. For a time, working people got their news from labor sources, attended union social events, and listened to their union leaders before casting their electoral votes. Union jobs were coveted because they were secure and well compensated. Being in the union meant that working people did not have to face the boss, the government, or the economy alone. Today we live at a time when most working Americans cannot name the president of the American Federation of Labor – Congress of Industrial Organizations (AFL-CIO), get their news from sources owned and influenced by corporate America, and identify more with the values of consumption than with class. Many will ask: Unions may have made sense for some bygone era of factory worker, but haven't all those issues been worked out and no longer apply to me? Don't unions mean conflict, and do we need to be so confrontational? And why do we need unions when they cannot guarantee security of any kind?

This book is intended to explain how workers and the labor movement got from there to here, and why this story is so important today. It is an attempt to explain what those in the field of labor and working-class history have uncovered in their scholarship and where points of disagreement still exist. I have organized it chronologically, but within each chapter I emphasize the themes discussed above. Chapter 1 shows how World War I – era hopes that democracy would be realized at home, at work, and in the world failed to materialize and instead inspired working-class movements that would ultimately result in the New Deal and the movement for industrial unionism. Chapter 2 traces ways in which World War II and the Cold War reinforced the role of the state in workers' lives, giving the union movement new life, and new problems. Chapter 3 outlines the tensions and promises that the 1960s and 1970s movements for civil rights, broadly defined, brought to the union movement, and discusses the rise of public sector unionism. Chapter 4 focuses on the decline of the industrial sector and its impact on the labor movement from the 1970s to the turn of the twenty-first century, and the Epilogue follows the story through to Barack Obama's presidency.

The narrative is based on the newest scholarship to emerge in the field, which presents its own challenges for today's student. Today labor and working-class history is still interested in the traditional story of the labor union, but the field has expanded in innovative ways to include much more. In fact, many of the assumptions of an earlier generation of scholars (the most important "workers" were male, factory workers; the industrial workplace was the most important area of their activity; and unions were the most representative voice of working people) have fallen out of favor. They have been replaced by a more robust attempt to understand the lived, dynamic experience of working-class people in all their racial, ethnic, and gender diversity. But the problem that still exists in telling this story is that much of what shapes working Americans' lived experience is a plethora of laws and institutions, unions and corporations, and long lists of acronyms and work-related lingo. It is difficult for the uninitiated to keep all the names of laws, institutions, and economic terms straight. I have done what I can to make these things understandable in an attempt to acquaint the reader with what sometimes feels like a foreign world. In general, when I use the term "labor" as a noun throughout the book, I am referring to the formal union movement (federations, labor leaders, internationals, and locals). I have also tried to be clear about what kind of working person I am discussing when using the term "worker," rather than assume the white, male, factory kind.

This story begins with World War I and its aftermath because this pivotal period launched changes in the US economy, state, and work force that would influence the modern era. Even though the United States was involved in the fighting for less than two years, wartime mobilization exaggerated and compressed economic, political, and social developments that had led up to the period and would have a profound effect on working people. Progressive reformers divided over the question of joining the war effort. Those, including President Woodrow Wilson, who ultimately backed US participation in the conflict, did so at least in part hoping that wartime initiatives would reflect a spirit of reform and democratic principles. In these ways, despite the fact that the United States emerged as the leading world power, US participation in the war was a complete failure. Previously weakened labor groups did receive national attention and short-term power, but Wilson and wartime federal agencies also unleashed nationalist propaganda that equated economic and political dissent with potential criminal activity, actions which reverberate loudly in our current wars against terror at home and abroad.

1

"Everyone Was Ready For Unionism"
The Precursors, Promises, and Pitfalls of Industrial Unions in the 1930s

In the middle of the Great Depression, industrial workers across the United States demanded the right to join a labor union. In teaching Americans what this meant, the press focused on such influential labor leaders as John L. Lewis, head of the United Mine Workers of America (UMWA) and leader of the Congress of Industrial Organizations (CIO). Cartoonists emphasized Lewis's full head of wavy hair, bushy eyebrows, and solid jaw; editorialists quipped about the dictatorial way he led the UMWA and the CIO. Lewis was indeed central to the 1930s labor movement: he bankrolled organizing drives and made unilateral decisions about which workers to assist. But there is a problem with relying on Lewis to tell the story of the rise of industrial unionism. Focusing on one or two such colorful characters distracts from the reasons why millions of Americans demanded union representation. Workers did not put their jobs and their families' livelihoods on the line because Lewis or any other leader told them to; they demanded union rights because their daily work lives were insufferable and they were newly empowered to do something about it.

Working Hard for the American Dream: Workers and Their Unions, World War I to the Present, First Edition. Randi Storch.
© 2013 John Wiley & Sons, Ltd. Published 2013 by John Wiley & Sons, Ltd.

Press reports also failed to convey the personal sacrifice and act of faith demonstrated every time a person went on strike for union recognition. Strikes in these years were high-stakes affairs. Employers were dead set against allowing unions into their workplaces. In a single year, 1937, in a single industry, steel, eighteen Americans died trying to bring unions to their factories. Workers carefully weighed the cost of losing their jobs, as the price for striking. Without unemployment insurance or union strike funds, workers questioned how they would buy groceries or pay rent. After all, was not any job – no matter how bad the conditions – better than standing on bread lines? They also had to wonder if they could trust workers in other departments and of other ethnic, racial, and gender groups to stick together. In a strike, might one group undermine another by returning to work prematurely? It is no wonder that, at times, the decision to join a union broke lifetime friendships and divided families. Labor educator Jack Metzgar, in *Striking Steel: Solidarity Remembered* (2000), presents these dilemmas and tells how his Aunt Ruth refused to speak to Jack's father for weeks after she learned Jack had signed her husband with the steelworkers' union. To Ruth and others, her husband's signature represented a betrayal of the family's security. Nonetheless, to minds of millions, the time for unions in the industrial workplace had come.

Many of those Americans who did not earn their keep by punching a timecard were perplexed. Why would working people demand union rights in the middle of the worst economic crisis of their lives? The answer is rooted in the hopes, betrayals, and battles that occurred during World War I and into the 1920s, experiences that prepared them for the 1930s drive to establish industrial unions. The fight for industrial unions did not come out of the blue. Changing political and economic conditions, new corporate policies, and creative forms of worker protest between 1914 and the early 1930s pushed government leaders and a generation of industrial workers to look to unions as a solution to their problems. The new unions they built stood on the foundation established during and after the Great War.

Political Prelude: Industrial Democracy Betrayed, from Wilson to Hoover

Woodrow Wilson came to the US presidency in 1912 from the New Jersey governor's office; before that he was president of Princeton University. Trained as a political scientist and historian, most comfortable behind a desk or a podium, Wilson was not to be confused with a labor hero. Still, his wartime policies would benefit those employed in war industries, inspire workers to demand workplace protections, and help grow trade union membership. He also supported some of the harshest policies against civil liberties and First Amendment rights in the twentieth century. The contradictory nature of Wilson's policies played out most dramatically in the world of wartime workers.

On April 2, 1917, Wilson delivered a war message to Congress, arguing that the United States needed to join the war that had been raging in Europe since 1914 "to make the world safe for democracy." In other words, Wilson claimed, US participation in the war was not about self-enrichment; it was driven by America's responsibility to uphold democratic principles worldwide. One arena where this goal was tested was in US industries where workers made or harvested war materials and government footed the bill. With its vast purchasing power and its commitment to fight a war, the federal government was in a strong position to demand that corporate America – at least those companies wanting lucrative government contracts – abide by new wartime federal policies that guaranteed industrial workers new protections.

Previously when workers struck, government generally acted to protect business's property through the use of court orders, mandating workers end their strike. Government officials also approved the use of state and federal force, sending in police or troops to "quell" strikes and get businesses back to business. Politicians agreed with industrialists that the legal and physical force used to end work stoppages was a small price to pay for companies being able to turn a profit. But in 1917, when one million workers in such war industries as copper, lumber, and meatpacking chose to withhold their labor in 4,500 strikes around the country, Wilson chose not to use the heavy hand of the state to crush them. Instead, he turned to his newly established Presidential Mediation Commission. The charge of the commission was to investigate labor conflicts in industries deemed vital to war production and recommend solutions. It was headed by Felix Frankfurter, a Jewish immigrant who grew up on the Lower East Side of Manhattan, taught law at Harvard University, and took an early interest in trade unionism, socialism, and communism. The commission, in its final report to the president on January 9, 1918, concluded that workers and management needed to develop a "collective relationship." According to Frankfurter, both "autocracy and anarchy" were basic evils. But the "central cause" of war industry conflict was due to unequal power in the workplace when it came to settling industrial conflict. Workers needed representation in the workplace. To that end, commission members also recommended that employers set up grievance procedures before problems led to strikes and that government establish a maximum eight-hour work day and more coherent wartime labor policies.

For the first seven months that the United States was at war, agencies making and recommending labor policy proliferated, and at times worked at cross-purposes with one another, with their congressional critics, and with court rulings. To put a stop to the confusion and conflict, in January 1918 President Wilson issued an executive order that created the War Labor Administration, headed by Department of Labor Secretary William Wilson, and charged it with reorganizing war labor agencies. The most important war labor agency to emerge, composed of an equal number of labor and business representatives, was the War Labor Conference Board (later renamed the National War Labor Board), which established wartime labor principles intended to guide peaceful and plentiful production in war industries and eventually, enforce them. Frank Walsh, a public school dropout who taught himself enough law to pass the bar and had a staunch reputation as a working-person's advocate, accepted appointment to the National War Labor Board (NWLB). He co-chaired with former President William Howard Taft, a man business leaders vainly pleaded with to defend their interests against labor's encroachment. Taft was inclined to help them out, but Walsh and the country's wartime productivity needs won out. A new relationship between labor and the state was in the cards.

Walsh and Taft oversaw an agency that miraculously turned the wish list of pro-labor reformers into government policy. The agency called for an eight-hour day, equal pay for women for equal work, the right to join a union, an end to employers' union-busting activity, and support of a living wage. The right to join a union was a prized victory for workers because it suggested that government believed in the legitimacy of collective bargaining and saw it as a fair exchange for workers' commitment to maintain high levels of war-related production. Collective bargaining rights allowed workers, under government protection, to advocate for better pay and treatment; and it forced employers to negotiate and then spell out their policies relating to pay, hours, and conditions of employment in a legally binding contract. If collective bargaining did not exist in a plant before the war, employers did not have to recognize unions during the war, but they did have to create shop committees of worker-elected representatives empowered to negotiate on all workers' behalf – a process that looked a lot like collective bargaining. The NWLB created such worker-elected shop committees in 125 war-industry factories.

The idea of "industrial democracy," which the NWLB made popular, carried with it the notion that war-production workers were patriots serving a vital national function and, as such, deserved fair treatment. (Not all war-industry workers benefited from "industrial democracy"; women who sewed for war industries from their homes were excluded from NWLB provisions, a hint of shortcomings in labor policies that used factory workers as their standard.) The new policies shifted power relations in war industries, supporting industrial war workers' challenge to what had been management's unilateral power. Under the protection of wartime agencies and supported by wartime propaganda, working people previously leery of identifying themselves as union members grew comfortable speaking as patriots in need of democracy.

The results were dramatic. During the war, one million new workers joined unions, and by 1920, five million workers belonged, more than double the prewar number. Union protection and government support resulted also in improved work conditions: by 1919 almost half of the nation's workers enjoyed a 48-hour week and only one in four worked over 54 hours.

Ironically, at the same time Wilson was giving speeches and making government appointments that tied democratic rights to war work, he also supported policies that suppressed free speech, targeting those critical of capitalist business practices and US participation in the war. The federal Committee on Public Information (CPI), led by journalist, hyper-patriot, and war enthusiast George Creel, worked feverishly to unite a divided country behind an unpopular war. Press releases, posters, movies, advertisements, and over 70,000 public speakers manipulated Americans' emotions and implored them to buy war bonds, conserve resources, enlist in the military, and report their antiwar neighbors to the Department of Justice. Creel used hyperbole and fear to build a more pro-war, anti-German society; rumors trumped facts in his war for Americans' hearts.

The problem – for both Creel and Wilson – was that the public was divided over whether to participate in combat overseas. Wilson had won reelection in 1916 as "the man who kept us out of war," but with government forces committed to bringing democracy to the world, Wilson needed unity of support at home. At first he hoped his government could wrestle critics' support through the CPI's propaganda, but quickly he fortified the CPI's messages with federal legislation. CPI propaganda was emotionally manipulative, jingoistic, and urgent, but ultimately only suggestive; federal legislation, however, restricted civil liberties under the threat of the law. The Espionage Act of June 1917 and the Sedition Act of May 1918 banned antiwar mailings and authorized imprisoning those who spoke against the war. Under these laws, 900 people went to prison and the government deported hundreds more.

15

Government curtailment of civil liberties also negatively affected those who advocated for workers' rights, especially those who connected workers' problems and unnecessary wars to the same source, the profit-driven capitalist system. To these radicals, capitalism ravaged workers, whether in work or at war. Many with these beliefs joined the American Socialist Party, formed in 1901, since it was the only political party opposed to US participation in the war. Between 1901 and 1917, American Socialist Party members recruited members and successfully elected candidates to city, state, and national office. In the context of war, however, Wilson's war goals chafed against socialists' antiwar beliefs, so few were surprised when socialist leaders became federal targets.

Victor Berger of Wisconsin is a case in point. Before winning a seat in Congress, Berger was a socialist leader of the Milwaukee local of the International Typographical Union and editor of the city's Federated Trades Council's newspaper. Through his union activity and editorial capacity he appealed to those who joined craft unions affiliated with the American Federation of Labor (AFL), offering information on socialist principles. In 1918, with the country at war, Berger won reelection as a representative of his congressional district, but the federal government indicted him under the Espionage Act for his antiwar position. Regardless of the wishes of his constituents, the House refused to seat Berger in 1918 and again in 1920, when he re-won the seat. The Espionage Act also kept all major Socialist Party newspapers from circulating through the US Mail, preventing antiwar advocates from communicating and organizing; it also provided the basis for the Justice Department to indict 27 socialists.

No socialist of the day was better known or more admired than Eugene V. Debs, the American Railway Union leader who in 1894 emerged into the national spotlight at the head of a strike against railway-car maker George Pullman. Imprisoned for his role in the conflict, Debs spent much of his jail time reading socialist writings and wondering why a government that presumably stood for democracy consistently protected the rights of big business over those of workers. Debs became convinced while in jail that neither the Democratic nor Republican Party represented working people, so, once released, he joined the Socialist Party and four times ran on its ticket for President of the United States. After winning almost one million votes in 1912, Debs ran again in 1920 from his prison cell, having been sent there this time for making what the government considered an antiwar speech. Delivered in Canton, Ohio's Nimisila Park before a thousand supporters and a few federal agents, the speech was labeled in the Terre Haute *Plain Dealer* as "treasonably-inclined blatherskite." In fact, it was a call to broaden citizens' civic rights. Carefully choosing his words, since he was aware of the government's crackdown on free speech, Debs questioned the morality of waging war on the backs of America's workers, without their support:

> They have always taught you that it is your patriotic duty to go to war and to have yourselves slaughtered at command. But in all of the history of the world you, the people, never had a voice in declaring war...The working class who fight the battles, the working class who make the sacrifices, the working class who shed the blood, the working class who furnish the corpses, the working class have never yet had a voice in declaring war...If war is right, let it be declared by the people – you, who have your lives to lose; you certainly ought to declare war, if you consider war a necessity.

The Supreme Court ruled that Debs had gone too far. Satisfied with the court's ruling, Wilson told his cabinet, "Suppose every man in America had taken the same position Debs did. We would have lost the war and America would have been destroyed." The broad, vocal movement that formed in Debs's defense saw things differently. To them, American principles were already being destroyed by the government's protection of capitalism and its willingness to send working-class people to fight in a war waged for its leaders' profits. Government's willingness to defy the Constitution and curtail free speech spoke volumes to them. Debs became a working-class hero because, though he did not need to, he aligned his fate with that of the oppressed.

Figure 1.1 Eugene V. Debs speaking in Canton, Ohio. National Archives and Records Administration/Great Lakes Region, Chicago.

Even more than members of the Socialist Party, those belonging to the Industrial Workers of the World (IWW) faced repression, even though their leaders did not take a formal stand against the war. Formed in 1905, the IWW was an organization determined to organize all workers, regardless of skill, gender, or race, into "One Big Union." Their greatest successes came in the West among lumber workers, agricultural workers, miners, and seamen. During World War I, federal troops in Montana and Washington monitored railroads and utilities to prevent their destruction from German and other enemies. In 1917, troops expanded their patrols to places where IWW members were recruiting: copper mines, forests, and farms. In the West, often with the aid of local, self-styled patriots, federal troops used violence to break strikes, help strikebreakers cross picket lines, commit unlawful search and seizures, and detain vocal labor advocates. That summer, deputized vigilantes in Bisbee, Arizona, rounded up 1,200 striking copper miners and dropped them off in the middle of a New Mexico desert, and vigilantes in Butte, Montana, caught up with IWW member Frank Little and left him dangling by his neck from a railroad bridge.

Officials in Wilson's government lent support to these people who took the law into their own hands, believing that strikes and labor militancy were acts of subversion rather than reflections of workers' call for democratic rights. When Wilson tasked a federal judge with investigating the IWW in August 1917, the Justice Department leapt to the charge in its zeal to quiet labor unrest. On September 5, Justice agents raided every IWW headquarters in the nation and eventually convicted 184 members of espionage and sedition. A US attorney boasted that the government raids were intended to "put the IWW out of business," which they nearly accomplished.

While World War I raged in Europe, government forces encouraging democracy in the workplace existed in tension with those bent on violating basic civil rights. The problem facing war industry workers was that the balance of forces was about to tip against them since government protection of their workplace rights was a temporary, wartime-emergency measure meant to last only as long as the war. When the conflict ended on November 11, 1918, so did pro-union, labor agreements and the public's willingness to support them. Government repression continued, however. For example, through the fall and winter of 1919, in response to a coordinated bombing of US officials' homes and offices in eight cities across the country, the US government acted in an heavy-handed, overzealous manner. Without concern for specific evidence linking individuals to the bombings, United States Attorney General A. Mitchell Palmer sent federal agents to seventy cities across the country to detain and deport people identified as communists or aliens with radical ties. The government held 10,000 people for questioning and deported 500. These Palmer raids and deportations sparked a "red scare" throughout the states, causing state officials to draft their own criminal syndicalism laws and to seek out "subversives."

So, between 1919 and 1922, when prices soared and wages stagnated, it was without government protection and public support that workers fought to maintain their shop-floor power and protect themselves against inflation. Through those years, eight million workers tested the limits of industrial democracy by participating in 10,000 strikes. The most militant year was 1919, when four million people walked off the job. The effects were felt broadly: Seattle workers supported a general strike that crippled the city; Boston police vacated their posts; and 300,000 steelworkers took to the streets. In 1922, hundreds of thousands more textile workers, railroad workers, and coal miners went on strike, sometimes for a day or two, other times for months – or in the case of coal miners, for years.

Whereas Seattle's general strike went off peacefully, violent conflict characterized most of the others. Hints that the steel strike of September 1919 would turn bloody appeared before the strike began. The *New York World* reported:

> In the Pittsburgh district thousands of deputy sheriffs have been recruited at several of the largest plants. The Pennsylvania State Constabulary has been concentrated at the commanding points ... At McKeesport alone 3,000 citizens have been sworn in as special police deputies subject to instant call. It is as though the preparations were made for actual war.

By the end of the strike's first week, 365,000 men stayed away from work, effectively shutting down the iron and steel industry in seventy major centers. That is when politicians and employers unfurled their attack plan. Part of it involved the media, with accusations that "bolsheviks" were behind the strike. Newspapers pried apart strikers' solidarity. On September 27, Pittsburgh's *Chronicle-Telegraph* instructed, "The steel strike will fail. Be a 100 percent American. Stand by America...GO BACK TO WORK MONDAY." Employers joined propaganda with violence. One company manager admitted that his spies operated within the union leadership and used their posts to provoke riots. Union steelworkers added to the tussle by chasing off individuals who attempted to cross picket lines and take vacated jobs (unionists called these strikebreakers "scabs"). They were no match, however, for state troops, national guardsmen, the army, and deputized forces sent to send striking workers back to work. On January 8, 1920, in defeat and with two dozen of their fellow unionists dead, steelworkers returned to their jobs.

Coal companies' assault on striking miners was equally cruel. When mineworkers in Matewan, West Virginia, demanded union recognition, coal operators paid detectives to evict them and their families from their company-owned homes. In an armed battle, seven detectives and two miners were shot dead. The "Battle of Blair Mountain" followed a few counties distant, when the company reportedly hired private planes to drop homemade bombs and federal troops swarmed in to quell a group of miners marching to demand their right to form a union. By the time the melee ended, over 500 miners faced charges of insurrection and dozens more of those with murder and treason. They did not get their union.

Without government protections and public goodwill, postwar labor uprisings did not win favorable results for workers. Striking throughout the 1920s proved ineffective because of the way judges handed out legally enforceable orders from the court, known as court injunctions, to stop them. Illinois Federal District Court Judge James Wilkerson handed down the most limiting injunction against a 1922 railroad strike, declaring it illegal to strike against wage cuts. Some hope for labor emerged when Supreme Court Chief Justice Taft led a majority that interpreted the 1914 Clayton Act in a way that favored unions. The Act prohibited activity that threatened free-market competition. Even though the point of the law was to crack down on business practices that undermined competition, anti-unionists hoped to use the law against the right of unions to exist. Taft, along with a majority of the justices on his court, excluded unions from antitrust litigation and went a step further in declaring injunctions inappropriate in regard to legal unions and strikes. But by 1930 this small victory had proved to be a hollow shell. Taft's court limited picketing during strikes, declared pro-worker state labor laws unconstitutional, and forced trade unions to jeopardize their treasuries by holding them responsible for actions of individual members during authorized strikes.

Through the postwar decade, leading Republicans deepened labor's woes. In 1919 President Warren G. Harding called for a return to "normalcy." To that end, while speaking in Boston on May 14, 1920, he reminded Americans that "all human ills are not curable by legislation" and society's problems could not be "solved by a transfer of responsibility from citizenship to government." Any hopes of continuing Wilson's pro-worker policies were doomed. Harding's call for "not revolution, but restoration; not agitation, but adjustment" was an attack against the millions of industrial workers who went on strike in the postwar period.

Between 1925 and 1929, President Calvin Coolidge's labor policies were no different. As governor of Massachusetts in 1919, Coolidge had made a name for himself when he fired Boston's striking police force. As President, Coolidge appointed Herbert Hoover as Secretary of Commerce to work with John L. Lewis and the United Mine Workers to negotiate a contract with mine operators: the Jacksonville Agreement of 1924. The contract prevented a strike, but it did not preclude operators from shutting down. Then, when asked to step in and coax mine operators to uphold their end of the deal, Coolidge asserted that government had no power to enforce the agreement. He also warned Lewis that if the UMWA struck, it would be violating a contract and undermining collective bargaining. Meanwhile Hoover, aware of the anti-union nature of the courts, suggested that the union take its grievances to the judiciary.

Little changed when Hoover became President in 1929. As head of the Food Administration during World War I and as Secretary of Commerce under Harding and Coolidge, Hoover shared the former presidents' perspective on workers' rights: they did not need any. During World War I Hoover was impressed with the positive effect of charity and voluntary business cooperation in stabilizing communities and industry. So when the Great Depression hit after 1929, in the face of growing desperation, Hoover continued to promote private solutions to the nation's crisis. Rather than force governmental intervention in banking policy when the stock market crashed, Hoover pleaded with Americans not to remove their deposits. In the depths of the crisis, he said that hoboes were "better-fed" than ever and in a moment of delusion asserted to the press, "no one is actually starving."

In 1932 Hoover called in the military to clear the streets of Washington, DC of 20,000 jobless war veterans who marched on the capital. Many of them mobilized in DC in hopes of winning an early payment of a promised $50–$100 government "bonus" for their wartime service. Embarrassed by the veterans' protest, Hoover turned to the US Army to end the march with bayonets, tanks, teargas, and fire that burned to the ground the protestors' tent city. The images of soldiers on horseback chasing veterans down Pennsylvania Avenue and military personnel brandishing bayonets at the marchers symbolized how far removed the government had become from the suffering and struggle of ordinary people.

To be fair, Hoover and Congress took unprecedented steps to address human problems associated with the Great Depression. For one, they established the Reconstruction Finance Corporation, which offered loans to companies large enough to secure their collateral so that they could expand and hire more workers. They also provided money to local governments and supported a few federal construction projects. In 1932 Congress passed the Norris-LaGuardia Act that outlawed "yellow-dog" contracts that employers forced employees to sign, indicating that they were not in, and would not join, a union. It also barred injunctions against union pickets and strikers.

In the early Depression years, neither effort mattered much. Working people realized they had no real, federal protection should they refuse to sign a yellow-dog contract. It made more sense to have a job and sign the illegal contract than to cling to convictions and stand, unemployed, on a breadline. Through the end of Hoover's administration and some time afterward, the Depression worsened, unemployment rose, hunger spread, and employers succeeded in their attacks against organized labor.

Congress also undermined workers in this period by passing historic legislation that reshaped the meaning of citizenship. In the context of war, the agricultural lobby won the right to bring farmworkers to the United States from Mexico, Canada, Cape Verde, and the Bahamas. As long as agricultural workers signed contracts with clear dates of departure and as long as growers agreed to send their workers back home at the end of the contract or the war, the government agreed to ignore immigration restrictions already on the books (a head tax and a literacy test in the workers' own language). In the postwar period, however, partly as a result of the Palmer Raids and ensuing red scare, the United States restricted its immigration policies. The Johnson-Reed Immigration Act of 1924 established a quota system that drastically reduced the number of immigrants from southern and eastern Europe and slammed shut America's doors to Asia's immigrants. US diplomatic, trade, and agricultural interests succeeded in keeping Western Hemisphere nations out of the reaches of the new immigration law, but the law still established barriers to American citizenship. New surveillance mechanisms created a new category of person – the illegal alien. Entering the country without a newly required visa meant that many immigrants' first act in the United States was to commit a crime. Migration of wartime agricultural workers continued informally (and now illegally) after the war, and throngs of Mexicans fleeing the Mexican Revolution augmented their numbers. Over half of formal deportations in this period involved aliens without proper paperwork. Over time illegal immigration status would became equated with general criminal activity; in effect Mexicans in the United States would increasingly be identified as illegal and criminal.

By creating racial and ethnic hierarchies through legislation, the state reinforced one of the unsavory ways in which America's wartime propaganda manifested itself in the postwar period. Henry Ford's rants against Jewish bankers and steel magnates' attacks against Bolsheviks resonated among the ranks of white, native-born Americans, who feared foreign influence and looked at the increasing number of African-American migrants from the South with trepidation and horror. Those who believed that wealthy Americans were genetically predisposed to succeed subscribed to the ideas of Social Darwinists, who were certain of the inability of eastern Europeans, Mexicans, and Japanese immigrants to assimilate. Such vocal hyper-patriots as eugenicist Madison Grant and Theodore Roosevelt were afraid that high fertility rates of "inferior groups" and low fertility rates of native whites would lead to the end of the Anglo-Saxon race, or "race suicide."

Not surprisingly, with government leaders supporting these notions, the 1920s witnessed the proliferation of racism, manifested most clearly in the activities of the newly risen Ku Klux Klan (KKK). Shopkeeper associations boycotted foreign-born competitors, and white, working-class neighborhoods witnessed a rise in Klan membership. Its members feared economic concentrations of wealth, believing that monopolies had the power to upend republican values and individual liberties. They also had no regard for what one Klan leader described at "a great mass of incompetent, unprincipled and undemocratic voters from below," namely African Americans, Catholics, and the foreign. And this time around, the KKK spread its hate outside of the South. In 1924 Detroit housed 35,000 Klan members, Chicago 50,000. In August of that year, 50,000 Klansmen made their way to Washington, DC, for a march past the White House in full white gowns and pointed white hats. In the postwar period, this reborn Klan took the government's patriotic war campaign and its rhetorical excesses to their logical conclusion. Klan members, after all, claimed to be the purest patriots. The flip side of Wilson's war campaign blazoned with hatred.

Corporate Prelude: The Unintended Consequences of 1920s Corporate Policies

At the beginning of the 1920s, two hundred companies owned one-fifth of the nation's wealth and their leaders helped shape a pro-corporate American foreign policy. State Department loans encouraged American exports while federal troops defended US investments and interests in China, the Caribbean, and Central America. Rich and powerful American investment houses – J. P. Morgan, Goldman Sachs, and Lehman Brothers – funneled international wealth into stocks, generating cash windfalls to corporations whose leaders spawned a slew of corporate mergers, consolidating their assets and operations, and filling sprawling factories with new technologies and grand department stores with merchandise.

Corporate leaders used their new economic riches to win back the unilateral control over workplace decision-making that they had lost during the war. With easy access to capital, corporate leaders pushed industrial production into the "machine age," where they found technological innovation to be their friend. Put simply, machinery cost less than workers. A new era of sheet-steel and tinplate production emerged, for example, when each continuous, strip-sheet rolling mill had the capacity of forty to fifty hand mills. Cigar-rolling and glass-tubing machines appeared along with mechanical coal-loading devices, power shovels, pneumatic tools, switchboards, and teletype machines. Developments related to improved technology resulted in one million industrial workers losing their jobs.

New technology also led to debilitating injuries and death. In steel mills, men worked with massive pots of hot metal and fiery blast furnaces. Molten steel sometimes spilled over, and occasionally furnace dust kicked up and landed on workmen. In these cases, workers were literally cooked while the unlucky ones lived with excruciating burns. Overhead cranes provided another menace: one whack could mean permanent disability. In factories with heavy machinery, most accidents occurred on quick-moving belts that easily pulled out limbs. Jack Metzgar grew up listening to stories about his grandfather, a skilled turner at one of Bethlehem Steel's Johnson rolling mills, who lost both his arms in the mills in 1917. The man got good at picking up dimes with his mechanical arms, but could never scratch his own nose, let alone work in the plant, again. With no protective guards, sawmills cut men in two. Slippery knives in meatpacking plants meant missing fingers and acid often burned away the skin of those in the pickling departments.

To make matters worse, in corporate leaders' fury to increase production and profit, companies paid managers to stand over workers with stopwatches and bully them. Regularly speeding up the assembly line led to fatigue as well as bloody, disfiguring accidents. Safety gear and disability insurance would have improved workers' lives, but they were expensive, so they did not exist.

New technologies also gave managers new ways to undermine once-independent craftsmen by pitting them and their skill against

26

easily trainable, low-paid workers. With new and better machines in their reach, managers created jobs that required less training and more, low-paid and easily replaceable people. The new jobs created as a result often were relabeled "unskilled" or "semi-skilled," since they did not require as much training or decision-making.

In addition to dividing workers by skill, another way managers asserted their authority and kept workers from seeing that they shared similar grievances was the sexual and racial segregation of jobs. On sugar and pineapple plantations in Hawaii, growers turned to mainland whites to fill management and skilled jobs and to Chinese, Japanese, and Filipinos to provide the backbreaking labor. They used racial stereotypes to justify the ethnic division of workers. Because Chinese were believed to be reliable but less energetic, irrigation work suited them best; Japanese workers were considered to have more strength, so growers used them for loading. In another example, Chicago's meatpacking employers turned to Germans, Irishmen, native whites, and smaller numbers of Bohemians when they needed skilled butchers, whom they paid well and who worked regularly. At the other extreme stood common laborers hired from the masses of recently arrived, southern and eastern European immigrants, and Mexican migrants, often hired by the day or hour with no job security. Meatpackers hired few African Americans, but did employ them, according to Rick Halpern in *Down on the Killing Floor: Black and White Workers in Chicago's Packinghouses, 1904–54* (1997), as a "powerful element of fear and mistrust in a situation already tense with ethnic friction."

In the 1920s, regulated wartime shop committees lingered, giving workers a forum for their voices on the job. In the postwar period, however, industrial leaders used the shop committees as a tool to keep tabs on, and steer workers away from unions. Rather than crush labor with force, the biggest corporate leaders formed their own company unions in which representatives from each department met directly with management to resolve grievances. Employers who recognized company unions believed their efforts would make government reform and union representation bygone efforts. For his part, AFL president Samuel Gompers, a one-time socialist who rolled cigars from the young age of 12 and built the federation on the principle of skilled workers' self-organization, saw representation committees of company unions as a "pretense admirably calculated to deceive."

In company unions, management supervised elections, determined which workers could act as representatives, and dominated committees that made decisions on grievances. Frank Schlieman, a pro-union worker at Emmerson Electric in St. Louis, was not convinced his employer would make changes through their company union. He gave it a chance, however, after his foremen threatened "repression." Schlieman quickly learned its limits when management refused workers' requests for wage increases and ignored their complaints about speedups. Taking each grievance as an opportunity to instruct, management shrugged off requests for higher wages with discussions of what other companies paid. Schlieman eventually stopped taking the company union seriously because he "couldn't get far with it." Others who pushed against the company union simply got fired.

Despite their limitations, company unions did give workers opportunities for collective expression. Occasionally, department representatives were successful in forcing management to make concessions. And unlike AFL unions, whose membership discriminated against women and those who worked unskilled jobs (especially those of certain ethnic groups), company unions often included immigrant, African-American, and women representatives, offering training and experience to a new generation of leaders.

In addition, experience with company unions sometimes politicized workers and sparked their interest in more authentic representation. When employers refused grievances, they helped workers accept the union principle that employers did not share their priorities. Some of those who had faith in company unions but experienced their limits became the best organizers for real union drives. When outspoken Emmerson Electric unionist Frank Sulzer lost his job, his department refused to elect another representative to replace him, prompting his co-workers to turn in blank ballots. Such actions provided a means for workers to act on mutual complaints. Company unions thus slowed what might have been a surge of union growth in the 1920s, but they still gave workers a voice and a degree of experience with efforts to improve their work conditions.

Company unions often worked with a series of other programs, known collectively as welfare capitalism, to tame calls for the formation of real labor unions. Throughout the 1920s, management in large capital-intensive firms turned to industrial psychologists to develop procedures to turn potentially conflict-laden labor–management relations into cooperative efforts; their goals were to show employees that management cared and to convince them that the most important relationship at work was the one between them and their employer. Chicago's Hawthorne Works of Western Electric, in collaboration with Harvard Business School Professor Elton Mayo, attempted to accomplish these goals when they instituted an interview program and had private conversations with each of their 25,000 hourly employees. The hope was that these once-a-year chats would keep employee grievances low in number and help foster the sense among workers that management cared. Other large industrial companies varied the number and combination of their programs. At times welfare capitalists tried to win workers' loyalty away from their fellow workers by mixing racial and ethnic groups within departments and luring ethnic workers to company life and death insurance policies and away from those offered by their community associations. Others relied on stock ownership plans that allowed employees to invest directly in the company for which they worked, encouraging a capitalist identity and a sense of junior partnership. Other programs retrained foremen to supervise with a gentler touch, offered workers wage incentives for productivity increases, and revealed a new respect for workers' seniority. The most comprehensive welfare capitalism included health and safety programs; educational, recreational, and social activities; such financial benefits as pensions, shares of company stock, life and health insurance, and profit-sharing plans; and such shop-floor relationships as personnel departments, supervisor training, and company unions. Loss of any of these benefits came when workers engaged in strike activity, showed union interest, or faced regular business layoffs, which hit semi-skilled and unskilled workers (including women) disproportionately. Therefore, the threat of lost benefits always loomed large.

All plans reflected what historian Alice Kessler-Harris in *In Pursuit of Equity: Women, Men, and the Quest for Economic Citizenship in the Twentieth Century* (2003) calls employers' "gendered imagination": whereas employers built loyalty among men through sports clubs and mortgage loans, they reached women through sewing and cooking classes, dances, and summer camps. Reflecting mainstream notions of women primarily as family members and only occasional workers, these programs gave women "sociability rather than security."

The idea that welfare capitalism would blind employees to the need for unions was shortsighted. Actually, few laborers in the 1920s, perhaps one in five, worked for an employer that provided a comprehensive welfare plan. Instead, most who experienced piecemeal welfare capitalism saw its uneven underside because employers could not afford or did not buy into the pro-worker pieces of such plans. Employers in the auto, rubber, and steel industries used personnel departments rather than foremen's favorites when hiring employees on a seasonal basis, but rarely incorporated other programs. Meanwhile, the smallest firms, especially those in stagnating industries, generally lacked any of welfare capitalism's procedures and programs.

Even those companies committed to welfare capitalism could not consistently implement policy. Many corporate leaders planned to reform their managers' leadership style, but foremen notoriously maintained harsh practices. Foremen were not uniformly monsters, but as Metzgar writes, "they all had this power over your life and the life of your family, and most of them used it in both big and little ways, sometimes with a purpose, sometimes just out of meanness, but always with the same humiliating result." In the 1930s, when the Great Depression dried up employment, workers competed aggressively for a day's pay. The opportunity to grab a woman's backside or gifts of money, booze, and homemade treats were a few of the bribes foremen took to assure the donor a work assignment. Corruption oozed over into job assignments that segregated minorities into industry's least desirable jobs and women into its lowest-paying ones.

The result was pent-up frustration and bitterness that brought workers to unite against a common enemy. In department stores and meatpacking plants, workers undermined their foremen's productivity schemes by limiting their output (also known as stints). Monitoring stints kept workers in communication and skilled in expressing collective power. Welfare capitalism's programs meant to build workers' company loyalty sometimes worked to make them more loyal to one another. Sports programs, cafeterias, and recreational events, for example, allowed men and women to develop friendly relations across racial and ethnic divisions.

Corporate leaders hoped their welfare plans would keep workers faithful and real unions out, but they knew better than to rely on hope alone and made arrangements in case their plans failed. The flip side of welfare capitalism was coercion. Detective and security agents routed out union-friendly employees and built blacklists of persons deemed best not to hire. Pretending to be average working people, spies kept their ears open to identify workers sympathetic to union activity and gave regular reports on them to management. Meanwhile, security agencies stockpiled weapons to use against workers in the case of a strike. In 1936 a special Senate committee exposed corporate America's disregard for workers' rights. Between 1933 and 1936, 2,500 corporations spent $9.4 million to hire labor spies and pay for firearms. The leaders of corporate America might be speaking softly, but they carried a big stick to silence dissent and ensure that their employees tolerated dangerous and humiliating workplace conditions.

By the end of the 1920s, 1.25 million Americans worked for employers who required them to sign "yellow-dog contracts" and deprived them of basic constitutional rights. If welfare capitalism's programs held out the promise of worker representation and raised employees' expectations, their failed delivery opened workers' minds to the possibility of effective unions. Many times, management's ineptitude proved to be the union organizer's best weapon.

Working-Class Prelude: Activism

In 1924, after almost forty years with the energetic Gompers at its head, AFL leadership passed to a less dynamic personality, William Green, who would serve as president of the federation until his death in 1952. Whereas Gompers grew up with an appreciation for the teachings of socialists and the principle of class conflict, Green was reared with a commitment to organized religion and the belief that employers and workers could reach mutually beneficial agreements.

Organized as a national federation of trade unions with national federation leaders having little ability to influence the policies or actions of its member unions, the AFL, by tradition, was decentralized and Green, a man of tradition, kept this alive. In regions where a number of AFL locals functioned, each would send a representative to sit on their city federation. There they would meet with delegates from the city's other AFL unions. Members of city federations kept one another abreast of local political developments, and every once in a while they joined forces to push for the city's government to abide by one or another demand. Delegates from striking unions informed other AFL unionists of the location of pickets and asked the others to support their job actions, but they were not *required*, just because they were AFL affiliates, to do so. Structure facilitated communication, but in the end it was every union for itself.

A few AFL affiliates, the International Ladies' Garment Workers Union (ILGWU), for instance, were organized industrially, which meant that within a unionized garment factory the spectrum of workers in all job categories could be signed up as members. The union included unskilled and skilled workers, women and immigrants, as well as white men. Most AFL unions did not operate that way, however. The majority was built around a craft, its knowledge and traditions. AFL bakers, electricians, barbers, or boilermakers were proud breeds. They were also exclusive ones. For those on the inside, that is what made union membership such a privilege.

Few people not related to a union member were allowed formal training in the craft, so individual, local craft unions tended to be family affairs, dominated by one ethnic or religious group. Silvio Burgio, an Italian orphan from New Rochelle, New York, knew this well. The United Association of Plumbers and Steamfitters Local 86 began as a German affair but gradually shifted to a largely Irish one. During Burgio's tenure, a small Italian group was allowed to join. In Burgio's case, a plumber in the Bronx agreed to take him on as a helper. Once the young man completed his apprenticeship, he earned the title of mechanic and then his initiation into the union. By his early twenties, the lean and muscular Burgio had sharp mechanical skills and a determination to measure with exactitude. The knowledge he acquired through his apprenticeship gave him power on the job. Contractors needed men like him to get pipes laid right, and Burgio, and other skilled craftsmen in the trades, relished the respect that gave him. Burgio identified strongly as a union man, carried his card, attended weekly meetings, and credited the union with his ability to buy a radio and a used car. For Burgio, one of the union's biggest victories was protection: he never had to bribe a contractor for a job. The contractors with the best jobs went through the union to hire men like Burgio. Working along-side others who shared a similar heritage, he never questioned the system's logic. Why shouldn't a father help a son into a trade? Why wouldn't one member of the North Italy Society pass his skill on to another? People of color in Chicago complained about these discriminating policies to city federation leaders, but their complaints went unheeded.

When these AFL unionists worked in manufacturing plants, they refused to consider broadening their membership to unskilled workers whose jobs required no formal training and who could easily be replaced. So at least part of the reason a surge of industrial unionism never took place in the 1920s was because the main labor federation of the time was not interested; its member unions understood the political climate, benefited from the 1920s economy, and did not want to be associated with women, African Americans, or unskilled industrial workers. In non-industrial workplaces where the vast majority of women and minority workers labored – department stores, office buildings, farms, laundries, white and middle-class homes – AFL unions did not exist, and federation leaders were not about to attempt to create them in those places. Female clerical workers were among the largest-growing segment of the workforce as a result of increasing demand for bookkeepers, typists, stenographers, and receptionists in industry, but no AFL organizing drives worked to represent them either. In the factories of 1920s industrial America, unskilled and semi-skilled workers had almost no union representation. Where unions did exist, such as in the aforementioned ILGWU, men led and controlled them.

Fania Cohn, a young Belarus immigrant and member of the ILGWU, represented the kind of person who began to challenge traditional union culture. Within her union, she saw that women juggled workplace and family responsibilities and helped develop innovative strategies to cope with the complexities of working women's lives. ILGWU women activists such as Cohn also broadened their union work to include worker education programs, community organizing, and political lobbying. In 1920 Cohn made alliances with labor activists and educators outside the union and established the Workers' Education Bureau, a central office to support correspondence courses, traveling libraries, and conferences. In 1921 Cohn joined forces with Rev. A. J. Muste, Rose Schneiderman, and other working-class activists to form Brookwood Labor College in New York, the first residential school for union organizers offering one- and two-year programs for its adult students. Fifty union-activist students a year attended Brookwood from the Mine Workers, Machinists, and Ladies Garment Workers unions as well as some railroad brotherhoods. By the end of the decade hundreds of activists had left these schools and returned to their locals to build democratic unions and consider establishing broader networks within labor's community.

Like Cohn, Nels Kjar was bent on changing the character of his AFL local. But unlike Cohn, Kjar was a member of the Workers Party of America, which later changed its name to the Communist Party USA. He was also a skilled carpenter, held an

AFL membership card, and in the early 1920s had supported the Communist Party's trade union, the Trade Union Education League (TUEL). The purpose of the TUEL was to provide an outlet for AFL members to strategize and act upon tactics that would convince members of their AFL affiliates to abandon their craft loyalties, shift to broader industrial-based ones, and support a Labor Party. For those like Kjar, a TUEL membership was *not* to replace his AFL one; the TUEL strategy, called "boring from within," involved TUEL members using their AFL union membership to push fellow union members to adopt TUEL policies. Kjar's membership in an AFL carpenter's local and his ability to cajole, persuade, and ultimately convince his fellow AFL brothers to care about those who lacked union representation – the unorganized – made the TUEL particularly threatening to traditional AFL craft-union diehards.

By 1928 Kjar's union leaders were fed up with him. Apparently he went too far when encouraging his fellow union members to reduce the "fat salaries" of local union leaders. For this and similar activity he was expelled, as were hundreds of other communists like him, and TUEL was all but doomed. To such communists as Kjar, all workers deserved rights and dignity, but capitalism would not grant them. If communists could point out how the system corrupted people, they believed, they could win loyalty among workers and, once united, change the system.

Through their brazen and outspoken style, communist trade unionists alienated many, but their efforts were not completely in vain. Participants in TUEL had learned a great deal about how to motivate and organize working people. They also published an impressive radical labor magazine, *Labor Herald*, supported a labor party based on unions, led striking textile workers in Passaic, New Jersey, and developed a network of labor militants who encouraged organization of workers of all crafts in the same industry. This move of structurally uniting industrial crafts (what was known as amalgamation) would bring them closer to what would become industrial, CIO unions of the 1930s. According to James Barrett in *William Z. Foster and the Tragedy of American Radicalism* (1999), in 1922 and 1923 the TUEL succeeded in getting their amalgamation resolution adopted by "perhaps half of organized labor in the United States."

At decade's end the Communist Party scrapped the TUEL and started the Trade Union Unity League (TUUL). Part of the rationale for the new organization had to do with AFL unions' expulsion of TUEL members. Another was that communist leaders in the Soviet Union had called for communists worldwide to form a new federation of independent communist unions that would operate separately from their AFL competitors. This new communist-led federation provided a model and experiences that would fuel 1930s CIO organizing drives. Expelled from the AFL and its local affiliates, communists set out to win over unorganized, semi-skilled, and unskilled workers in factories and restaurants, on fields and building sites, and along the rails. To do so, communist labor organizers reached across gender and racial lines, built community support for workers, and trained a generation of labor militants. By 1930 the American Communist Party's membership remained small – about 7,500 – but was committed and increasingly effective at organizing.

TUUL activists channeled workers' grievances into action and, when possible, encouraged strikes. In 1933 in California, the Cannery and Agricultural Workers' Industrial Union led 24 walk-outs of over 37,000 field workers (cherry, tomato, and cotton pickers) over low wages and poor conditions. That same year, in textile towns of the southern Piedmont, workers protested speedups and wage cuts. Often, calls for improved conditions were met with violence at the hands of employers and even the state. The National Miners' Union, for example, led coal strikes in four states in 1930 and 1931, including one in an eastern Kentucky county where the intense and brutal violence of coal-mine managers, vigilantes, strikebreakers, and the National Guard against armed, striking miners resulted in the county being nicknamed, and long remembered, as "bloody Harlan County." In Tallapoosa county, Alabama, a communist-led sharecroppers' union attempted to win the right to plant gardens, improve local schools, have rest periods, and of their pay in cash, to name just a few of their demands; but the actions of the county sheriff and a posse of armed citizens he deputized, curtailed their plans. On July 15, 1931, the posse shot and killed one of the union's local leaders, Ralph Gray, burned his house to the ground, and displayed his corpse on the courthouse steps. Their numbers were small, but the willingness of TUUL unionists to take great risks to fight against the odds spoke to the desperation of the times.

Communists quickly found that the most responsive members of the working class were the unemployed; future union activists got some of their best organizing experience outside of factories. Communist-organized councils of the unemployed formed at the neighborhood level in major cities were connected by a national network. In 1930, the first full year of the Great Depression, one million working people joined in communist-led "hunger marches." These marches were characterized by thousands of unemployed people who marched to the offices of state officials, local relief agents, or corporate employers and presented demands for jobs, improved relief assistance, and better homeless-shelter conditions. While communist leaders organized national activity and guided the general contours of council activism, Unemployed Councils were mass organizations with local latitude. With banners in hand and choruses of chants, council members descended on neighborhoods where families were evicted, returning furniture to apartments, cutting through red tape at relief stations, and illegally turning on a neighbor's electricity. Sometimes, as in Detroit and Chicago, police gunned down council members in a rally or at an eviction protest. More often, police arrived with batons and whacked at protestors before arresting those in reach.

More than a few Communist Party council members would eventually build on their organizing skills in the labor movement: Chicago's council leader Joe Weber in steel; council leader and law school dropout Jack Spiegel in the boot and shoe union; and council members and African-American churchgoers James Samuel and Richard Tate in packinghouses. Chicago packinghouse union leader Herb March recalled borrowing tactics from unemployed organizers when he and others built the United Packing House Workers of America. One evening a week, employees forced their employer to deal with their grievances. "Beginning at 4 or 4:30 p.m., one by one a hundred or so aggrieved workers would take their turn confronting the plant bosses with their problems," March remembers. "Nobody's getting out until we settle all these cases. These guys have all been waiting here all this time and you can't treat us this way."

Unemployed councils were also places where communists made their biggest impression on African-American workers. Highly successful in black urban neighborhoods hit hard by unemployment, the councils gave black men and women a vehicle to stand up against racist landlords, employers, and government officials. Surprisingly to many, councils did this with a commitment to civil rights and interracial activity, which leaders would later carry into their union activity. Lowell Washington, an African-American member of the Unemployed Councils in the 1930s, remembered, "[I] never really even talked to a white man before, and I certainly hadn't said more than two words to a white lady, and here I was being treated with respect and speakin' my mind and not having to worry about saying something that might rile 'em up...Let me tell you it changed the way I thought about things."

Another important influence that shaped working-class activity in the 1920s and developed future labor activists was the black nationalist movement inspired by Marcus Garvey. A stout Jamaican whose fast-paced and moving speeches gave voice to the indignities of life in a racist society, Garvey counted half a million members in his Universal Negro Improvement Association by 1921. Garvey awakened African Americans to World War I's failed promise to spread democracy at home and abroad, the cost of the violent postwar race riots to black communities, the hope of African peoples elsewhere to thwart the rule of their white, colonial oppressors, and the promise of black nationhood bolstered by black capitalism and a strong black entrepreneurial class. Garvey was not a communist, nor was he a trade union militant, but like communists and trade union militants, Garvey drew on the symbolism of militaristic culture, emphasizing assertiveness and self-defense. Women participated in the movement and helped shape the meaning of black nationalism.

Garveyism challenged the racist view within US society that black women were immoral and sexually loose, idealizing black women and presenting them as beacons of morality who thrived in the traditional male-led family.

Even though Garvey's business plans did not call for it, his black nationalist ideals entered the workplace through race-based union activism. According to Beth Bates in *Pullman Porters and the Rise of Protest Politics in Black America, 1925–1945* (2001), "New Negroes," the growing group of militant African Americans frustrated by the empty wartime promises of democracy and the reality of postwar racial violence, included in their quest for full citizenship the demand for unions. When white unionists excluded them, as typically happened, blacks formed their own unions. Under the guidance of A. Philip Randolph, a gifted speaker, socialist and civil rights activist, the Brotherhood of Sleeping Car Porters (BSCP) pushed the New Negro Movement forward by tying the winning of union rights to African Americans' "unfinished task of emancipation."

In 1925 the drive to organize the porters spilled over into the community. In Chicago the Pullman Palace Car Company employed the largest number of porters and maids in the city (4,000 and 100, respectively). In response to Randolph's union, Pullman officials hired spies, fired union supporters, and rewarded *anti-union* black male leaders. To win the respect of Pullman's African-American workers, Chicago's union organizers turned to African-American clubwomen. By the end of the decade, led by journalist and anti-lynching crusader Ida B. Wells-Barnett as well as some union-friendly ministers, a movement developed among those who supported porters and maids in their union drive. Its leaders reached out to influential persons inside the offices of Chicago's African-American newspaper, *The Defender*; the National Federation of Colored Women's Clubs; the YWCA; and Chicago's National Association for the Advancement of Colored People (NAACP) and Urban League chapters to develop a powerful network of union supporters.

This "New Crowd" who came to support the BSCP in the second half of the 1920s, writes Bates, became leaders of a new generation of African Americans ready to "assert rights and make collective demands rather than appeal to white benefactors on an individual basis for relief for subordinate status." The new crowd called for "applying direct pressure using the power of mass collective action."

Like Cohn and her worker education programs, communists and their unemployed councils, and Garveyites and the New Negro movement, working-class activism that bridged the workplace and the community characterized consumer struggles in cities across the country. When A. Clement MacNeal of Chicago's NAACP helped direct a "Don't Buy Where You Can't Work Campaign," he did so in the face of his organization's refusal to support direct action. Targeting Woolworth's Five and Ten on Chicago's South Side, MacNeal joined a new generation of activists who mobilized a boycott, established pickets and propaganda, and held public meetings to change the corporate policies of a national chain that refused to hire black clerks, even in black neighborhoods. Similar activism emerged among African-American men and women in Cleveland with a Future Outlook League that withheld their dollars from places that did not hire them. Feeling unrepresented by predominantly white unions and the standard, middle-class NAACP and Urban League, Cleveland's black working-class activists organized boycotts and pickets of neighborhood stores, eventually succeeding in getting work for African Americans in local businesses.

By the time of the 1932 presidential election, many industrial workers must have felt as if they had been on a roller-coaster. In the fifteen-year period that preceded Franklin D. Roosevelt's election as president of the United States, industrial workers tasted government-enforced "industrial democracy," only to have it yanked away from them after the war. They watched as their employers installed welfare capitalism and quickly learned there was nothing democratic about it. Many lost their jobs; many others feared losing their jobs. A small fraction held a union card and an even smaller one had the foresight to imagine how these exclusionary and largely craft-based unions might become more inclusive, democratic, and powerful. Only a tiny number had the experience to make it happen. But through shared workplace grievances, new community organizations, and experimental unions, some were beginning to believe that joining in a union with other working people from different backgrounds and sexes was exactly what they needed to do if they wanted to have a meaningful voice on the job. From 1932 until the decade's end, for industrial workers, a perfect storm was brewing.

A New Deal for Workers: A Failed and Flawed Start

In the early 1930s General Motors workers were fed up with how the company was treating them. Gage Russell worked a line ten feet away from a water fountain, but foremen increased the pace of the belt he worked on to the point that even short water breaks were impossible. Every time GM worker Leo Connelly had to use the bathroom, he had to get the permission of his foreman, who timed his bodily function. In 1932 the company cut Connelly's pay. When asked why, his foreman told him that he did not know; that money decisions were made by upper-management in the main office. When Connelly got up the courage to inquire at the main office, he was told that decisions over pay were in fact made in his department. When he returned and told this to the foreman, the man got angry. Did he want his job? If so, he must stop asking questions. Why were GM workers ready for a union? Connelly knew: the company "treated you just like a dog, you know."

Still, changes had to occur in the White House and the union movement before Russell, Connelly, and thousands of others could channel their grievances into the creation of viable industrial unions. But change was on the way. The 1932 election was a complete routing of Hoover and those who championed business as a knee-jerk reflex. Franklin Delano Roosevelt (FDR) won 89 percent of the electoral vote and 57 percent of the popular vote. At the Democratic nominating convention, FDR had argued that Americans deserved a "New Deal." No one at the time, including Roosevelt, was sure what that would mean, but in the end the broad range of New Deal agencies and policies would

41

reorient the role of the federal government in such a way as to guarantee working people security.

Committed to bringing economic recovery and stability to the nation, Roosevelt took a pragmatic approach to reform, one premised on the notion that government owed working people a safety net and protection from capitalism's chaotic whims and shifts. In this vein, Roosevelt's administration helped create a modern labor-relations system that early scholars of the era credit with benefiting the organized labor movement. Democratic-led Congresses passed pro-worker legislation in part because New Deal supporters believed that secure jobs, minimum wages, and union rights would encourage workers to spend their wages on American-made consumer goods, which in turn would keep factories running and jobs plentiful. Economists, lawyers, and public administrators agreed with such union leaders as Amalgamated Clothing Worker (ACW) President Sidney Hillman, Roosevelt's closest labor advisor, that workers' inability to participate in consumption underlay the current economic crisis. Policies that supported workers' and consumers' rights turned private, corporate decision-making into a public matter with national consequences. Labor's demand for a rising standard of living no longer fit in to the national discussion as a selfish end. Collective bargaining combined with fair pricing put working people at the center of the nation's economic recovery and its future stability.

Roosevelt's presidency represented a new promise to workers, but in its early years, Roosevelt addressed that promise unevenly. The president's speeches asked Americans to return to the unified determination mustered to fight foreign enemies in the Great War, using the comparison as a basis for expanding his federal powers. He then relied upon many of the same advisors Wilson had consulted on labor policy, none more so than Felix Frankfurter. And as he had under Wilson, Frankfurter worked with other government officials who operated under conflicting political philosophies concerning power, labor, business, and the state. Business-friendly advisors hoped to support cooperation between labor and capital without fundamentally redistributing power.

Worker-friendly advisors hoped to redistribute power by giving unions the tools to remake society's economic and social relationships. Roosevelt vacillated between the two, always feeling vulnerable to fiscally and socially conservative Democrats who held power firmly throughout the South. Such tension in Roosevelt's administration helps explain the disagreement among scholars interpreting the nature of the New Deal – whether it was liberal or corporatist, radical or reformist. In the end, Roosevelt was capable of supporting far-reaching, progressive change for working people as well as undermining it.

The initial major piece of New Deal labor legislation that passed in 1933 during Roosevelt's first 100 days in office, the National Industrial Recovery Act (NIRA), reflected both tendencies. Concerned with economic recovery, the law excused industry from antitrust legislation and encouraged business cooperation to plan and predict their share of sales, then limit their production accordingly. In exchange, companies had to guarantee minimum wages and maximum hours and stop using child labor. In addition, Section 7a of the act supported workers' right to form unions and bargain collectively without employer intimidation. Companies that complied were awarded the Blue Eagle to post publicly, a signal to consumers that purchases from these sellers were safe contributions to a better economy.

For workers, the NIRA was better on paper than in practice; it gave the appearance of government support without providing any way to enforce its rules. Section 7a, especially, had no teeth. When employers fired employees for talking about unions, the jobless individual had no recourse. Moreover, the NIRA excluded field workers and domestic servants from collective bargaining rights, establishing troubling precedents.

And there were other problems with the NIRA. Believing labor's place at the bargaining table to be an illegitimate intrusion, employers were set against the act's labor provisions. New Deal union legislation was based on craft unions' governance structures and contractual arrangements, but corporate leaders viewed craft unions as illegal fronts that engaged in extortion – in other words, a racket. Everyone knew that illegal rackets bribed businesses to pay for protection against such crimes as arson or murder that the racket itself might inflict, but business leaders also believed that craft unions fit this category, since they saw unions as illegal businesses that forced companies to pay for union "protection" from strikes. The influence of organized crime in such unions as the teamsters, whose union organized truck drivers and warehouse workers, meant that many in the public also negatively identified craft unions with mobs, violence, and extortion.

New Deal reformers challenged these long-held views, arguing that union members should be allowed to engage in constitutionally protected, voluntary activity. With Roosevelt in the White House, federal authorities used state power to make unions legitimate. In the case of the NIRA, New Deal officials invited craft unions to participate in the creation of codes that set wage scales, hours of work, and terms of business competition.

Naturally, employers fought the provisions of Section 7a, and they had their day in 1935 when the Supreme Court ruled the law unconstitutional. Even though the court's technical problem with NIRA was with how the law dealt with monopoly-like business practices and not in its support of unions, the decision ended the entire experiment three weeks shy of its second year.

Fighting for Unionism in the 1930s Without Meaningful Federal Protection

Working people's widely shared belief that the president of the United States supported their struggle to gain rights in the workplace overshadowed weaknesses in the NIRA. Workers participated in a spate of strike activity that spread like wildfire. "Man-days lost due to strikes, which had not exceeded 603,000 in any month in the first half of 1933," writes the historian Irving Bernstein in *The Turbulent Years: A History of the American Worker, 1933–1941* (1971, reissued 2010), "spurted to 1,375,000 in July and to 2,378,000 in August." From heavy industry to filmmaking, workers demanded the right to collective bargaining. Despite

Roosevelt's willingness to exclude farm workers from the NIRA, in 1933, 56,000 of them in 17 different states went on strike – 47,000 field workers in California alone. Come 1934, Bernstein notes, "Anybody struck. It was not just auto parts workers in Toledo, truck drivers in Minneapolis, longshoremen in San Francisco, or mill hands in the South. It was the fashion."

By fashion or necessity, 1934 was the most militant year of the decade, with 1.5 million workers involved in strikes. General strikes broke out in three major cities – San Francisco, Minneapolis, and Toledo – and 400,000 textile workers along the eastern seaboard supported an industry-wide strike. Each of the General Strikes had elements in common: they were led by radicals determined to increase workers' control; strikers won support from AFL unions and the public; and the strikers used the opportunity created by the NIRA to demand union representation while not depending on the federal government or the AFL to win the day. The San Francisco waterfront strike extended up the West Coast to Seattle. In San Francisco police fired shotguns at picketers and lobbed tear-gas canisters into crowds. The governor brought in the National Guard; Roosevelt put the US Army on alert. Workers stuck together in the face of violence, sometimes in opposition to their union leadership, and in the end the longshoremen were victorious, and won the right to union representation.

In Minneapolis, Teamsters local 574 shut down the trucking industry and eventually the city by using "flying squadrons" of pickets who moved from worksite to worksite. A month of violence-initiated against strikers by police, private guards, and deputized citizens-ended when employers surrendered, leading teamsters to continue organizing drives throughout the Midwest. The successful workers in Minnesota took their cues from a core group who identified politically as Trotskyists, a splinter group from the Communist Party who believed that their leaders and doctrine were the purest expression of Lenin's Russian Revolution.

Workers in the Auto-Lite plant in Toledo, Ohio, striking for union recognition, were stymied by a court injunction. Thousands of picketers, led by the Unemployed League – a group organized by the radical American Workers' Party – trapped scabs when they tried to leave the plant. National Guardsmen demanded the pickets scatter, and when they refused, guardsmen shot and killed two and wounded hundreds more. The city's unions voted for a general strike, but around-the-clock negotiations resulted in the union winning recognition, a grievance system, and increased wages. Not all was won, however, as the hated scabs were allowed back in the plant. Nevertheless, the company union had been routed and union fever spread in Northwest Ohio.

Some scholars argue that 1934 was the most important Depression-era year in reversing labor's decline. Union membership increased 20 percent that year, sending a message to lawmakers and AFL leaders that industrial workers had power and were willing to exercise it by striking in mass.

Not all labor activism sprang from NIRA promises. The Agricultural Adjustment Act of 1933 (AAA), a pillar of early New Deal legislation, required landowning farmers to leave their land unplanted in exchange for a government payment. By subsidizing acreage reduction (paying farmers to keep fields unplanted to reduce supply and raise prices for crops) the government would be increasing the ability of farmers to buy food and consumer goods. The government allotted funds for tenant farmers and sharecroppers who lost employment when the land they worked on for their landlord went unplanted, but local authorities in sparsely populated rural areas did not believe such people, many of whom were African American, were worthy of federal payments, so few of them actually received money. Instead, hordes of poor farmers and their families were simply kicked off the land and sent packing.

Taking their cue from factory workers and teamsters, tenants and sharecroppers organized unions and struck over the unintended effects of AAA. According to Robin Kelley in *Hammer and Hoe: Alabama Communists During the Great Depression* (1990), thousands of Alabama's evicted tenants turned to the Communist Share Croppers' Union (SCU) for help. Local protesters grew in number as landowning farmers booted tenants and sharecroppers from their land. As these AAA-triggered evictions surged, SCU members demanded immediate relief, along with investigation of local New Deal officials. "The SCU in places where [it] has been slack [is] beginning to wake [people] up," said one SCU leader, "and people don't wait for the comrades to come as they used to." Local officials not only refused to distribute federal payments to tenants and sharecroppers, but they also undermined SCU activity by taking evicted tenants and strikers off relief rolls. Without a job or federal payments and no chance of earning relief, the evicted farmers found the SCU one of their only allies in their fight for survival. In 1934, after winning increased cotton payments and credit allowances, the SCU numbered eight thousand.

The energy released from New Deal promises and workers' attempts to organize spawned union growth. The UMWA could barely keep up with demands from miners wanting to sign union cards; by 1934 its membership had reached half a million. Clothing workers in the ILGWU welcomed new, predominantly Mexican-American locals in Los Angeles and San Antonio. By the end of 1934 the AFL had added 2.5 million workers, including those in one of its 1,400 newly chartered, federated locals. Communist TUUL unions also had success, although not as much as the AFL. By 1934, membership in TUUL locals numbered 125,000. New independent organizations also formed among black sharecroppers in Arkansas and Tennessee, pork butchers in Minnesota, tool-and-die makers in Detroit, professional actors in Hollywood, and journalists in New York.

However, union interest did not translate into consistent union victories. In such highly competitive industries as garment making, collective bargaining was successful. But in the larger steel, auto, and electrical manufacturing firms, which had not traditionally dealt with unions, employers refused to bargain in good faith and continued to fire union militants – all activities that went unpunished so long as NIRA officials had no policing powers. Company unions were most employers' first line of defense against Section 7a. GM worker Clarence Lisher remembered the fear he and fellow workers felt when their only

Figure 1.2 Reverend W. L. Blackstone, union organizer and member of the president's Farm Tenancy Commission, inducts a new Southern Tenant Farmers Union member, 1937. The string symbolizes the tie between the member and the union. Kheel Center for Labor-Management Documentation and Archives, M. P. Catherwood Library, Cornell University (#5859pb2f22ep800g).

recourse was to go to the company's "hand-picked representative." GM worker Irving King recalls, "everywhere their authority was absolute. You had no recourse if you disagreed with anything on your job." Employers claimed they were happy to negotiate but believed they should choose which employees to sit down with, and only they should determine the parameters of the discussions.

The Wagner Act and Industrial Unionism

As the dust of the 1934 labor uprisings settled and the Supreme Court ruled the NIRA unconstitutional, lawmakers began debating a new labor bill. New York Democratic Senator Robert Wagner, led the charge against employers and for workers' right to unionize. The strength of working-class activism in the early 1930s pushed legislators like Wagner to pass the National Labor Relations/ Wagner Act (NLRA) of 1935 in an attempt to rectify the NIRA's weak nod to unionism.

The NLRA was a landmark piece of legislation for many working people. Expressions of workers' unionization rights were not new, but legal enforcement of these rights was. Such enforcement was crucial, the preamble to the act indicated, since collective bargaining rights and "the exercise by workers of full freedom of association, self organization and designation of representatives of their own choosing" was understood as fundamental to healthy employment, wages, and the "free flow of commerce." According to law, "the denial by employers of the right of employees to organize...leads to strikes and other forms of industrial strike or unrest, which have the intent or the necessary effect of burdening or obstructing commerce." Employers' resistance to negotiate, explained the NLRA, caused strikes and labor unrest, which in turn harmed the nation's economy. Employers, therefore, had to cease actions that undermined union organization.

Section 8 of the NLRA defined some of these activities as unfair labor practices (ULPs), actions the law precluded employers from taking, such as refusing to bargain collectively, coercing or intimidating employees who supported unions, firing workers who filed ULP charges against their employer, and dominating or interfering with labor organizations. Section 10 of the act established the National Labor Relations Board (NLRB), a body of three appointees (later five) empowered to make sure that when outlawed labor practices occurred, those behind them were prosecuted.

One of the Wagner Act's (as the NLRA was commonly called) most significant contributions was to empower the NLRB to designate units of exclusive representation, thereby undermining employers' use of company unions (and their hand-picked favorites) that previously had helped them skirt the provisions of

49

the NIRA. Using collective bargaining as a weapon to fight for the economy's recovery and stability, Wagner went to war against company unions on the principle that workers should be protected from employer coercion and have the right to choose their bargaining representatives, in effect protecting the tradition of self-organization that dated back at least to the 1840s. To that end, representation elections were not mandatory; the NLRB would only hold them when workers filed for them. To file, workers needed to gather their co-workers' signatures on cards that indicated their support for a union. Once they had enough signatures to convince them that they could win an election, they turned those cards into the NLRB. During a card drive and in the period leading up to an election, employers were not permitted to coerce employees or intimidate those who were pro-union.

US business leaders reacted against the Wagner Act swiftly and with a heavy hand. In St. Louis, electrical employers organized into anti-union groups and argued that higher wages would scare off industry and business. These business associations dated back to the 1910s and maintained power through their anti-unionism. The St. Louis anti-union business associations were not unique. Coal operators turned to private deputies; southern cotton textile operators wielded power by controlling public officials, newspapers, and police forces; steel employers stockpiled tear gas and ammunition in preparation to break strikes; while others infiltrated their workforce with spies. Key corporate leaders believed if they resisted long enough, they would withstand this "undignified affront."

It would take a while for the Wagner Act to make a difference. In 1935 a foreman caught General Motors worker Robert Gibbs with a union card. Switching before Gibbs's eyes from a "nice guy" to a tyrant, the foreman fired him on the spot, refused to pay him, and gave him two minutes to exit the building. Seeing the Wagner Act as an unnecessary intrusion of federal power into private negotiations, the business community, aligning with conservative citizens, dug in their heels, fired workers suspected of having union loyalties, and waited, believing that the Supreme Court would set things right. This time it did not.

While business united against the Wagner Act, labor divided over the old question of which workers were worthy of union representation. Labor militancy in 1934 gave way to membership losses in early 1935. By that time, thousands who had joined AFL unions a year or two earlier had lost their jobs, changed employers, or left town. Such a high rate of turnover convinced some AFL leaders that it was not worth going after largely unskilled and semi-skilled mass production workers, who did not have enough experience with unions, were often of different ethnic backgrounds than the Anglo, German, and Irish workers already in the craft unions that dominated the AFL, and were too easily provoked to strike.

But some AFL leaders disagreed. John L. Lewis of the UMWA, Sidney Hillman of the ACW, and David Dubinsky of the ILGWU came to the AFL from industrial unions, supported the addition of new federated locals, which would be organized industrially and comprised of workers from a spectrum of skill levels. They also believed that the organizational separation of skilled from semi- and unskilled workers was a mistake. While affiliated with the AFL, these leaders argued for reaching out to the unorganized in creative ways, including the need to dispel craft loyalties and jurisdictional claims that taught that all butchers, for example, belonged in a meat cutters'-only local, that sausage stuffers could fend for themselves. Under the craft-based organizational structure, it was considered blasphemous to suggest folding meat cutters into a broader, packinghouse workers' union. In the jurisdictional world of the AFL, craft unions had proprietary rights to organize all workers claiming a trade. After a year of pleading and arguing with his craft-bent colleagues, Lewis had enough. He had entered the mines at age 15 and at 39 held the presidency of the UMWA. A powerful speaker and effective strategist, the stocky, confident Lewis commanded a strong presence. When at the AFL's 1935 convention in Atlantic City the burly William L. Hutcheson of the Carpenters' Union moved to silence dissent among a group of rubber workers over the question of jurisdiction, Lewis lost his temper. The two men parlayed insults, Hutcheson called Lewis a "bastard," and the latter landed a thereafter famous, crushing fist onto the face of the 61-year-old Hutcheson, knocking him across a table.

Lewis's push for industrial unionism within the AFL seemed odd given his career, which rested to this point on his ability to use bureaucracy to maneuver to the top of the UMWA. During the 1920s, writes historian Robert Zieger in *The CIO: 1935–1955* (1995), Lewis was not open to democratic union control and "clamped a rigidly repressive personal control over the union." He also supported Republicans Coolidge and Hoover. At the same time, however, industrial unionism struck close to home for mine-worker Lewis. As long as steel mills remained without unions and steel corporations owned and operated their own coalmines, they threatened the existence of the UMWA. Even though the union won victories in these so-called captive mines, non-unionized steelworkers made the wins vulnerable to backsliding. On a more socially conscious note, Lewis feared that the economic changes of the 1920s threatened the social order of the nation. Against the conspiratorial machinations of financiers, bankers, and the corporate elite, the labor movement stood as the best fortification against corporate domination of the United States. To him, the time for industrial unionism had arrived.

And he was right. Beginning in 1935, Lewis and other union leaders formed the Committee for Industrial Organization (CIO) within the AFL. In 1938, they would break from the AFL completely and call themselves the Congress of Industrial Organizations or, more simply, the CIO. CIO hired organizers to travel to industrial centers, where they explained to workers how industrial unions would differ from craft ones. CIO unions would represent all workers in the core industries, from the most to the least skilled; they would include women, ethnic minorities, and African Americans. At its best, CIO unions would bring democracy and its principles into the walls of US industrial workplaces. More generally, a union federation with a commitment to organizing all workers, regardless of skill, meant that an entire organization would be committed to shoring up the rights of the working class and advocating on their behalf in city halls, state capitols, and Washington, DC. A core number of these CIO recruiters were communists, fresh from battles in Unemployment Councils and eager to advise workers about how best to spread the union movement throughout their company. Despite facing threats and uncertainty, industrial workers listened.

With the Wagner Act facing a court challenge, NLRB police powers frozen, and employers' heightening resistance to unions, workers rose to the call. Between February 18 and March 21, 1936, in Akron, Ohio, workers led a struggle at the Goodyear Tire factory that involved picket lines of 5,000 strikers and supporters. Building on the momentum created by rubber workers, the CIO formed the Steel Workers' Organizing Committee (SWOC) in June 1936 and urged the AFL's Amalgamated Association of Iron and Steel Workers (AA) to organize the unorganized. When the AFL and the AA showed little interest, Lewis hired 200 organizers from the ranks of the UMWA and the Communist Party and prepared for battle.

One of the more dramatic episodes in the early days of the CIO occurred when workers sat down in Flint, Michigan's General Motors factories and ceased work from December 1936 to February 1937. In this famous sit-down strike, rather than picket GM from outside the factory gates, a thousand employees camped inside two of the huge Fisher Body Plants for six weeks. Such a tactic prevented GM's management from bringing strikebreakers through picket lines and into the factory, where they would take strikers' jobs. It also forestalled excessive violence: strikers had a hunch that GM would hesitate to invoke violence inside the factory's walls – the equipment was too valuable to risk.

GM management (and others in the period like them) fundamentally opposed the principle and exercise of collective bargaining. GM's workers agreed that they should collectively have a say in how they would be paid, the order in which workers should be laid off in slow times, and the number of hours they should be expected to work. As US citizens, they expected to be able to vote for candidates, push for legislation, and freely speak and gather. Why should they have to forfeit these rights when they punched in for work each day? Workers' productivity drove corporate profits and CEO salaries. Didn't their labor earn them the right to expect dignity at work and security during hard times or when they became too old to work the line? Collective bargaining legally protected their right to send representatives to negotiate with GM's representatives over matters critical to their lives.

At the end of 1936, United Auto Worker (UAW) President Homer Martin tried to negotiate with GM's Executive Vice President, William S. Knudsen, but Knudsen showed no interest in bargaining with a person whom workers authorized to represent them over wages, hours, and other business decisions. Knudsen said, "Grievances of individuals or groups of individuals can only be handled locally where the employe[e]s and the plant management are familiar with local conditions as well as the basic general policies of the corporation concerning employe[e] relations." He told the *Detroit News* in January 1937 that UAW leaders could not understand the complexity of GM's 200,000 employees who lived in "35 separate communities in 14 states." Knudsen also argued that it was impossible to bargain collectively as long as workers were striking. "We cannot have bonafide collective bargaining with sit-down strikers in illegal possession of plants." To win the public's support, GM took out full-page newspaper advertisements claiming that the UAW was illegitimate and only had workers' support because union thugs coerced and intimidated people. Collective bargaining would open the door to a "labor dictatorship," the nation's largest automaker alleged, running roughshod over businesses in America at the same time Adolf Hitler and German forces were expanding their reach across Europe. To GM's corporate leadership, collective bargaining was simply un-American.

Of course, nearly all of GM's workers disagreed. In a response to Knudsen, Martin made clear that the UAW was not trying to run GM unilaterally because that was not what collective bargaining meant. To Martin and GM's workers, collective bargaining would allow better wages so they could do such basic things as purchase GM's most inexpensive cars, an act that was out of reach for many, but one that would be good for individuals, the company, and the US economy. But beyond a wage increase, Martin and GM workers believed that bringing union rights to their workplace connected them to Americans who fought for political freedom in the Revolutionary War. Martin said:

We today are fighting for social and economic freedom. This is a struggle against the inhuman speed-up which has made man the slave of the machine; it is the fight against the vicious espionage system which deprives the automobile worker of those legal rights to join any organization he desires (keeping in mind that the General Motors Corporation paid $167,000 to the Pinkerton strikebreaking agency in 1935); it is an endeavor to shorten the hours to a working day which will enable the automobile worker to enjoy his wife, his children, and his leasure [*sic*] time. It, in short, is an effort to obtain those things of which every true American can be justly proud . . . Organization can be labor's only reply to conditions which are subject to the whims of management. Only through the effective medium of a national agreement can dictatorship by management be avoided. (*Detroit News*, January 7, 1937)

As for coercion and intimidation, the *Detroit News* of January 22, 1937, told the story of George Culley, a six-year employee at Chevrolet Gear and Axle in Detroit, whom GM fired after he refused to sign a company-drafted petition stating he opposed the union effort. In Flint, company officials told Buick and Chevrolet workers that if they did not sign anti-union petitions they would not be able to get company loans during the season when the plants closed and workers were laid off. In Saginaw, Michigan, a vigilante campaign openly supported in the local press resulted in union representatives receiving threats of physical violence. Responding to such tactics, union leaders sent word to workers in non-striking plants to sign the petitions to protect their jobs.

Meanwhile, the workers in the Fisher Body plants in Flint continued to sit and wait, writing and singing songs, forming committees to clean up after themselves, leading exercises, safe-guarding company equipment, and keeping one another inspired. They also read newspapers and ate food delivered by a group of a thousand wives, mothers, and supporters, who organized themselves into a women's auxiliary. From the strike's beginning, organizers agreed that the sit-down was a male affair. If women and men co-mingled in the plant, the company and the press would have a field day spreading rumors, discrediting the strikers, and distracting attention from collective bargaining. Outside the plant, however, women performed vital functions to support the strikers, including generating publicity, staffing picket lines, organizing first aid, cooking meals for the men in the plant, keeping an eye on workers' children, and giving support to women whose husbands were inside.

Women were limited to this auxiliary role until January 11, 1937, when Flint's police tried to force their way into the plant to dislodge the men. The unarmed men inside turned on fire hoses and threw car parts from windows at the approaching officers, who were armed with rifle shells and buckshot, tear gas, and firebombs. In the end, it was one Genora Johnson who turned this skirmish into a union victory. As the leader of the women's auxiliary, Johnson stayed close to the occupied plants when the police arrived, and she refused to be led to safety. When the battery on the sound truck used by male union organizers began to run out, Johnson took charge. She recalls:

> That's when I got to take the mic [*sic*], and again, circumstances you lose yourself; you go beyond yourself and think of the cause. I was able to make my voice really ring out on that night because I knew the battery was going down and we had only a few minutes left. That's when I appealed to the women of Flint. I bypassed everybody else then and went to the women, and told them what was happening. That's when I said, there are women down here, the mothers of children, and I beg of you to come down here and stand with your husbands, your loved ones, your brothers, your sweethearts.

Her call encouraged other women to confront the police, which ultimately turned the tide.

According to Johnson:

> And when I made that appeal...A hush came over the crowd the minute a woman's voice came over the mike. It was startling!...then I saw the first woman struggling and I noticed when she started to break through and come down, that a cop grabbed her coat – and this was in freezing weather, freezing weather, there

were icy pavements and everything was frozen – and she just kept on coming. And as soon as that happened other women broke through and then we had a situation where the cops didn't want to fire into the backs of women. When the women did that, the men came naturally and that was the end of the battle.

After what was dubbed "The Battle of Bull's Run" (after the attempted assault by the police), the sit-down strikers held strong for another four weeks.

In early February 1937, union members occupied an additional plant, Chevrolet Number Four, in hopes of pushing GM to the negotiating table. GM fought back in court and won an injunction ordering the strikers out of GM plants, but the workers still refused to budge. Michigan Governor Frank Murphy sent

Figure 1.3 Crowds gather outside of the Fisher Body Plant no. 1 to show support for the sit-down strikers inside, Flint, Michigan. Walter P. Reuther Library, Wayne State University (#3890).

National Guard troops to Flint, but, fearing bloodshed, he did not order them to enforce the injunction. With both sides holding firm, President Roosevelt tipped the scale on the side of the union and asked GM representatives to meet with the workers' representatives. On February 11, 1937, they did so.

As a result, GM employees at 17 plants won pay increases and recognition of their union as the sole bargaining agent. Workers emerged victorious and inspired a generation to consider the power unions gave workers.

In the wake of their triumph, the industrial union movement swept into the Packard, Hudson, Murray Body, and Chrysler auto plants. In an unexpected turn of events, US Steel signed a contract with the SWOC on March 2, 1937, and Lewis declared at a 1937 SWOC conference, "If we can break the Hindenburg line of industry – steel – everyone knows how far we can go in organizing millions."

Corporate Resistance and Workers' Unity

The CIO would go on to organize millions of workers, but not right away. Corporate resistance kept the Wagner Act tied up in the courts in the hope that the Supreme Court would rule it unconstitutional, as it had the NIRA. In April 1937, to the chagrin of corporate America, the high court upheld the constitutionality of the Wagner Act.

CIO organizers wasted no time in getting back to work, only to run up against the vicious anti-unionism of Tom Girdler and other leaders of "Little Steel" – the name given to the five independent, mid-sized steel companies that were "little" only when compared to the size, productivity, and geographic reach of US Steel. On Memorial Day, 1937, the bloodiest attack of the year was caught on film as Chicago city police, fed and armed by Republic Steel, swung clubs wildly against unarmed marching workers, their families, and supporters. Bashing limp bodies and shooting into the backs of retreating workers, the police killed ten persons and wounded many more.

Even in the face of public scrutiny, neither Republic Steel's Tom Girdler nor Chicago's police showed remorse. Before the Congressional La Follette Civil Liberties Committee, a committee formed to investigate ways employers avoided collective bargaining, the Chicago police demonstrated what *Time* magazine called disturbing "comedy" in the face of "otherwise, grim, gruesome business." When shown a picture of the riot, a Senator on the committee asked Police Sergeant Lawrence J. Lyons "what that [police]man was drawing." Lyons replied, "I don't know. He may be drawing his handkerchief." The Senator asked, "Out of his holster?" Quick on his feet, Lyons responded, "We have left-handed policemen." Then Captain James Mooney laid the blame for the police slaying of ten protestors at the feet of communists. According to Mooney, "the purpose of communists is to overthrow the Government and attack policemen, and they are getting money from Russia to help them do it." When asked if he really thought that the Republic steel strikers were paid by Russia, Mooney replied, "I wouldn't be surprised...A lot of people in my district went back to the capital of Russia." When asked where that was, Mooney answered, "I don't know – wherever Lenin is." When senators showed the photo of a policeman clubbing an unconscious body, William V. Daly, Chicago's assistant corporation counsel, argued, "you got to consider the human element, Senator. They was all excited." Apparently, to Daly, only Chicago's police had a "human element" worth considering. Paramount released the amateur film as a news reel to the public after the La Follette Committee held a viewing of it for 700 witnesses, mostly senators and congressmen. Upon its release, Chicago police banned it from the city. In other cities, audiences had a hard time making sense of the chaotic scene put before them. But when shown close-ups of the dead, dying, and wounded, they began to hiss, boo, and shout.

Still, the event did little to unsettle Girdler, who faced the press and insisted that 21,000 of his 50,000 workers remained at work and that his mills were shipping thousands of tons of steel every day. As far as spending a million dollars on arms and ammunition, Girdler quipped, "I never knew a steel plant that didn't have guns and ammunition to protect its property." For Girdler, the workers in the Memorial Day massacre got what was coming to them.

Steelworkers wanting union representation in Cleveland, Youngstown, and Massillon, Ohio, also met with violence. At the notoriously brutal, anti-union Jones & Laughlin works in Aliquippa, Pennsylvania, workers on strike for union recognition engaged in a two-day battle against the company. Family and supporters took to the streets, blocking plant entrances, as horse-mounted and armed police blasted them with tear gas. In the end, 18 workers were killed in the struggle during the summer of 1937.

In November 1938, when the CIO formally established itself as the Congress of Industrial Organizations, the number of mass production industries resisting unionization blossomed. Even in such corporations as GM and Firestone, where the union had won victories, employers worked overtime to limit collective bargaining's scope – racism and sexism would still apply in hiring and job assignments, for example. International Harvester hired a team of lawyers to maneuver around the NLRB and stall union recognition.

It turned out that despite the Wagner Act, workers could not simply rely on the state to see their union to victory. They had to keep pressure on the shop floor to rout out company unions, defy obstinate foremen, and pressure their employers for recognition. Shop stewards, the union representative in each factory department, led these efforts. In Chicago's Armour meatpacking plant, workers participated in "whistle bargaining" whereby every grievance came with a steward's secret signal to stop work. Slowdowns, stoppages, and walkouts showed workers' initiative in winning recognition and built loyalty and trust among co-workers in a plant.

For workers, the taking of these collective actions made for heady moments. Standing with fellow workers against their foremen and the companies they represented was as thrilling as it was terrifying. Winning was historic. That is why steelworker Johnny Metzgar and other CIO unionists like him spoke of John L. Lewis and the miner's union "with the same reverence and gratitude that [they] usually reserved for God." Lewis and the UMWA paid the bills, sent out the organizers, and allowed men like Metzgar to fight for dignity in places as undignified as the shop floor of US Steel. "All this ferment, militancy, radicalism, violence and perhaps even an altered working-class consciousness," writes historian Melvyn Dubofsky in *The State and Labor in Modern America* (1994), "were part of American reality during the 1930s."

Workers' sense of power had indeed been altered, but by no means were most workers radicals or persons seeking revolution. In 1937, when strikes affected every mass production industry in the nation, a mere 7.2 percent of employed workers participated in walkouts. The capitalist system might have stumbled, but it never completely collapsed. In fact, under the guidance of New Deal policies and programs, it seemed to be improving without fundamental changes. In fact, workers were not trying to change the system in the late 1930s. Instead, surveys and polls from the decade show a leftward movement among workers and working-class voting patterns that betrayed new levels of class-consciousness. Most workers remained committed to what Lizabeth Cohen in *Making a New Deal: Industrial Workers in Chicago, 1919–1939* (1990) refers to as "moral capitalism." Rather than revolution, Cohen argues, workers "looked to the state and the union to create a more just society within a system that still respected private property and many managerial prerogatives." Most workers viewed the New Deal as favorable to them. In the end, they sought a fairer capitalism and were drawn to the CIO in part because of its legitimacy in the eyes of the state.

Extending the New Deal for Workers

As CIO workers fought to make their working lives more just, they felt a partnership with President Roosevelt and the Democrats in Congress and pushed them to address not only the workplace but also unemployment, healthcare, and old-age security. To achieve these ends politically, a coalition grew among national unions, union locals, city and county governments, ethnic fraternal organizations, and members of the Communist Party. In

1934 the Lundeen Bill, named for Ernest Lundeen, the Minnesota congressman who introduced it, proposed that *all* workers, including part time, agricultural, domestic, and professional, should be guaranteed unemployment benefits paid for by federal government revenues, which would be enhanced by taxes on the richest individuals and corporations – not payroll taxes. Such a plan connected the welfare of US citizens to the state rather than limiting coverage to particular workers in specific job categories. Bold on its face and backed by a wide base of supporters, the Lundeen Bill was ultimately displaced by the Social Security Act, a landmark piece of legislation in its own right.

The Social Security Act of 1935 is largely remembered for its government support for the elderly; but the legislation was more comprehensive, broadening the role of the federal government to include unemployment insurance and aid for poor families. Under this law, federal or state payments to the poor, the elderly, and the unemployed represented new ways of thinking about the government's responsibility to society; if capitalism created vulnerable categories of people, then it was the government's job to provide support and security to all. The legislation suggested that the poor and unemployed should not be blamed for their condition, as they traditionally had. Because there was a structural element inherent in the capitalist system that created winners and losers, the federal government had a responsibility to protect the welfare of society against the vicissitudes and misfortunes such a system created. Old Age Insurance, moreover, would ease older workers out of jobs with the guarantee of a pension, which would allow older citizens to maintain their consumer purchasing power. It would open their freshly abandoned positions to younger workers, who would no longer have to support their aging parents alone, and it would put an end to costly state-based, means-based, old-age programs.

The legislation, however, created a new set of winners and losers. When it came to old-age insurance, lawmakers chose to fund it through a tax shared equally by the employer and employee, a payroll tax. By raising money to support the program in this way, most citizens would see their payment as something they earned, an entitlement, not a government handout. If a person worked in an industry covered by the law, they directly paid for their government-supported pension in the future. Workers' contributions, lawmakers argued, "would purchase dignity." Because the idea of equity was so pervasive among lawmakers, the notion that investors would get a fair return on their contribution was central to the act. Those who worked irregularly, or whose contributions would be too low to earn an old-age benefit that would induce them to leave the workforce, undermined the program because lawmakers cared primarily about opening jobs to younger people. Framers of the legislation kept their gaze on industrial workers whose retirement would mean employment for the next generation. Their motivation meant that several job categories, including agricultural laborers and domestic servants (together representing approximately three fifths of the nation's African-American population), were excluded from social security taxes and their pension benefits.

The notion that wage work was rightly a male preserve also shaped this legislation that treated women as second-class economic citizens. According to Alice Kessler-Harris in *In Pursuit of Equity: Women, Men and the Quest for Economic Citizenship in 20th Century America* (2003), lawmakers imagined that women lacked a commitment to work, worked irregularly, and primarily labored outside of the industrial sector. Women's retirement, therefore, would not improve the labor-market problems inherent in the Great Depression. When the law was amended in 1939 because it was excluding nearly half of the working population (60 percent of excluded workers were women), lawmakers extended benefits to fatherless children, wives, and widows of male wage earners who contributed to the program. Such a move bolstered the benefits of those who were already covered rather than opening up opportunities to excluded categories of workers; women and children got benefits as men's dependents. These new benefits reinforced society's belief that male dignity was tied to a man's ability to provide for his family and that a woman's virtue was linked to her dependency on a man.

Other Social Security benefits were problematic as well. Unemployment insurance, established through a federal and state partnership, was administered through the states. From state to state, workers faced widely varying eligibility requirements and benefits. Southern states had more restrictions regarding eligibility and paid less than northern states. When it came to the part of social security that dealt with single mothers with children, government oversight and scrutiny took on an even more oppressive character. Aid to Dependent Children put mothers under the watchful eye of state social workers, who determined benefits based on their understanding of what a particular woman needed, how stable her home life was, and whether her sex life was appropriate.

Once the president signed the Social Security Act into law, broad coalitions of labor leaders and liberals then turned to redefine health security as a relationship between citizens and the state and not one between employees and employers. The New Deal's promotion of personal security paved the way for all reformers to make the case that security against sickness was a matter of justice and every citizen's right. A 1938 national health conference sponsored by the Roosevelt administration brought 150 activists to Washington, sparking what one scholar refers to as a grassroots health security movement. Activists designed and constructed community health programs and pushed for wider local, working-class access to health facilities and services. In addition, unions and organized community groups in six cities launched educational programs and experimented with local health plans. The late 1930s was a period of ferment and experimentation, seeing many unions and employee groups deciding to subscribe to health plans independent of their employers. Workers' demands for power and security did not have to be an either/or equation: these goals were often combined.

As the pace of economic recovery slowed in 1938, Congress passed the last major New Deal initiative directly affecting US workers: the Fair Labor Standards Act (FLSA). The FLSA called for a 44-hour work week, reduced to 40 by 1941, and overtime pay after that. For the first time, it included a minimum wage that would increase over time with no regional differences; and it stopped the shipment of goods made with child labor.

As a matter of principle, the FLSA made enormous strides, expanding the role of government into the world of wages. Unfortunately, it did so in a way that established wage minimums rather than wages levels that would allow families to live above the poverty line. The rate negotiated was tied to the low-paying southern textile and lumber industries as a concession to conservative congressional representatives from the South; it was too low to actually improve the livelihood of most wageworkers. Of course, AFL leaders preferred it that way. They believed that the government had no business trying to control wages: that was the job of unions. They only backed the law once it was clear to them that its mandated wage minimum would not interfere with the contracts they negotiated through collective bargaining and would only affect those workers outside of traditional union strongholds. In the end, the FLSA excluded 20 percent of the labor force from its provisions, among these domestic servants, seamen, and workers in agriculture, retail and service, food processing, packing and transportation, government, and non-profit enterprise. Only 20 percent of women who worked for wages were employed in sectors of the economy covered by the FLSA. Four out of five African-American men worked in agriculture in 1935 and more than one third of African-American women worked as domestic servants. Taken together with the NLRA and the Social Security Act, the FLSA represented a new, if flawed, partnership between the federal government and society.

Assessing Workers' New Deal and Industrial Unionism

Roosevelt's New Deal was no small undertaking: the federal government inserted itself into workers' relationships with their employers, removed the job of regulating hours from employers' hands, and guaranteed workers security in their old age. The labor movement, unleashed by New Deal policies, agencies, and protectors, brought protections to millions who had suffered without them. These were not small advances by any means.

As inclusive as they were, both the labor movement and the New Deal shared limitations, leaving many unprotected. Taking industrial workers as its model, the NLRA assumed that all employees worked in the same worksite. But women and minorities working as homecare workers, for example, were often dispersed. New Deal policies also entrenched racism by excluding those working in certain sectors of the economy – like farming and domestic service – and supporting segregation in several of its other programs. Because the New Deal was narrowly conceived as a federal project to revive the capitalist economy and get people back to work, women, African Americans, and ethnics were dealt with as potential workers rather than in ways that would address prejudice and discrimination. Because women were imagined as homemakers, dependents, and only marginally tied to wage work, they received less than equitable treatment in government programs.

The CIO treated women and minorities better than did New Deal policy, but not always. Committed to closing the gap that divided workers by ethnicity and race, CIO leaders tried to reach out to African Americans by demanding promotions for black workers, challenging racist company practices, and forcing the hiring of more black workers. The labor movement's rhetoric convinced Canadians, Mexicans, and other foreign-born workers that unionism was an important way to express ones' identity as an American. Wearing union buttons to create a public presence, frequenting taverns and restaurants to unite different groups in a social atmosphere, using radio spots to promote a unified message, and providing supportive roles for union wives and family activities, the CIO created an alternative community based on the union. Reminding workers that their fates were connected, union leaders encouraged a spirit of unity.

The problem was that this culture of unity was always limited and tenuous. In particular, it was limited, like the larger New Deal, by a masculine notion that the primary worker was the man. Women, whether they supported families or not, were auxiliary. The culture of unions was also limited by ethnic and racial tensions that were malleable but present despite the culture the official CIO promoted. UAW leaders who talked about "working-class Americanism" in their broad appeal to ethnic and racial workers, at the same time used the rhetoric of "working-class Americanism" as a weapon to constrain black workers' fight for racial equality within the UAW. When black workers pushed for an African-American seat on the union's executive board, for example, UAW leaders used the rhetoric of "working-class Americanism" to turn them down. No one group should get special treatment, the argument went, over the others. In such cases, civic nationalism brought black workers to unions, but once they were members, racial hierarchy and white control limited conditions and prospects for advancement.

The New Deal unleashed labor activism, but it would take another world war to consolidate the gains of the new labor federation, as well as for the limitations of the Wagner Act to be fully felt. In the meantime, the CIO continued to vie with an equally large and growing force in the AFL. AFL locals maintained emphasis on male, craft-exclusive membership and kept its business–union parochial practices. At the same time, crime organizations scared a handful of AFL union leaders – in Chicago's teamsters, construction employers' associations, the Building Service Employees International, and Chicago's Bartenders Union – into opening their union's bank accounts to illicit ends. When the head of the coal teamsters refused to admit gangsters, he was shot in each leg in front of his wife and children. In the 1930s, gangsters murdered thirteen Chicago labor leaders.

As corruption dotted AFL unions, CIO campaigns continued, and the federal government expanded its responsibilities, a conservative backlash coalesced. Republicans and southern Democrats, intolerant of federal interference in private businesses' economic policies, redoubled their efforts to thwart union organizing and government involvement. AFL leaders joined anti-New Deal groups, particularly concerned (without clear grounds) that the NLRA favored CIO industrial unionism over their form of craft unionism. Also, they pushed to limit the wage provisions of the

Social Security Act. That year, the NLRB came under federal scrutiny for being a communist-run agency, and the House of Representatives formed the House Committee on Un-American Activities (chaired by Martin Dies, Jr. of Texas and known as the Dies Committee) to investigate and expose the suspected subversion.

In the last years of the 1930s, political forces were aligning to redirect the fortunes of workers. Liberty League members (conservative Democrats opposed to the New Deal's pro-labor provisions) as well as anti-labor business leaders in the National Association of Manufacturers mobilized to defend management rights against unions and New Deal liberalism more generally. They saw a major victory in the Supreme Court's 1939 Fansteel case ruling. Workers in Chicago at Fansteel Metallurgical tried to form a union in 1936, but their employers did everything they could to stop it, including hiring spies to infiltrate union planning meetings and setting up a company union, which was illegal under the Wagner Act. In response, Fansteel workers organized a sit-down strike in the plant and stayed put even after management got a court order to force them out. After a second order, police removed the workers, management fired them, and they appealed their case to the NLRB. In 1938 the NLRB ruled that the company had to hire 90 of the workers back because the company had broken the law, thereby inciting the sit-down. A majority of Supreme Court justices, however, did not agree and ruled that the NLRB could not force employers to rehire workers who had broken the law. Since sit-down strikers violated the terms of a court order, they were the ones at fault according to the court. Hereafter, sit-down strikes would no longer have the same workplace sting (although civil rights activists would use them to creative new ends in the postwar period). Employers may have lost the battle, but they were not planning on losing the war.

Conclusion

In the end, the 1930s left US workers with a mixed legacy. Rising to the challenges of the Great Depression, working-class activists built new movements and organizations and pushed the federal government to extend its eye to the world of work, where the labor movement began to establish itself as an equal player. CIO union activists pushed labor organizations to expansive social, political, and economic ends, as well as for inclusive, interracial union membership. Individuals committed to the idea that the state had the responsibility to step in to help the individual when the capitalist system could not brought into the open the issue of healthcare, old-age pensions, and the persistence of unemployment. The new role of the federal government as responsible for the security of US workers meant that many working people, including women and minorities, turned their loyalty to the Democratic Party and committed themselves to the New Deal order. New government responsibilities, social-democratic union agendas, and reconfigured political alignments were just some of the changes to emerge from an otherwise tragic period in the nation's history.

And yet, the government's oversight of the world of work came at a cost to women, minorities, and ultimately the labor movement itself. Roosevelt's negotiation between his liberal base and those more racist, southern Democrats meant that New Deal programs and policies were developed in ways that perpetuated racial and gender discrimination. They also were unquestioning in their support of individual spending as the solution to capitalism's crisis and helped promote working Americans' identity as upwardly mobile consumers. Finally, whereas the state's willingness to assert itself into the relationship between workers and employers worked to the advantage of newly forming unions during the Great Depression, only a few years later, the cost of state intervention would begin to be felt. World War II and its aftermath would reveal just how strongly and widely.

2

Big Wars, Big Labor, Big Costs

World War II began on September 1, 1939, when Germany invaded Poland; it expanded to the United States on December 6, 1941, when Japanese forces bombed the US naval base at Pearl Harbor. US soldiers fought the war in Europe and Asia, and in colonial holdings throughout the world; at home, Johnny Metzgar, a CIO steelworker, and a generation of US workers like him, were engaged in their own battle for democracy. Johnny Metzgar and his co-workers participated in the life-defining struggle to wrestle union recognition from US steel; other workers in wartime industries demanded the same right to union representation from their employers. These calls for collective bargaining rights were transformative wartime experiences. In *Striking Steel: Solidarity Remembered* (2000) Johnny's son Jack recalls the moral significance that union recognition held for his father and those of his generation:

> Those who think that labor negotiations and strikes are simply about money have never met anybody like my father...For many of my father's generation, a lot of the moral intensity of their

Working Hard for the American Dream: Workers and Their Unions, World War I to the Present, First Edition. Randi Storch.
© 2013 John Wiley & Sons, Ltd. Published 2013 by John Wiley & Sons, Ltd.

unionism was about achieving justice for past as well as present wrongs – and that part came with an obligation, a duty that required you to do your best to right the wrongs. One way to measure how you were doing in performing this duty was in pennies per hour. But the basic moral issue was about power. We – our family as a whole and everybody in the valley, not just the men who worked in the mills – not only "owed the union" for the good life we were living, but we also had an obligation to make sure that the power of the companies to control every jot and tittle of our lives was never allowed to return. This, not only for its practical benefits to us, but for general justice's sake.

The New Deal gave unionism its initial surge, but it was within the context of World War II that Johnny Metzgar, those "in the valley," and millions more throughout industrial America got a taste of "general justice" through the union movement.

Nazi atrocities, Hitler's sweeping military campaign, and Japanese military aggression combined to make World War II an all-consuming worldwide fight requiring an unprecedented wartime mobilization. Soldiers needed uniforms, food, and training; the military needed ships, parachutes, airplanes, trucks, fuel, guns, and bullets; and civilians needed to figure out how to skimp and conserve for the greater good. Industries that produced war materials and the workers who filled them became the central focus of the nation's domestic concerns. War production brought hope, employment, and paychecks into the homes of millions of previously unemployed and underemployed working people and ended the Great Depression. Both CIO and AFL union leaders understood the opportunity war production created to build their organizations and launched campaigns to sign up members. They also worked tirelessly to develop these new members by teaching them union principles and acting on those principles collectively. Through their union, working people learned how to win against their employers on shop floors, at hearings before federally appointed government agencies and boards, and in the media. In the period of the war, union membership surged and union leaders attained new-found power. The AFL and the CIO developed into formidable institutions.

For at least a generation after the war, journalists and scholars referred to the period of World War II and its aftermath as a time of "labor's forward march." These were the years when labor and the Democratic Party worked hand in hand and corporate America and big labor negotiated good union contracts that increased workers' pay and benefits. When unions delivered the goods to their members, non-union employers often matched the union standard and large segments of working America earned, saved, and spent more than ever before. Productivity, profits, and stability in the workplace not only translated into bigger paychecks, but also into health benefits, job security, and community prosperity. Union recognition and members' shop floor power allowed Johnny Metzgar and workers like him to appreciate the direct connection between the New Deal's pro-labor promises and their unions' ability to bring justice to themselves, their families, and society more generally.

At the same time, not all was well in the world of work, including in Johnny Metzgar's union. The New Deal's contradictions simmered during World War II and exploded with great force in its aftermath. Since the early 1930s, workers throughout the country depended on spontaneous action and militant showdowns to pressure foremen who put workers in harm's way or otherwise violated accepted work practices. But as war spread through Europe, labor's representatives were called to Washington, DC, and appointed to wartime agencies to develop labor policies that would ensure smooth wartime production (without strikes to slow it down). Boardroom politics in Washington, DC, undermined the power of union members on shop floors; at the local level, union leaders increasingly found their hands tied by contracts (shaped by federal policy) that forced them to police their members and keep them producing. Moreover, the labor movement was not unified and divisions between the AFL and CIO as well as within the CIO led to public confrontations and internal battles that tried the public's patience. In addition, an influx of women and minorities into war industries meant that unions recruited new members to the chagrin of their old ones. Prejudice within union memberships demonstrated that many union members did not intend "general justice" for all.

All the while, the fact of labor's growing size and the positive federal attention it received gnawed at conservative politicians, business leaders, and community members who worked diligently and creatively to put Pandora back in her box. Full production, rising wartime profits, and a scarce labor supply convinced such anti-union stalwarts as Tom Girdler and Henry Ford to sign union contracts and keep the peace in industry. But at heart, even those who did recognize unions viewed them as illegitimate organizations led by outsiders who unjustly threatened managerial rights to workplace decision-making. When the war ended in 1945 and inflation soared, unions used their newly developed communication structures to lead a highly coordinated and disciplined strike wave. This show of power was the proverbial straw that broke the camel's back. To business leaders and the new group of conservatives who were swept into Congress in 1946, unions clearly had too much power, and they successfully pushed back with a crushing, labor-weakening blow in the form of the Taft-Hartley Act.

Between 1945 and 1960, union membership peaked, and those workers fortunate enough to be covered by union contracts won some of the best benefits of their – or any US workers' – lives. But the limits and legal requirements that came with government protection increasingly became a liability for workers. The AFL and CIO's (and AFL-CIO when they merged in 1955) social vision, moreover, had eroded. By the 1960s the idea that unions would bring "general justice" or real and sustainable power to working people – both union and non-union – rarely was the ideal most average people pondered and believed possible.

Wartime Mobilization, 1939–1941

As Hitler spread war through Europe between 1939 and 1941, his enemies increasingly turned to the United States for supplies. After Germany's march into the heart of France in 1940, Roosevelt quickened the pace of US support. Government contracts sent defense industries into motion and millions of people to work, who then quickly joined in the ongoing struggle to bring union recognition to their workplace.

In the first four months of 1941, workers in steel, auto, electrical, and agricultural implements industries laid down their tools and walked off the job to pressure employers who continued to deny them CIO recognition. At Bethlehem Steel, 19,000 workers struck their Bethlehem, Pennsylvania, mill. Their employers continued to rely upon their company union as a way to prevent dealing with a CIO one. They also harassed union supporters and encouraged police violence, but workers' unity prevailed, and Bethlehem management finally agreed to an NLRB-supervised election. In the end, over 21,500 of the company's 28,500 employees voted for the CIO's Steel Workers Organizing Committee (SWOC), which during the war would establish itself as the United Steel Workers of America (USWA). Bethlehem workers' victory opened the door to success at Youngstown Sheet and Tube and at vehement union-hater Tom Girdler's Republic Steel, site of the 1937 May Day massacre. In an emotional victory, 70 percent of Girdler's 40,600 employees chose SWOC representation. Ford's employees followed suit after United Auto Workers (UAW) activists succeeded in forcing an NLRB election at Ford's River Rouge, Michigan, complex, where one giant factory housed the entire auto-production process and its mind-numbing work pace that paid low wages. The May election resulted in the UAW winning 70 percent of 74,000 votes cast.

Just as important, AFL unionists shifted into an organizing mode. The Teamsters extended their representation to over-the-road truckers and goods handlers, and machinists increased their membership in aircraft industries. Between June 1940 and December 1941, organized labor grew by 1.5 million members. By the end of 1941, ten million workers (or 27 percent of the non-agricultural workforce) carried union membership cards and by 1945 union membership stood at fourteen million or 35 percent of the non-agricultural workforce.

74

For the first time in their working lives, these union members felt a rush of victory over their employer and the sense of power that came from being part of a group of people with the ability to voice their demands at work and actually be heard by those in management, those who previously did not care to listen. Jack Metzgar recalled a story that was retold in his union family because it was extreme and demonstrated his family members' vulnerability before the union came to US Steel. In the story, a good worker tried to ensure his steady employment by regularly bringing his foreman homemade kielbasa, mowing his foreman's lawn in the summer, and shoveling his snow in the winter free of charge. One day the foreman, a married man with a family, asked the worker to set up a date for him with the worker's 16-year-old daughter. When the worker refused, his foreman fired him and the worker spent the rest of the year unemployed at a time when no unemployment insurance existed. In remembering the significance union representation held for his father, this story loomed large. Unions meant that workers would be able to stand up for themselves and protect their dignity. According to Metzgar, "though it didn't happen all at once, the union eventually stripped not only the foremen but even the company of this arbitrary power."

The problem for workers, however, was that these union victories were made possible, in large part, by the growing war emergency. Henry Ford and Thomas Girdler did not hesitate to flout the law protecting unions in the 1930s, but wartime mobilization and its potential profits changed them: both bit their tongues and signed union contracts. Roosevelt, for his part, supported unions as long as they served the US government's need for uninterrupted war production by keeping their members off picket lines and at work. In other words, war industry union victories came conditionally. While war spread in Europe between 1939 and 1941 and US industry supplied war materials to Germany's enemies, union workers watched their leaders get called to Washington, DC, to serve on federal wartime planning boards and develop workplace procedures and economic policy with big business. They were finally part of organizations with national power, but quickly learned that such power came with strings attached.

Federal wartime agencies, like those that functioned during World War I, were established to oversee the massive coordination and production of war goods required to support troops around the world. Even before the United States declared war against Japan and Germany, the federal government created agencies to plan the nation's mobilization, develop wartime labor policy, and dampen workers' willingness to walk off the job. Many of these agencies took on a tripartite structure, including representatives from the labor movement, management, and the public, which had the appearance of balance. In practice, however, corporate America's influence overwhelmed the agencies. Even when Roosevelt appointed business and labor representative as co-directors of the Office of Price Management, General Motors executive William Knudsen and his corporate appointments made policy while the CIO's Sidney Hillman and his labor appointments served in advisory capacities.

"Dollar-a-year" executives, corporate leaders who continued to draw their corporate salaries but who were on loan to the federal government for a symbolic sum, made clear that US industries would not mobilize for war on the cheap. Instead, corporate America demanded serious government enticements: depreciation allowances, excessive profit, new tax arrangements, and relaxed antitrust laws. Roosevelt might have nationalized war industries, built new government-owned ones, or taken a more active management role for the federal government, but he did not. James Atleson in *Labor and the Wartime State: Labor Relations and Law during World War II* (1998) coined the term "profit patriotism" to describe the new power of business leaders in the mobilization period and the primary role Roosevelt afforded to them and to capitalism.

So once appointed by Roosevelt, Hillman and other labor representatives prepared to shape the direction of the nation's war planning, but they never had the power that corporate America had to influence policy. They quickly found that board rulings were no more powerful than Roosevelt and his conservative southern supporters wanted them to be. Hillman served as a member of the National Defense Advisory Commission (NDAC), whose members advised in 1940 that the federal government should refuse to give defense contracts to businesses in violation of federal labor laws, but Roosevelt was not so sure. The White House urged caution in light of upcoming elections and congressional and military pressure eventually forced the NDAC to retract the ruling completely. That year, when Ford was under indictment in six different cases for violating the National Labor Relations Act (including one involving a murder in the company's attempt to stop unionization), the government awarded Ford a contract for $122 million to labor's dismay.

More problems followed in March 1941 when Roosevelt replaced the NDAC with a tripartite National Defense Mediation Board (NDMB) whose charge was to "assure that all work necessary for national defense shall proceed without interruption and with all possible speed." In response, labor's representative worked to develop procedures that would allow for production to surge ahead without the possibility of a work stoppage. In other words, members of the NDMB worked to substitute workers' stinging strike weapon with the blunt poke of forced arbitration. As labor–management negotiations dragged on, workers would be required to work rather than wait for the outcome of the negotiation (and potentially influence it) from the vantage point of a picket line.

Eager to prove their leadership and patriotism to the nation, union leaders guaranteed that their members would stay on the job in the face of industrial conflict. But they could not follow through consistently. In June 1941 workers at North American Aviation in Inglewood, California, who produced approximately 20 percent of the military's airplanes, refused requests from the NMDB that they continue producing while board members attempted to resolve their conflict over wages. Roosevelt ordered the Army to operate the plant only after he got support to do so from leaders in the CIO and the UAW. Over 2,500 troops marched with bayonets and dispersed the striking picketers. In this case, war workers paid for CIO and AFL leaders' thirst for respectability with their dignity.

Twice when companies refused NDMB recommendations, the federal government seized plants, but overall the board did not strengthen workers' hand. Its decisions were not binding and its members were unable to involve themselves in conflicts directly until the Secretary of Labor informed them that they had authorization, creating time lags and bureaucratic confusion. Unfortunately for workers, the future of federal government involvement in their work lives would include such NDMB processes as the federal government's ability to remove workplace problem solving from workers' hands.

In the name of smooth war production, the NDMB took the bold move to support union security in war industries, but this too came at a price. Until union security provisions were put in effect, unions were fragile operations that fought year-to-year to keep their members. Union stewards, or leaders in each factory department, had to collect dues person-by-person each month. Union staff had to train new members, develop new leaders, and create ways of communicating with their members. Union security, however, allowed unions to include "maintenance of membership" clauses into their contracts, which allowed employees who were already members of unions to remain in those unions should their company change owners. The logic went that as long as unions provided stability to workplace relations they were a social good and their presence should be supported. Union leaders argued that if the union was going to be able to ensure wartime stability and no work stoppages occurred, they should represent all the workers in the industry. The War Labor Board would later adopt this maintenance of membership concept and agree to a dues check-off to further strengthen union security. The fledgling CIO organization, hurt by the 1937–1939 recession, desperately needed the membership numbers and dues stream. As such, they had little patience for "free riders" in the workplace, those workers in unionized workplaces who refused to join and pay dues. The problem for unions was that union reps were still obligated to bargain on their behalf, so free riders got the

overall benefit of the union without sharing the costs of maintaining it. As Robert Zieger explains in *The CIO, 1935–1955* (1995),
"Unionists drew an analogy between political citizenship and
industrial citizenship. The majority in the shop, like the majority
in a political unit, made choices in free elections that bound all.
Thus the union shop was necessary to extend real democracy
from the civic books into the nation's mills and shops."

With union security, however, came the promise that unions
would shift wartime workplace dynamics from spontaneous to
stable. Such sentiment was deepened when the AFL executive
council and increasing numbers of CIO unionists called for an
end to strikes in defense industries. No-strike pledges served
as patriotic gestures that unintentionally undermined union
power: without the right to call strikes, management could more
easily take advantage of workers' weakened state; and they
did. Rather than fight management, union leaders argued with
their members, served as disciplinarians, and tried to keep their
members in line.

By supporting no-strike pledges, moreover, labor's leaders
aligned themselves with anti-union conservatives in the military
and the government: patriotism became the umbrella under
which assaults against militancy and political free speech took
cover. When the CIO's Industrial Union of Marine and Shipbuilding Workers went on strike against a New Jersey firm, Representative Eugene Cox of Georgia labeled the strike "treason" and
Representative Clare E. Hoffman of Michigan put forward legislation that would make striking illegal in defense plants. In the face
of such charges, the New Jersey strike ended after two days.
Patriotic posturing painted all war-industry job actions as
un-American. Roosevelt, for his part, increased FBI surveillance
of labor unions.

In the meantime, divisions between AFL and CIO unionists
continued to fester. CIO drives in steel, auto, and meatpacking
awakened the AFL to the need to grow its numbers in mass
production industry before the CIO shut them out. AFL unions
had always included some semi- and unskilled workers but new
drives and commitment brought thousands of these workers into

such AFL unions as the machinists, meat cutters, restaurant employees, teamsters, and laborers. CIO unions, in the meantime, reached out to craft workers in their commitment to organize entire industries. Enormous and sometimes violent jurisdictional feuds between AFL-affiliated and CIO-affiliated unions occurred in electrical, paper, woodworking, aircraft, and food-processing industries. Which union should rightfully represent the workers in each industry? Should workers sign with AFL carpenters or CIO woodworkers? Bitter battles erupted, unions raided each other's memberships and crossed one another's picket lines. The public looked on in disgust.

AFL and CIO leaders also sparred over the National Labor Relations Board (NLRB), whose members had the power to determine the appropriate composition of bargaining units, oversee union elections, and rule on unfair labor practices. According to AFL leaders, the NLRB's system of determining which workers would be represented in a single local favored the CIO's industrial structure over craft unionism. They also attacked the NLRB's ruling that prevented AFL unions from signing agreements with employers before they won a majority of employees' support. Publicly attacking the NLRB, AFL leaders aligned with those anti-union forces in government and the business community who also sought the end of this overwhelmed but proindustrial union government agency. The CIO, for its part, tried to convince workers that the AFL negotiated sweetheart deals with employers that benefited the union leadership but not its members; that the AFL incorrectly, and underhandedly, painted most CIO activity as communist inspired; and, more generally, that the AFL embraced corruption.

In September and October 1941, AFL and CIO differences aired to a national audience. Lewis and the United Mine Workers of America (UMWA) shut down the "captive" mines – owned and operated by steel companies – and demanded a closed shop. The NDMB voted 9–2 against Lewis and the mineworkers. AFL board members George Meany and William Green were opposed to the government's granting closed-shop status, believing it a union principle that needed to be won through bargaining, not through government hand out. The two CIO board representatives who voted in support of Lewis, Philip Murray and Thomas Kennedy, both UMWA members, abruptly resigned from the board, killing it, and exposing the rifts that divided the AFL from the CIO.

In addition to these fundamental disagreements between the AFL and CIO that threatened the integrity of the labor movement were internal problems and divisions that lingered within the CIO. Throughout the mobilization period, the CIO's financial situation was precarious. Union drives were costly and unions did not collect dues until they negotiated contracts. Even then, stewards had to convince members of the value of paying their dues each time they came around to collect. Lewis and his UMWA bankrolled much of the organizing drives launched by CIO unions. In 1940, for example, UMWA supplied one third of the CIO's monthly dollars. This also meant that Lewis called the shots regarding which workers were worthy of his money and union support. Large sums supported affiliates whose lead organizers carried Communist Party membership cards. Later in life when Lewis was asked about the large number of communists on the CIO's payroll, he famously quipped, "Who gets the bird, the hunter or the dog?" Communist unionists were, as Lewis recognized, committed, uncompromising, and successful organizers. So while his decision to hire on a number of communists for organizers might be understood as a strategic move, the CIO's financial accounting largely depended on UMWA's fuzzy math.

Other divisions within the CIO centered around Lewis, who butted heads with Amalgamated Clothing Worker (ACW) head Sidney Hillman over CIO policy and US foreign policy. As the war escalated in Europe, Hillman aligned himself with Roosevelt and his foreign policy position believing that only a rapid US build up of military goods would defeat the Nazis. Hillman supported such government policies that promoted unhindered war production. Lewis, however, was antiwar and increasingly anti-Roosevelt and believed that Americans were being manipulated into supporting another unnecessary war. From his perspective, Roosevelt's war policies benefited capitalist profiteers at labor's expense. The two had words in the press and at labor gatherings.

81

In the 1940 election, with Hillman stumping for Roosevelt and Lewis for Republican candidate Wendell Willkie, the CIO endorsed no candidate.

UMWA leader John L. Lewis had been a Roosevelt supporter during the Depression, but as the president nudged away from neutrality and toward engagement, Lewis made a public break with him and ultimately with his CIO leadership position. His hubris got the best of him. On October 25, 1940, over the radio, when Lewis announced his support for Willkie, he pledged to step down as leader of the CIO if its members backed Roosevelt. A few days after Roosevelt's inauguration, Lewis kept his word and at the CIO convention turned the top spot of the federation over to his close ally, SWOC president, Philip Murray. Lewis was dictatorial, controlling, and central to the industrial union movement: his abdication as CIO president in 1940 dealt a blow to the organization.

Over the next year, Lewis's anger with the CIO and several of its leaders worsened. He attacked Hillman for his blind support of Roosevelt as well as what he perceived to be the weak policies Hillman backed as a member of NDAC. After all, Lewis pointed out, NDAC put forward labor policies without clear enforcement mechanisms and clear penalties. More generally, Lewis believed that Hillman and other CIO leaders collaborated with the federal government to undermine labor's freedom. Distancing himself even further from the CIO, Lewis sent the federation a bill for over $1.5 million for loans the UMWA had made to the CIO.

In the face of labor's lack of unity, business leaders and politicians increasingly demonstrated their anti-union sentiment. In the context of wartime mobilization, they focused their animus on unions' ability to disrupt production through striking. Business leaders attacked labor unrest as un-American and labor representation as unwelcome. Conservatives in Congress joined in, discussing legislation to weaken the Wagner Act and limit strike activity. Meanwhile, the Dies Committee opened investigations into communist infiltration into US society, with particular attention to the labor movement. Their logic implied that since strikes were un-American and communist inspired, then all unionists who led them must be reds, or at least pink, and worthy of being publicly exposed. Meanwhile, the Special Committee to investigate the National Labor Relations Board (the Smith Committee), chaired by Howard W. Smith of Virginia, attacked the operation of the NLRB.

As a result of mounting political pressure, Roosevelt appointed NLRB-critic and conservative Democrat William Leiserson to the board and instructed him to narrow its interpretation of the act. Roosevelt also refused to reappoint the NLRB's first chair, Warren Madden, a person who imagined great authority for the NLRB. Following widespread Republican congressional victories in 1938, Roosevelt, in need of conservative southern support for his initiatives, joined Congress's turn to the right. Even in the period of war mobilization, anti-unionists succeeded in slowing labor's march.

With conservatives' attention on union busting, they did not, however, halt activism among African Americans, which foreshadowed war and postwar militancy among this group of workers. As war mobilization extended into 1941, it became clear to African-American leaders that employers' discriminatory hiring practices and racially segmented workplaces would continue unless federal intervention made them stop. This was especially clear to the educated, charismatic, and well-spoken A. Philip Randolph, president of the Brotherhood of Sleeping Car Porters (BCSP), who the Attorney General of the United States once referred to as the "most dangerous Negro in America." Men such as Randolph had experienced the government's hypocrisy during World War I, when the nation's principles of democracy went unheeded in war industries at home. After that war, he continued to fight workplace discrimination without support from the federal government. In 1935, with the help of some industrial unions and the NAACP, Randolph forced the AFL to appoint the Committee of Five to Study Negro Discrimination in AFL affiliates. Their sessions publicized the pervasive character of racial discrimination in AFL unions.

Racist unions, however, were just part of the broken system Randolph hoped to repair. Entire defense industries were lily white and proud of it. In the South, where 17.6 percent of the total national defense budget was spent on defense-related industries, white southerners held firm to the principle that minorities were not capable of doing the same work that whites did; the closer a white southerner worked to a black person, the more degraded the former felt. Glenda Gilmore in *Defying Dixie: The Radical Roots of Civil Rights, 1919–1950* (2009) explains that "above all, Jim Crow rested on two fundamental beliefs: maintaining the 'integrity' of the white race and maintaining the southern labor system, which depended on a base of underpaid black labor to keep the wages down for all." Racism notoriously pervaded southern living, but it also thrived in other regions. In 1941, for example, a spokesperson from California's North American Aviation, an industry benefiting from war contracts, stated that African Americans would be hired only as janitors or in similar jobs. Racial exclusion from jobs created by government demand and paid for with government dollars raised Randolph and others' frustration levels to new heights. This time Randolph was determined to push for anti-discrimination policies from the president before the United States went to war, but Randolph's efforts to get Roosevelt to end discrimination in war work, and his meetings to discuss the matter, went nowhere.

So on a train ride south from another fruitless meeting with Roosevelt in Washington, DC, Randolph hatched a plan with a fellow BCSP member, Milton Webster, and consequently issued a "Call to Negro America" to march on Washington on July 1, 1941, if the president refused to give African Americans equal access to jobs in defense industries. Initially, Randolph estimated that 10,000 would march. How could black America fight fascism while living under Jim Crow conditions? In a short time, however, the March on Washington Movement (MOWM) brought together a broad national coalition of civil rights and religious groups with 36 local chapters whose members were ready to march. The swift and positive response from churches, NAACP chapters, and labor leaders pushed Randolph to increase his projection of marchers to 100,000 and send President Roosevelt a list of demands for laws that would end discrimination among government contractors, in defense training, the armed services, the federal government, and unions. On June 25, 1941, the MOWM won from Roosevelt executive order 8802, which required US defense contractors not to discriminate against workers due to race, creed, color, or national origin. On July 19 the president also established the Fair Employment Practices Committee (FEPC), a committee of seven including Milton Webster as one of two African-American representatives, charged with overseeing executive order 8802. Critics believed that the MOWM should have held out for more of their demands before calling off the march, but Randolph disagreed. His critics stewed but could not argue with the fact that the MOWM organized the first protest that put the federal government on record against racial discrimination in employment. The movement also spurred the creation of the FEPC, the first policy-making agency with black representation. "When the federal government condemned employment discrimination," Gilmore asserts, "it struck at the heart of white supremacy."

With meager staff and resources, and in the face of hostile conservative opposition, the FEPC's ability to enforce the order was limited – evasion was easy and epic – and the committee's jurisdiction did not extend beyond defense work. In 1943 it established a field office in Atlanta for southeastern District VII led by a native white Virginian who fought to find office space for his desegregated staff, stood up against a city council resolution that demanded the FEPC leave the city, and took on Senator Howard W. Smith of Virginia, who held hearings in an attempt to stall FEPC work and prove that the agency was overstepping its bounds. Investigating defense contractors and righting the wrongs of racism was an uphill battle and one that did not happen fully in the FEPC's short life (its authority ended on June 30, 1946).

The FEPC was authorized to do these things, but the organization lacked authority and resources. Working as a field examiner out of the Dallas FEPC office in 1943 and then as a director of the San Antonio office in 1944 and 1945, Carlos Castañeda observed the ways in which race prejudice and the treatment of

Mexicans as social inferiors led to their denial of equal rights and to what he referred to as the "destruction of the basic principles of democracy." Mexican oil workers on Texas's gulf coast, for example, faced hiring, wage, and job classification discrimination; it was not that Mexicans could not get jobs in the oil industry, it was just that when they did, it was as janitors, members of the cleaning crew, and assistants. The FEPC made little headway when CIO and independent workers' organizations stood by their racist contracts that limited the number of minorities who could be hired, the jobs they could be hired into, and the promotions they would receive. In Corpus Christi, Texas, the company Southern Alkali fought to maintain a Mexican-free workplace by instituting an English-language exam for its new hires and continuing workers. They would have liked to hire workers of Mexican heritage, Alkali's management contested, but their white workers just would not stand for it. Over two hundred workers of Mexican descent filed their complaints with Texas's FEPC between 1943 and 1945. They hailed from such war industries as food processing, shipbuilding, and oil refining; few saw relief.

Still, the fact of the order and the existence of the FEPC represented the federal government's new position on racism in the workplace; it would not be business as usual. FEPC members worked against employment discrimination practiced by such unions as the AFL's Boilermakers and the Iron Ship Builders and Helpers of America, in Portland, Oregon, and Los Angeles, California. In Detroit, UAW and black leaders succeeded in using an FEPC ruling to defuse tension that erupted when thousands of white workers walked off the job at the sight of newly upgraded African Americans. The FEPC also launched investigations and held hearings against employers. In some cases, such as in Fort Worth, Texas, airplane factories, FEPC members even got some help from all-white AFL unions whose officers relished the chance to challenge and showcase management's abuses. While the FEPC did not succeed in winning full compliance from either unions or employers, President Roosevelt's executive order and FEPC provided legitimacy and a focus to civil rights struggles at work.

The willingness of minority workers to fight for an upgraded place in war industries and the federal government's support of these efforts would lead to big demographic changes in employment in the years to come. In the summer of 1942, however, African Americans held only 5 percent of defense-related jobs. Women had yet to see openings. The government did not count the numbers of workers of Mexican descent; their presence was small. The fact that it was the job of a federal agency (and not labor unions themselves) to demand these changes is also telling. "General justice" would not be the experience of all war workers.

When bombs exploded in Pearl Harbor and the mobilization period rapidly came to a close, union membership in war industries had grown substantially and union leaders increasingly sat on federal boards. Rules outlining industrial production in war industries tied shop stewards' hands and removed workers' ability to act spontaneously. If employers violated any term of the contract, workers were committed to stay at work while legalistic machinery churned and attempted to resolve the problem. Productivity would not suffer – spontaneity, militancy, and a sense of solidarity would. At the same time, a growing resentment swelled in the business community and among anti-union politicians and the non-unionized public. Playing on fears of communist infiltration and "un-American" strike activity, the entire union movement was called into question.

Government Intervention: War Industries and Labor Policies, 1941–1945

Once the United States became an active combatant in World War II, the dynamics of the war mobilization period escalated. Federal wartime agencies reached deep into US households as they rationed such goods as sugar and gasoline, set prices for manufactured goods in order to help control inflation, controlled rent prices in cities where housing was short, coordinated military conscription, distributed propaganda, and built badly needed housing. With a more visible hand in industrial labor policies, the government recruited women and oversaw the hiring of African Americans, Mexicans, and Mexican Americans. The increased need for war production provided these new war workers with regular employment, overtime pay, and access to union representation.

The exigencies of war also meant that new federal agencies took over the job of overseeing management–labor relations, nudging the NLRB into the background. During the war years the NLRB continued to conduct union elections and investigate unfair labor practices, but cuts to its appropriations and Roosevelt's decision to shift wartime power to the newly charged National War Labor Board (NWLB), meant that the NLRB operated in the NWLB's shadow.

The NWLB's job was to get labor leaders and corporate executives to agree on the best path to a stabilized system of industrial production, or, plainly speaking, one that would keep labor's no-strike pledge lasting. Questions of union security and wage equity were its to hash out. To union leaders, the answer was clear: if they give up their right to strike, they should be guaranteed union, or closed shops. To corporate representatives, closed shops were pariahs, the first line of assault against management prerogatives and power, and therefore to be fought against with all weapons.

The NWLB continued NDMB traditions of supporting union security through maintenance of membership, believing that such provisions encouraged union members and leaders to act responsibly, cooperate with management, and abide by contracts' terms. They also extended their support for union security by backing dues check-off, which allowed unions to take dues monies directly out of workers' paychecks rather than requiring stewards to collect them in person every month from every member. NWLB advocates believed that union security gave union leaders an incentive to discipline wayward members who undermined smooth production systems and that management would respect the sanctity and permanence of unions.

As the NWLB helped to establish labor's permanence through union security provisions, they also undermined a union's ability

Figure 2.1 The 1944 send-off rally in Chicago for UPWA leaders going to Washington to pressure the National War Labor Board for a wage increase. Courtesy Hagley Museum, Herbert March.

to fight for better wages in the face of wartime inflation. Roosevelt himself gave speeches on the need for "equality of sacrifice" in the face of the war emergency, US deaths abroad, and inflationary concerns at home. Everyone would have to sacrifice, to give up something treasured, for the United States to mobilize fully and win the war. His administration sent a flurry of legislation to Congress to alleviate the surge of inflation the war emergency sparked – between January 1941 and May 1942 prices increased by 15 percent. The urgent request for agricultural subsidies, price controls, and tax increases required Congress to respond to the public's outcry. War workers' wages, however, fell out of Congress's purview and under the NWLB's authority, allowing its members to act on their own in their attempt to manage inflation. They did so in a policy created to deal with steelworkers, and then applied it more broadly to workers in other war industries.

The policy determined percentage wage increases for workers in various war industries, above which unions were not permitted to negotiate. Ultimately, it hurt war industry workers, undermining unions' chance to negotiate their members' wages at a time when the labor market was tight and union power was strong, handing that responsibility to the government. The complicated and problematic formula used to determine the percentage increase– known as the "little steel formula" – was conceived as a way to guarantee war workers' wage increases in the face of rising inflation. The hitch, however, was that the formula limited the possible wage increase of the steel union to a low percentage, and the cap was then applied to all wartime workers. Unions could get around the formula by negotiating fringe benefits –paid holidays, vacations, travel, incentive pay, bonuses, shift differentials – which they did. Still, union leaders pointed out, in normal times they would be able to strike for higher percentage increases; the wartime no-strike pledge, however, tied their hands. No caps were put in place to limit corporate profit, which grew exponentially during the war and might have been more fairly shared with war workers. Union leaders also used the government's own patriotic language against them; the little steel formula undermined the notion of "equality of sacrifice" when only union members sacrificed high pay as corporate America raked in profits. Their logic was strong, but it was to no avail.

The only labor leader to challenge this hardening system of stabilized labor–management relations directly was John L. Lewis, who led half a million miners of soft coal out of work in the spring of 1943 in a series of massive strikes. In congressional hearings Lewis vowed to fight for his underpaid members who died at the rate of 2,000 per year and who were injured at the rate of 270 a day in the context of speeded wartime production. The NWLB ultimately granted mineworkers a significant wage increase, but Lewis's leadership model did not influence fellow labor leaders.

AFL and CIO leaders grew increasingly frustrated by NLRB rulings that limited their power and authority, but they were not willing to jeopardize their new positions on federal boards or to appear unpatriotic. Once Hitler broke his pact with Stalin and invaded the Soviet Union in June 1941, most communist unionists joined AFL and CIO leaders in their support of the no-strike pledge and continuous wartime production. When Lewis flaunted his refusal to support the no-strike pledge, the AFL and CIO expressed dismay. The communist newspaper *The Daily Worker* charged Lewis with going to war against Roosevelt instead of Hitler. Maintenance of membership was too valuable to throw away by violating no-strike pledges. In addition, under the watchful eye of the federal government and in the context of a popular war, union leaders were able to negotiate some of the best contracts to date. As they ran larger, richer, and federally protected unions, the groups' leaders became increasingly invested in protecting their place in the web of what Nelson Lichtenstein in *Labor's War at Home: The CIO in World War II* (1997) terms "a Rooseveltian political consensus." Many union leaders became increasingly removed from the interests of their members.

While union leaders committed not to strike for the duration of the war, union members were not as willing. The number of unauthorized "wildcat" strikes increased as the war progressed. Whereas 1942 saw 2,970 strikes involving 840,000 workers, 3,700 strikes in 1943 included 1.98 million workers, in 1944 5,000 strikes involved 2 million workers, and in 1945 nearly 3.5 million workers walked off the job. Often these walkouts were spontaneous and short, lasting a few days. More than half of them occurred in rubber industries and the converted auto plants where more than half of all workers took part in wartime strikes in 1944 and 1945. A fifth of workers went on strike yearly in steel and shipbuilding factories and about 5 percent did so in textile and electrical machinery plants. While AFL unionists did not do so as often as those in the CIO, they continued to protest wartime conditions by walking off the job.

Once workers walked off the job, it was the duty of stewards, local officers, and ultimately the national union to cajole them back to work. In effect, the workers' direct action put their union's security at risk. Wartime employers pressured NWLB members: If national unions could not guarantee continuous production, why should they have union security?

The truth is that most union members did not want to undermine their union, but short, direct actions were the only way for them to exert their power at work. Working through the NWLB took too much time. In 1943 and 1944, NWLB members received over ten thousand grievances a month. In addition to having to rule on them, NWLB members also had to negotiate conflicts over wage differentials and other contract demands. Resolution of these matters could take over a year. Workers' direct action, however, was immediate and generally channeled their frustration into productive ends.

Workers in Armour's hog kill department demonstrated this in 1944 when they shut down the hog kill two hours shy of break time. The shut down, called by union stewards, happened because the company removed a union ballot box used for a steward's election in the hog kill. Workers would have voted in their meeting hall, but long wartime hours made that difficult. After three emergency grievance meetings that day had failed to win management over, the hog shacklers stopped work at their steward's behest. When together they returned to the floor 36 minutes later, the killing gang refused to handle the hogs, which then all spoiled on the line. In the end the workers stopped company interference with union elections in the plant.

On the face of it, this episode suggests that Armour's union stewards opposed the no-strike pledge, but this was not the case. In fact, several Amour leaders were members of the Communist Party who heartily supported full wartime production in support of those bent on defeating Nazi Germany. At the same time, these local leaders realized that if they did not act in their members' interest, small, departmental conflicts might explode into larger ones. Publicly, union leaders supported the wartime no-strike pledge, but as director of the United Packinghouse Workers District 1 and Communist Party member Herb March recalled, "if you got an obstinate management, and they won't do anything, the guys are understaffed, they want to get the production out, they start giving the guys hell – and . . . [the workers] wouldn't take it." To such union leaders as March, pragmatic action trumped wartime policy. So when International Packing House Union President Lewis J. Clark sent word to local unions to discipline their striking workers, no action ensued.

Such flouting of the rules was not always union practice and the UAW's international leaders took the no-strike pledge more to heart. This was especially the case in 1943 when the NWLB denied maintenance of membership to the Chrysler unions because local officials did not enforce the pledge adamantly enough. Swooping in to maintain their union security provisions, international executive board members directly investigated local job actions (taking the task away from local officers) and imposed discipline against direct-action-savvy workers and their union leaders. The International ended unsanctioned strikes in three different locals by unilaterally removing their democratically elected union officers and appointing officials who agreed to back the no-strike pledge. In this case, and others like it, the no-strike pledge exacerbated the fact that international unions were now enmeshed in federal bureaucracy. For a time UPWA officials balanced war pressures with the spirit of industrial unionism, but the demands placed on international unions by the federal government would make such balancing acts difficult to continue for long.

Wartime Demographic Developments

Government wartime measures caused dramatic changes in the demographics of work. The nation's pledge to fight against Nazi racism and authoritarian rule emboldened African Americans' fight for civil rights, dignity, and jobs. In February 1942 the *Pittsburgh Courier* launched the Double V Campaign; "The first V is for victory over our enemies from without, the second V for victory over our enemies within." African-American newspapers popularized black leaders' two-pronged fight against enemies of democracy abroad and threats to racial equality within. The fight against discrimination was one that all Americans should embrace, the paper read, because "We are Americans, too."

One front of the domestic war against discrimination was in defense industries, where African-American workers made significant inroads. By 1944, 1.25 million black workers (300,000 of them women) were industrial workers, an increase from 1940 of 150 percent. Their 1944 numbers in war industries were triple what they had been in 1942, with particular strongholds (5–13 percent of workers) in aircraft, military vehicles, shipbuilding, steel, and munitions. Unprecedented numbers, moreover, joined CIO unions; of four million CIO members at the height of the war industries, African-American unionists comprised 7.7 percent of the total, 300,000 members. The UAW took the lead with 100,000 African-American members, followed by the USWA with 70,000 African-American members.

Behind these numbers is a story of struggle; black workers had to fight for good war jobs as well as union representation. Building off of the MOWM, African-American workers mobilized protests and strikes to demand their place in defense industries. Their willingness to walk out of Detroit's Chrysler and Dodge plants in the summer of 1941, for example, convinced the UAW to support African-American workers' rights to department transfers and job upgrades. Three thousand black unionists also struck against Ford in 1943 for better job opportunities. Remarkably, such activity was not exclusive to the North. In Winston-Salem, North Carolina, for example, black workers led a strike against R. J. Reynolds Tobacco Company, forcing management to the bargaining table. In Memphis, communist-influenced United Cannery, Agricultural, Packing and Allied Workers of America (UCAPAWA) and the National Maritime Union led a spirited biracial union campaign, and in Birmingham, Alabama, a black majority of Mine, Mill unionists stood up for workplace rights. The International Longshore and Warehouse Union in San Francisco helped develop a network of activists committed to progressive racial politics, and in Baltimore, CIO unions backed black workers' rights in shipyards, steel mills, and electrical factories.

Mexican and Mexican-American workers, like their African-American counterparts, were also emboldened by wartime rhetoric that emphasized the morality of justice and democracy. And like the Double Victory campaign backed in the African-American community, Mexican activists, such as José de la Luz Sánenz, a founder of the League of United Latin American Citizens (LULAC), a Mexican middle-class civil rights organization that advocated for the rights of working people, connected the dots between the government's wartime democratic language and Mexican-Americans' call for equal rights. In the newspaper articles he penned, de la Luz Sánenz made the point clear: fighting Nazis around the world necessitated bringing democracy to people of Mexican descent. The International Union of Mine, Mill, and Smelter Workers of America agreed and integrated wartime declarations for democracy into their fight for equal rights.

As soldiers left the country to deploy for war and war industries searched for workers, Mexicans and Mexican Americans took their fight for dignity into the war industries of oil, garment, meatpacking, construction, and transportation. Still, discrimination slowed their movement out of agriculture and unskilled work and into semi-skilled and skilled wartime industrial work. In urban areas Mexican workers' ability to achieve upward mobility paled in comparison to African-Americans' achievements.

Slowing Mexican and Mexican-Americans' movement to better-paying jobs were farm owners who worked with state and federal agencies to regulate farm workers' mobility and keep them in agriculture. Sometimes this meant farmers wishing to leave farm work for industry would need to carry a clearance slip from the government indicating that they had authorization to leave; sometimes the government simply delayed gas or rubber allotments to families so they could not drive out of the region and to better jobs. Reaching out to Mexican immigrants at the war's start, the US government offered them temporary working papers for the war crisis if they would labor in US fields. This so-called Bracero program annually brought between 40,000 and 60,000 Mexican workers to US farms, and that is where farm owners and the government wanted them to stay. Another factor retarding job mobility was the fact that defense industry employers turned to white women first and only to black and Mexican male workers when their other options dried up. Minority women were even lower on the priority list of hiring in war industries. Their war industry job prospects never matched those of their male peers, let alone those of white women.

Not everyone in war industries was thrilled with the encroachment of African-American and Mexican-American workers. Sometimes, in both AFL and CIO affiliates, white and white ethnic workers participated in "hate strikes" and walked off the job when forced to work with workers of color. In Mobile, Alabama, whites assaulted black co-workers with pipes, clubs, and other weapons in response to twelve African-American workers getting upgrades to work as welders in response to an FEPC order. International Longshore and Warehouse Union and United Steel Workers members protected the use of their hiring halls to keep minority workers out of desirable jobs. Meanwhile, 31 AFL affiliates and most of the independent railroad brotherhoods refused to allow African Americans to become members. Other affiliates set up subsidiary locals that allowed black members the privilege of paying dues but disallowed them from voting. The Boilermakers and the Machinists, two of the largest AFL unions involved in military production, were among the most racist of the federation. Wartime racism in the workplace peaked when 25,000 white workers walked off the job at a Detroit, Michigan, Packard aircraft engine shop in 1943.

Certainly some of this racial conflict was motivated by whites' fear that minorities would undermine white workers' economic dominance. At the same time, with white women increasingly visible in traditionally male workplaces, some violence was perpetrated in white male workers' attempt to control access to white women.

Working-class racism extended from the shop floor into communities and formal political arenas. The federal government sent the National Guard to Detroit to protect the Sojourner Truth Housing Project's new black residents. Built in an attempt to alleviate Detroit's desperate wartime housing crisis, the project provoked racial controversy from the outset. Once completed, African Americans proved willing to take the government up on its promise for decent housing, even if it meant moving into an all-white neighborhood. Their decision to do so unleashed white mob brutality and racial tension. Similar racial violence was unleashed in June 1943 when fifty sailors stationed at the Naval Reserve Training School in Los Angeles pursued young Mexican Americans through a largely Mexican-American neighborhood that lay between the school and downtown, beat them, and stripped them of their "zoot suits," an ethnic fashion character-ized by wide-legged, tight-cuffed pants and long coats with wide lapels and padded shoulders. The result was more than a week of rioting as thousands more military personnel from area bases joined in the frenzied pursuit and beating of the so-called zoot suiters. The year 1943 was one when racial violence peaked; 47 cities experienced 240 racial incidents.

Such working-class racism had important political conse-quences in the urban North where white neighborhood associa-tions flourished. In Detroit, white working-class citizens went to voting booths and in 1945 (and again in 1949) defeated UAW candidates in place of segregationist Democrats and conservative Republicans. Such rank-and-file racism has caused some his-torians to question the potential for interracial working-class unity.

Whereas AFL affiliates and some CIO unionists brazenly embraced their racial exclusivity, CIO union organizers and their leaders were at least publicly committed to industrial, interracial unionism and willingly challenged their members to do better. Diffusing racially tense environments, CIO unions could also become vehicles for racial empowerment. In unions such as the United Packinghouse Workers of America, for example, African Americans used the structure of the union and the pressure of war production to open employment to African Americans, turn back racist shop-floor practices, and challenge manage-ment's authority. In 1943 African-American UAW men struck to get black women hired in departments outside the foundry,

97

such as sewing rooms; and CIO unionists and the black community of Winston-Salem, North Carolina, built a dynamic civil rights movement led by the left which focused on economic equality. In Los Angeles, moreover, the United Cannery, Agricultural, Packing and Allied Workers of America (UCAPAWA) became a force for bringing union rights to ethnic workplaces in the region. UCAPAWA's vice-president was the charismatic Luisa Morena, a Guatemalan-born activist who was only 34 when the United States joined the war. Coming to the union after years organizing for the AFL and then the CIO in Florida and Pennsylvania, Morena was a gifted public speaker in Spanish and English; she built local union organizations as democratic units rooted in the networks that women workers created in the plants. In building the second largest local in UCAPAWA, Local 3, Morena groomed Mexican women to play leading roles as officers, executive board members, and contract negotiators. As it turned out, their contracts were among some of the CIO's most fruitful, including free legal advice and hospitalization.

In less hospitable work environments, CIO organizers navigated tense race relations by talking up the union's fight for economic power rather than cheering racial justice. In Louisiana's sugar industry, CIO unionists succeeded in narrowing wage gaps between the North and the South and within Louisiana. This economic success paved the way for black and white workers to cooperate in locals, on local executive boards, and in daily struggles. Still, such union organizing failed to break down rigid racial and gender job segregation, and white racism kept social events lily white. Clearly, biracial unionism often had a tenuous nature. Still, the power of CIO unionists' interracial vision caused them to push for inclusion. With economic gains, white racists did not become multiculturalists, but they did share their workplace with minority workers in new and egalitarian ways.

Yet neither AFL nor CIO union leaders were committed to improving the status of women war workers, even though they did make gestures in that direction. In 1944, for example, the AFL's annual convention called for the organization of women workers. As early as 1942, the Machinists, Teamsters, Carpenters, Foundry Workers, and Shipbuilders opened their membership to women. Plumbers and Steamfitters followed suit at the direct order of their national leaders. The UAW, moreover, set up a women's bureau in 1944 to address special issues that women union members faced such as daycare, work conditions, and hostility faced from male managers and co-workers.

Even more than AFL and CIO union leaders, government wartime propaganda painted a rosy employment picture, targeting a white, female, middle-class audience and asking these women to sacrifice the niceties of middle-class living and tough it out in the world of work. These "Rosie the Riveters" were assured such jobs would be safe and similar to work done at home. Most important, they were told, war work was temporary. In reality, most women who went to work in war industries and in wartime business offices did so because they needed to work and these were the best-paying jobs. The majority of women war workers came from waitressing, domestic service, and other ghettos of women's employment. By the end of 1942, federal funds allowed public daycare centers to open to working mothers' children and while the number of centers was inadequate to meet the challenge, by war's end, over 3,100 centers gave care to 1.5 million children. In defense industries, women flocked to trade unions, participated as stewards and union officers, and developed a movement for labor reform; they were comfortably settling in to new jobs and union positions.

However, most male workers and their male union representatives believed women were only temporary workers to be tolerated in the wartime crisis. Men viewed women workers as interlopers who interfered with male work cultures. Carolyn Miller, a Ford worker docked pay for wearing red pants and allegedly distracting her male co-workers, felt the sting of employers' attempts to control sexuality through wartime uniforms. Women were still largely viewed as secondary workers without equal rights to employment. Shipyard employers in Mobile, Alabama, happily hired white women rather than African-American

Figure 2.2 Josephine Ledesma, airplane mechanic instructor, Randolph Field, San Antonio, 1941. Voices Oral History Project, University of Texas at Austin.

men because they believed women in the workplace was a temporary solution. African-American workers, they feared, would permanently subvert the social order.

Questions of equal pay for equal work and seniority hinted at most unions' lack of true commitment to women as workers. The UAW's wartime president, R. J. Thomas, only supported equal pay for women for cynical reasons. Such a policy, he believed, would protect men from managers who attempted to use women's lower wages as the measure of fair compensation for men. One might expect managers to pit women workers against male workers in war industries, and they did. What was surprising, however, was that the UAW's wartime contracts actually enforced it. UAW union agreements refused seniority to married women, assuming that they were well supported and most deserving of firing in the event of layoffs. One local contract had a provision that stated that when a man transferred to a woman's job he would keep the male rate of pay, but when a woman went to a male job, she kept women's pay. The racially progressive UPWA turned a similarly blind eye when it came to its women members. Unlike the UAW, the UPWA had no women's bureau or commitment to women activists and shunted its female members into a sex-segregated seniority system and a dual-wage system – women got paid at inferior rates than men.

A few unions went against the tide and committed to women. The United Electrical, Radio and Machine Workers of America (UE), with a female membership of 40 percent, hired women into one third of its national staff positions and filed winning cases with the NWLB against General Electric and Westinghouse for paying women less than men for the same work. Half of the stewards in the Morena-led UCAPAWA (renamed the Food, Tobacco, Agricultural, and Allied Workers in 1944) were women. With a strong female leadership and membership base, the union signed contracts supporting equal pay for equal work as well as leaves of absence, which women could take for pregnancy, without losing their seniority. Most industrial unions were not as progressive as these, but good union models had the potential to inspire others and gave women in those other unions goals worth fighting for.

Whether or not their unions backed them, increasing numbers of what historian Dorothy Cobble calls "labor feminists" emerged throughout the 1940s. These female union supporters and members prioritized working-class women's needs and worked to stop the sex-based disadvantages that hindered them. Some held influential national union offices or served in government positions. Others held secondary positions of leadership as local union leaders and representatives to district councils, as business agents, and in staff positions. Because of AFL unionists' hostility toward women workers, most of these women found their calling in CIO unions, but not always. Labor feminists worked through the Amalgamated Clothing Workers of America (ACWA), the UPWA, the International Union of Electrical Workers (IUE), the research department of the CIO, the Communications Workers

101

of America (CWA), the ILGWU, the UAW, the UE and the Food, Tobacco, Agricultural, and Allied Workers Union of America (FTA). Women could not rely on their union brothers to push their fight forward; wartime contradictions pushed labor feminists to the fore.

Bessie Abramowitz Hillman, a Jewish Russian immigrant who sewed buttons on garments in a Chicago factory as a young girl, was the first woman appointed to the ACWA's General Executive Board and a labor feminist. Having been politically schooled by Jane Addams and the women of Hull House, Hillman and labor feminists like her understood the importance of developing and maintaining female networks to advocate on behalf of working women. Her networks extended into the national Women's Bureau and the Women's Trade Union League, through the White House to Eleanor Roosevelt, and into the offices of such civil rights leaders as A. Philip Randolph. In her role as ACWA leader, Hillman championed civil rights, workers' education, and child welfare.

Such labor feminists as Hillman wanted working women to be treated with as much dignity and value as working men, which meant that they sometimes advocated for policies that gave women special treatment. Some argued that it was contradictory to call for equal rights and then demand ones different to those that men received. Hillman, and labor feminists like her, did not see it that way. Instead, they made distinctions between sex-based practices that hurt women and those that did not. "At times the route to equality was through differential treatment," writes Cobble in *The Other Women's Movement: Workplace Justice and Social Rights in Modern America* (Princeton: Princeton University Press, 2004); "at other times the path lay through rejecting such practices." Their focus was on redefining certain men's jobs as female or dissolving boundaries between men and women's work to expand women's work, but not necessarily ending the practice of dividing jobs into women's and men's.

Labor feminists from such unions with large proportions of women members as the ACWA, UE, IUE, and CWA put political muscle behind equal-pay efforts at the state and federal level.

Some equal-pay supporters believed that the policy would maintain men's earning power and traditional gender roles. But, for most supporters, equal pay was about fairness and women's ability to support themselves and their dependents. For many women, the injustice of doing men's work for half the pay was too much. In 1942 the War Labor Board passed General Order 16, which allowed unions to make claims for wage increases on the basis of equal pay for equal work. Subsequent board rulings favored the principle and legitimized the idea, but each case had to be taken up by a union and fought through the federal bureaucratic machinery. Despite General Order 16, many women continued to work for unequal pay.

Labor feminists broadened equal pay to the idea of comparable worth. Equal pay for equal work applied to a small number of women doing men's work, but not for the women in low-paying women's jobs. During the war, women unionists resorted to sitdowns and other direct actions to get pay rates adjusted based on equity. They also worked with women's bureau staff to pressure unions to push forward pay equity adjustments allowed under the WLB. Beginning in the early 1940s, UE women filed grievances and organized conferences around wage equity; they also went on strike and filed lawsuits. In 1945 the UE won a landmark case whereby the WLB sided with the union's call for equal pay for equal work, an end to sex differentials in wages, and the end to "women's" jobs. The problem, of course, was the victory came in 1945, just in time for the war's end and the return of male soldiers who expected to take back their industrial jobs from women workers. Union solidarity was about to be tested.

Crisis in Industrial Relations, 1945–1946

As soon as the war ended in August 1945, a new battle brewed over labor's continuing role in shaping the nation's economic, social, and political priorities. On the one side stood labor's representatives, newly emboldened by their federal wartime roles and responsibilities, the growth in their membership, and the resources in their treasuries. On the other side stood the business and anti-union community of vocal citizens who waited with great anticipation for the war's end, so they could rid themselves of government meddling and unions. CIO leaders hoped to expand the model of tripartite leadership that oversaw wartime labor relations, continue maintenance of membership agreements, and implement a reconversion plan that included government's ability to control price increases. Government price controls would slow inflation as real wages increased, insuring workers' prosperity into the future. The thought of such a plan made corporate leaders seethe with anger. The country's new president, Harry S. Truman, who found comfort among conservative Democrats, called a conference in November 1945 in which labor and management's fundamentally different ideas of the postwar economy and power were aired. The meeting ended inconclusively and previewed the battle ahead.

The public, not privy to the meeting's deliberations, got their own taste of the tensions that had built between management and labor at the war's end as industrial warfare spread across the country; pent-up frustrations from wartime restrictions bubbled over in militant displays of working-class solidarity. In 1945, 35 percent of US workers – 14.5 million people – belonged to unions. Entire sectors, including the industrial and transport industries, had representation, and working people agreed that they had had enough of the wartime no-strike pledge stranglehold. Their concern with reconversion to peacetime production, potential unemployment, depressed wages, and inflation encouraged them to support their union representatives, who called strikes in unprecedented numbers. CIO union strikes were large: 200,000 autoworkers, 300,000 meatpacking workers, 180,000 electrical workers, 750,000 steelworkers. And CIO unionists were not alone: the International Longshoremen's Association shut down East Coast ports for 19 days; AFL Machinists and lumber workers also refused to work. In Stamford, Connecticut; Lancaster, Pennsylvania; Houston, Texas; and Rochester, New York, rallies and strikes involved thousands of AFL and CIO members and labor supporters city-wide. In May 1946, railroad workers and soft-coal

Figure 2.3 John L. Lewis of the United Mine Workers and David Dubinsky of the International Ladies Garment Workers' Union converse at President Truman's Labor–Management Conference, October 1945. Kheel Center for Labor–Management Documentation and Archives, M. P. Catherwood Library, Cornell University (#5780PB18F4A).

miners walked off the job in the face of President Truman's threats to draft them into the military and his call for antistrike legislation.

While reconversion's uncertainty convinced many to strike, the central concern driving workers out of their worksite and into this strike wave was wages. Unlike strikes of the 1930s that called for union recognition, these postwar actions were premised on labor unions' permanent place at the table. Rather than call out goon squads and private police forces to terrorize striking workers with machine guns and bayonets, as in the past, employers turned to court injunctions and the press to sway the public.

Unionists were not criminals; they were asserting rights of citizenship, and they were here to stay. The question, however, was how much of a corporation's income could workers force from the hands of their employers.

Wartime profits were huge. One commentator calculated that war contracts allowed eight steel companies to more than double their 1939 profits in just one year; the United States had not even entered the war yet. In another case, the press reported on an aircraft company that in 1940 took in $5 million in profit in just a three-month period. Kim Voss in *Hard Work: Remaking the American Labor Movement* (2004) estimates that during the war, war industries saw 250 percent profit increases above prewar levels.

Certainly, many believed big business could afford to pay higher wages. To not do so, thought some, employers would establish threatening precedents. One *New Republic* writer wrote in "Labor and Defense" (February 17, 1941), "Today, when profits are swollen by defense contracts...we believe that a rise in labor's share of the national income is urgently required if the distribution of the national income is not to be become dangerously top-heavy." These concerns of threatening income disparity were common in the 1940s and 1950s, when Americans saw causation between Hitler's rise to power and widespread economic vulnerability among masses of Germany's people. Some believed that too few rich and too many poor was a recipe for a weakened citizenry and the rise of fascism.

Labor leaders, such as the CIO's Phillip Murray and the UAW's Walter Reuther, agreed that workers should be involved in production decisions: these were the choices that shaped the pace and character of workers' everyday life. They also argued that wage increases should be an important piece of labor's postwar fight. For his part, Murray wanted a broad CIO wage policy that would rationalize compensation across core manufacturing industries. Reuther took that idea a step further. Rather than argue for a wage policy in narrow terms – how wages would affect the workers who would earn them – Reuther argued that wage increases should be connected to overall economic activity for the public's good. Enormous wartime profits, he argued, would allow General Motors to raise their workers' pay by 30 percent without having to increase the price of their cars. If the price of cars remained flat but workers' pay increased, then workers would have more purchasing power. Since the dollars in their pockets would be able to go farther, working Americans would be apt to consume even more products. Demand for more products would mean boosted factory orders and full employment. Increased wages for working Americans would mean a stronger US economy and general prosperity.

At its heart, Reuther's plan was the boldest of the bunch. When it was lost so was hope that labor would see rising wages *and* the ability to hold down consumer prices. The belief that GM could afford both (wage increases and no price increases) convinced Reuther to push hard. In case GM representatives argued that they could not afford Reuther's proposal, he challenged them to open their books to the public to prove it. Claiming that they did not even open their books to stockholders, GM leaders refused, so on November 21, 1945, UAW workers shut down 92 plants in 50 cities. In January, a fact-finding committee appointed by Truman reported that the cost of living had increased by one third since 1941 and recommended that GM agree to an hourly wage increase that would cover half of that, which amounted to about 19.5 cents an hour for the average GM worker. GM refused to agree until it was authorized to increase car prices, which it ultimately was allowed to do. In the meantime, electrical, packinghouse, and steelworkers demanded the same wage deal (offset by inflated prices). The Office of Price Administration ultimately folded and authorized companies to raise prices on consumer goods. Only then did corporate representatives agree to settle national agreements, which set patterns for contract benefits in these four industries.

Business leaders understood that this strike wave required them to act decisively. It was one thing in a war crisis to accept tripartite arrangements and to tolerate union representation on federal planning boards; after all, union representatives were few and they were not even present on the most powerful agencies.

Moreover, wartime profits were large enough to distract from the nuisance of unions in times of crisis. But just as unionists looked forward to throwing off the no-strike pledge, business leaders looked forward to ridding themselves of union oversight. In the postwar world, they wanted back in the driver's seat, alone, and they wanted to reclaim their right to manage unilaterally.

When the dust of the 1945–1946 strike wave settled, industrial management emerged victorious. In exchange for wage increases, which consumers would pay for in the form of higher prices on consumer items, business leaders inserted telling new provisions into their labor contracts. One UAW contract with Ford outlined the rights of management to plan production and the responsibility of union leaders to discipline unruly members who did not follow management's plan. Workers' wage increases cost unions in the court of public opinion: companies made it clear to consumers that unions were to blame for higher prices. Unionists also paid for their wage increases with less power to determine which direction companies would take in the future, authority that would have proved useful in upcoming decades.

Postwar Politics and Taft-Hartley, 1946–1948

The postwar strike wave also stirred anger and resentment throughout the halls of Congress and in the White House. After Roosevelt's death in August 1945, Truman's support of conservative Democrats and his frustration with strike behavior did not serve unionists well. Truman needed labor support so he vetoed such anti-labor legislation as the Case Bill, which limited the powers of the NLRB and workers' right to strike. But he also wanted the public and his conservative congressional critics to be clear that he was no labor coddler. In the 1946 miner's strike, Truman put the mines under government control. When they reverted to private hands and labor once again reached an impasse with management, Truman obtained a federal court injunction stopping the miner's strike. Meanwhile, the 1946 congressional elections established Republican control of both houses, and conservative Democrats joined them in denouncing union power. For almost a decade, anti-union lobbyists and their congressional representatives had been discussing ways to limit the Wagner Act. Now with their numerical advantage assured, anti-union members of Congress were able to push forward.

The 1947 Labor Management Relations Act, known as Taft-Hartley for its sponsors Senator Robert Taft and Representative Fred A. Hartley, redefined the relationship between labor and management and between workers and unions in ways that were detrimental to the most democratic unions and the power of all workers in the workplace. Lewis called the law "the first ugly thrust of fascism in America." Whereas the Wagner Act explicitly gave federal support to collective bargaining, the Taft-Hartley Act redirected the government's protections. Under Taft-Hartley, the government would act as a neutral body that would oversee employers' rights to resist unions as well as employees' rights to gain them. In the name of neutrality, employers would have the right to turn workers against unions, and union shops would be subject to referenda to ensure that workers were not being bullied into joining the union.

The assumptions that underlay Taft-Hartley were those that had been discussed in business boardrooms, chambers of commerce, and conservative political offices since 1935. Labor unions were rackets with unfair advantages and coercive powers that included the strike, business leaders argued. They asserted that workers, employers, and the public were victims of their excesses, and unions, especially CIO unions, were infiltrated by communist traitors, whose loyalties lay with Moscow. Employers were sure that, once talked to, no worker would *really* want to pay his or her hard-earned money to a union. In the name of liberty, they argued, the worker should not have to. Taft-Hartley gave employers their chance to prove their convictions had merit.

The law's provisions revealed the pickle that labor had gotten itself into: government meddling in industrial relations might have raised concern to the most militant during the war, but at least it ensured labor's security and place at the policy-making table. In the postwar period, however, government interference was about to get downright menacing for all union members. One of Taft-Hartley's biggest blows came in outlawing mass picketing and sympathy strikes or secondary boycotts. A sympathy strike or secondary boycott occurs when workers take action against any person or company who is not their direct employer, and before Taft-Hartley it was a powerful way for unionized workers to show their support and solidarity with one another. If construction workers found that their building owner was contracting out to non-union electricians, plumbers, or janitors, for example, the construction workers could go on strike to pressure that owner to pay union wages and offer union jobs. Taking that power and ability to demonstrate class solidarity away from unionists weakened their collective force.

And that was not all. According to Taft-Hartley, closed shops (where in workers would be hired only from among union members) would be no more. According to the courts, closed shops forced employers to "discriminate" against non-union workers. In maritime and printing industries this part of the law created particular disruption. In New York, newspaper owners who had not been opposed to closed shops now agreed to restore them only when the "law permits." In maritime unions, union-run hiring halls provided union workers to employers, this to supplant the pre-New Deal era system – a daily humiliation that played out on the docks, where in bribes, kickbacks, and foremen's demeaning physical exams determined who worked and who did not. Now two trial judges ruled that hiring halls constituted illegal closed shops under Taft-Hartley. Basic protections were under siege.

Taft-Hartley also overrode the country's custom whereby federal laws take precedence over state laws. According to the law, as long as state statutes go farther than Taft-Hartley in prohibiting "agreements requiring membership in a labor organization as a condition of employment," states were permitted to rule. This open invitation found twenty takers from Arizona to Maine who passed "little Taft-Hartley" acts throughout the country with some provisions more restrictive to labor than the original, including laws prohibiting striking and picketing, laws requiring all kinds of financial disclosures, and "right to work" laws. These right to work laws were (and are) particularly damaging to unions because they made membership voluntary for workers; and while "voluntary" sounds like a democratic principle, it actually worked the opposite way when it came to bettering workers' overall conditions. Even in "right to work" states, union contracts benefited all workers in a workplace (and, more generally, a region); and once a union had a contract with an employer, they were required to represent all of the workers in their bargaining unit, whether they were a member or not. But, only union members footed the bill for this benefit; non-members, or free riders, got all the benefits with none of the sacrifice. So while unions worked on behalf of all workers in a bargaining unit, individuals in right to work states could opt out of paying their dues and undermine the front of solidarity that unions relied upon. On the one hand, then, these right to work laws defended the rights of workers who do not want to join unions, including protecting individuals' rights to job opportunities in unionized workplaces. On the other, however, they limited the union's power to better the conditions for workers more generally. Without dues from those who opted out, how would unions pay organizers, develop organizing materials, and effectively educate potential members about their function? Underfunded and under siege, unions gave up on entire regions of the country, and workers faced employers union-free.

The federal law tied labor down in other ways. It ruled that supervisors could no longer form unions, and it forbade federal employees from striking. It authorized the president to issue an 80-day injunction if a strike represented a national emergency on the assumption that workers struck impulsively and irresponsibly. At the same time, it gave employers broad rights to free speech when addressing their employees regarding unions, and judges broad authority to issue antistrike injunctions. Anti-labor assumptions – maybe unions were running a racket after all; did not unions coerce workers? Are not most strikes irrational and unreasonable? – slanted media coverage and won the day.

The legal and bureaucratic nature of the legislation gave new life to the field of labor law. The NLRB was now the tool for decertification elections and would only provide its services to unions that required every officer, from the local on upward, to sign and file an affidavit that promised they were not members of the Communist Party. Tools to challenge unions were sharp and multiplying.

Against the pleas of Senators Robert Wagner and John F. Kennedy, Taft-Hartley passed both the House and Senate with large majorities. Truman vetoed the bill, arguing that it stuck the government into what should be a private and voluntary negotiation between workers and their employers, would fan the flames of class warfare and increase communist influence in unions, and weaken unions and punish the majority for the crimes of a minority. While the president's message was strong and hit the notes that most labor supporters wanted to hear, both Houses of Congress overrode his veto. Truman knew they would, and according to Melvyn Dubofsky in *The State and Labor in Modern America* (2004), this was a result that Truman may have even wanted. He had been on record as speaking against labor's power; his veto, however, might keep unionists voting for him in the upcoming 1948 election.

Organized labor labeled Taft-Hartley the "slave labor act," viewing it as a gateway to fascism. Pro-union advocates rightly anticipated ways in which the law would open employees to employer intimidation and unions to legal fights. Most of the unfair union practices that Taft-Hartley outlined were already illegal, but the new law allowed employers to build cases for NLRB proceedings that would require investigation and rulings that would draw out proceedings and cost unions seeking representation rights and their members lots of money. While most AFL unionists did not mind signing non-communist affidavits, at least one, George Q. Lynch, president of the AFL Pattern Makers' League, did. Lynch was an AFL union leader who was opposed to communism and happy to admit it. Still, he demanded his right as a citizen to join any legal party he liked. Signing the affidavit, to him, violated his rights and those of his fellow unionists. Leaders of CIO unions whole-heartedly agreed and called this affidavit-signing craze a violation of their civil liberties. John

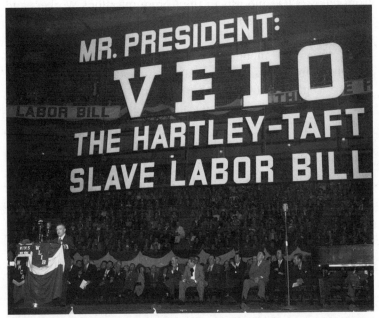

Figure 2.4 David Dubinsky of the International Ladies Garment Workers' Union gives a speech against the Hartley-Taft Bill, May 4, 1947. Management Conference, October 1945. Kheel Center for Labor–Management Documentation and Archives, M. P. Catherwood Library, Cornell University (#5780PB17F25D).

L. Lewis and Philip Murray flat-out refused to sign affidavits and willingly gave up NLRB representation. Communist Party union leaders and their supporters relished the solidarity, for a time.

The larger problem, however, was that it was virtually impossible to survive without formal NLRB recognition and groups within the labor movement began immediately to take advantage of the situation. UAW locals challenged UE locals to representation elections because UE officials refused to sign the required affidavits, stating that they were not members of the Communist Party. The UAW won in Hartford, Connecticut, and Brooklyn, New York. They also "raided" non-signing locals in industries making machinery and farm equipment. The UE also faced raids from fellow CIO unionists in the Communications Workers and the Steel Workers and by AFL machinists and those in the International Brotherhood of Electrical Workers. AFL unionists also went after CIO members whose union leaders were non-compliant in metals, lumber, and white-collar work. Without NLRB recognition, unions whose officials refused to sign non-communist affidavits were not allowed a place on the election ballots. Recertification elections became confusing campaigns with one-time established unions encouraging their members to vote "no union."

The raiding convinced CIO leader Murray to shift course and no longer support fellow CIO union leaders who resisted Taft-Hartley. He threw his support behind the law and called on all CIO local union officers to sign affidavits stating that they were not members of the Communist Party. The union movement, he conceded, would have to fight against Taft-Hartley at the ballot box – not on the shop floor, nor in the streets.

Political (Mis)calculations: Operation Dixie, CIO Purges, and International Alliances, 1946–1950s

Labor unions, with 15 million members in 1945 and heady in the wake of workers' postwar strike wave, believed they could turn out the vote and unseat anti-union politicians. Their confidence also came from the past success of their Political Action Committee (CIO-PAC). Formed in 1943 and with women playing a significant role, CIO-PAC successfully turned out labor's vote to reelect Roosevelt in 1944. As the largest organized group in the Democratic Party, labor had much at stake when it came to bringing liberal politicians back to Washington, DC.

Within labor's big political picture, however, sat the conservative South, with its anti-union leanings and refusal to bend on racial justice. One-party southern rule meant that anti-union, segregationist southern Democrats had the power to force domestic servants and agricultural workers out of New Deal legislation;

they also successfully filibustered an attempt to make the FEPC a permanent organization.

Dixie's political representatives consistently resisted federal intervention, but found they would have to accommodate themselves to a few major inroads. The Fair Labor Standards Act, wartime spending in defense industries, NLRB rulings, and the Tennessee Valley Authority, which dramatically transformed the region through electrification and economic development, represented just a few of the ways southern living was being changed and brought up to northern standards. Perhaps, thought CIO leaders, union drives could help extend these efforts. If the CIO could bring union protection to unorganized workers in the South, they would in effect shore-up support for pro-labor southern Democrats in political office. To achieve this end most effectively, though, white workers would have to be won over; it would not be easy. White workers imbibed the hatred and fear headlined in the southern press and spoken by their employers, neighbors, and ministers: the CIO was just a communist front, a bunch of outsiders, who did not have the interests of the South at heart and who played with fire when they dared to advocate for racial equality.

Operation Dixie was the informal name given in 1946 to the CIO's effort to organize southern workers. Technically, the campaign lasted until 1953, but in reality the failure of the drive was apparent to anyone paying attention by November of its first year. CIO leaders anticipated southern organizing pitfalls, prevented communists from participating in the campaign, and kept their message focused on wages, hours, and workplace conditions. Unions would bring economic security; racial equality would take a back seat. CIO organizers set their eyes on the largely white textile industry and sent white men to hand out leaflets at gates, ask workers to sign membership cards, and talk to workers at their homes to avoid violating racial and gender proprieties, but no good came of the effort. AFL unionists, employers, politicians, and Ku Klux Klan members called out union organizers as "reds," and Operation Dixie amounted to a failure both for southern workers and the CIO's political strategy. The CIO still had beachheads throughout the South among tobacco workers in North Carolina and Memphis; oil workers in Louisiana and Texas; iron, foundry, and aluminum workers in Alabama and Tennessee; pulp and paper workers in Virginia; rubber workers in Memphis and Gadsden; and aircraft workers in Georgia and Texas; but these locals largely had been organized during the war. The southern campaign claimed small victories, but was not powerful enough to turn the southern political tide. By the time of the 1948 election, the CIO had largely abandoned the South. CIO-PAC mobilized in key industrial states, waged a get-out-the-vote campaign peopled by a million volunteers, and celebrated Truman's razor-thin victory in 1948.

Communists had been some of the CIO's most effective organizers during their 1930s drives for new members, but CIO leaders' concerns over how their politics would play in the South and their determination to organize among white workers signaled that the CIO leadership was preparing to move in a new direction. Their waxing reluctance to back their union brothers and sisters who held Communist Party membership cards solidified when internal fights concerning Truman consumed the organization. CIO leaders backed Truman because they hoped he would help them blunt the excesses of Taft-Hartley; but throughout Truman's campaign, they faced communist opposition in their ranks. Communist unionists were less convinced that Truman or those in Congress wished to help labor. Communists, moreover, had other political reasons to oppose Truman. In the context of the growing Cold War, the Truman administration moved ahead on a direct anti-Soviet path. The 1947 Truman Doctrine provided US aid to corrupt forces in the governments of Greece and Turkey in the hopes that they would defeat communist-led guerrillas vying for power. The 1948 Marshall Plan provided millions of dollars to Europe in order to rebuild its economy along capitalist lines. That year, communist unionists and their supporters publicly came out against the CIO's support of Truman and put their backing behind former Vice President Henry A. Wallace. Why should they support a man who spoke out against labor during its postwar strike wave, who supported European colonial powers, and who participated in red baiting? Did CIO resolutions supporting Truman mean that communist-influenced unions were precluded from advocating for his challenger?

The 1948 election and political questions surrounding it brought the issue of communists in the CIO to a head. To anti-communist labor activists, support for Wallace and against the Truman Doctrine and Marshall Plan was just more of the same: blind support for Soviet doctrine and willing manipulation of unsuspecting union members in the name of Stalin. To many, communists had little integrity. First, in 1935, they supported the Soviet Union's campaign against the spread of fascism, but then switched lines in 1939 when the Soviet Union signed a Nonaggression Pact with Germany, and then changed their position again in 1941 when Hitler violated the agreement and invaded the Soviet Union. The House of Representatives Committee on Un-American Activities (HUAC) held hearings into communist union activity; Truman's Loyalty Program screened federal employees for communist sympathies and applicants for communist leanings; and business leaders publicly equated CIO union activity with communist (which was code for un-American) activity. Communists in the CIO were more of a liability than ever.

In the end, CIO leaders stood behind Murray's decision to force locals' executive board leaders to sign non-communist affidavits. Their fighting days were over. When UE leaders withheld their CIO dues in protest of the federation's insistence that their leaders sign their non-communist affidavits, the federation kicked them out and joined anti-communist forces by chartering a rival organization, the International Union of Electrical, Radio and Machine Workers (IUE), which proceeded to raid unprotected UE locals for membership.

In 1949 and 1950 the CIO's leadership established procedures for CIO staffers to follow when bringing charges against communist-influenced unions, which were similar to those used by anti-unionists in Congress. Staff members did not need to prove that union leaders were communists, only that they followed

117

the party line. Did they support Wallace in 1948? Did they pass resolutions against the Marshall Plan? No matter what kind of shop-floor leaders these unionists were, CIO leaders only wanted to know how red their politics were. In the end, CIO leaders believed they had enough evidence to expel eleven of its unions for having policies that were too pro-Soviet. In addition to the UE, the CIO expelled the FTA; United Office and Professional Workers of America; Mine, Mill and Smelter Workers; Farm Equipment Workers; Fur and Leather Workers; International Longshoremen and Warehousemen; United Public Workers; American Communications Association; National Union of Marine Cooks and Stewards; and International Fishermen and Allied Workers.

The expelled unions, which were among those most committed to racial and gender equality, were now without NLRB protection and the most vulnerable to raids of their membership. So when the United Steelworkers accused a fellow CIO affiliate, the Mine Mill workers in Alabama's Bessemer and Red Mountain, of being run by reds and successfully won a representation election over Mine Mill, they did so without the support of the black workers and allegedly with the support of the Ku Klux Klan. Similar dynamics played in the FTA, whose members were Mexican-, Filipino-, and African American, and in the ILWU, which represented workers from Japan, China, Puerto Rico, Portugal, Hawaii, and the Philippines. Between 1951 and 1953, AFL and CIO unions carried out over 1,200 raids. The UE and the ILWU were the only unions identified in the CIO's purge of its "left-led" unions to survive the onslaught. While AFL membership grew to 10.2 million in this period, the CIO's membership fell from a postwar high of 6.3 million to a 1954 total of 4.6 million.

The purge successfully wedged out the CIO's soul. The loss of these eleven unions was a major blow to moving forward against racism and sexism within the labor movement. Those unions identified as "left-led" were also the ones that negotiated the most democratic contracts and the ones most likely to put limits on the power of capital. Regardless of where the Communist

Party members stood in relation to political position in the period between the Nazi–Soviet pact and the Cold War, their contracts were more consistently pro-labor than those not left-led. And unlike those who were convinced that wartime enthusiasm encouraged communist unionists to betray workers' interests (since they supported no-strike pledges and full production), in fact wartime contracts by left-led unions were less likely than those of their rivals to give in to management prerogatives or to have complicated grievance procedures. By expelling its left-led unions, the CIO, pushed by Taft-Hartley, the business community, and public pressures, eviscerated the main players in the fight for workers' power on the shop floor and main groups who openly challenged management's unchecked authority. Union leaders' politics made a difference on the shop floor. Reuther's UAW encouraged stable labor relations; Farm Equipment Workers' representatives flamed class conflict.

Moreover, Cold War pressures caused the CIO to withdraw from progressive international commitments and get involved in undemocratic and strangely anti-worker ones. At first labor representatives from the United States, Great Britain, and the Soviet Union believed it possible to build a just social-democratic postwar world through a worldwide labor federation, the Workers Federation of Trade Unions (WFTU). With the Cold War brewing, however, labor's leaders abandoned internationalism in the face of domestic pressures and the hopes of shoring-up support from their governments. While it took the ranks longer than their leaders to abandon international alliances, nationalist and anti-communist Cold War goals ultimately prevailed. Most non-communist unions withdrew from the WFTU in 1949 and soon joined with AFL leaders to found the International Confederation of Free Trade Unions (ICFTU). This turn of events was a tragedy. In the name of the Cold War, the international organization undermined worker movements around the world that its leaders suspected of being connected with communists. For example, in 1951 ICFTU set up the Inter-American Regional Organization of Workers (ORIT), a US-funded organization that shut down strikes against the United Fruit Company in Honduras and helped the company establish a company union. Later, the Kennedy administration would help the AFL-CIO establish the American Institute for Free Labor Development (AIFLD), back it with federal dollars, and support its efforts that promoted pro-Western governments and business deals. Through the AIFLD, the union movement became complicit in suppressing militant and communist union movements throughout the world, with a focus on Latin America. Both federations also sent in organizers to challenge Puerto Rico's Confederación General de Trabajadores, since its leaders refused to comply with Taft-Hartley; and they both expressed support for US troops sent to fight in Korea. No longer forums in which to debate and question such issues as US foreign policy, both labor federations became partners in the federal government's Cold War.

Big Labor, Big Costs, 1955–1960s

It was like-thinking that encouraged the AFL and CIO to join in their own partnership. William Green and Philip Murray both died unexpectedly in 1952, and their replacements – George Meany and Walter Reuther – established a Joint Unity Committee, called for an end to raiding, and in 1955 merged the federations. The AFL-CIO represented 145 unions and 16 million workers. In 1956, with almost 24 percent of the labor force organized, the union movement reached its largest share of the workforce to that date. While their size was impressive, it was not the focus of news headlines dealing with labor: union corruption took that honor. Senator John McClellan's Select Committee on Improper Activities in the Labor or Management Field opened televised hearings in 1957. Teamster President David "Dave" Beck came under fire for rigging elections, associating with criminals, and participating in extortion. His replacement, Jimmy Hoffa, was already headline news for welfare-fund fraud and setting up sweetheart deals that went easy on employers, lined union officials' pockets, and left workers powerless. Hoffa was dirty, but he was not alone. McClellan's committee paid attention to corruption in such unions as the Hotel and Restaurant Workers, United Textile Workers, and Bakery and Confectionery Workers. The AFL-CIO did what it could to expel the criminals in its midst, but Congress still passed the Landrum Griffin Labor Management Reporting and Disclosure Act of 1959, which required pension and welfare-fund administrators to report on the funds. The act established standards for how unions were to behave: contracts for their workers, procedures for elections, local disciplinary measures, a five-year cooling off before convicted felons and converted communists (equally suspicious characters under this law) could hold union office.

In the face of Taft-Hartley, AFL and CIO consolidation, and Landrum Griffin, the nature of the labor movement changed. On the one hand, important examples persisted that demonstrated labor unions could still promote a social-democratic vision in the postwar United States. Between 1958 and 1966, for example, Reuther developed strong relationships with anti-communist liberals and middle-class labor allies to push the United States' economic future along social-democratic lines – full employment, federal urban policy, and civil rights legislation. Reuther ultimately failed at restructuring the political economy, but his efforts suggest not all unions had given up the larger fight to improve the lives of working people, even when they were not union members. Even more successful than Reuther in shaping a social democracy in the 1950s were workers in New York City who achieved low transit fares, rent control, various health, educational, and cultural institutions, and a free city university.

On the other hand, the majority of the labor movement turned inward, away from a larger social responsibility to bring dignity to both union and non-union working people in the United States and instead settled on their own union members and what they could win. As it turned out, there was much to be gained. It was during this period that the provisions unionized labor won allowed millions of workers and their families to live with more peace of mind and a new level of comfort. By the 1960s these provisions had established a virtual private welfare system for unionized workers that included real wage increases, vacations, holidays, pensions, health insurance, disability insurance, and all kinds of job security in the form of seniority systems. GM's 1948 contract with the UAW established a Cost of Living Adjustment (COLA), which guaranteed raises based on increased consumer costs, and through the 1950s more than half of the major union contracts included COLAs. In heavily unionized industries, regional and sometimes national contract patterns became established – wage settlements at one firm became the pattern for agreements throughout the industry. Stability was further entrenched in union contracts. Usually, industrial relations experts recommended that contract agreements allow for binding arbitration during the life of the agreement. This meant that when the contract was in effect, workers would not resort to strikes. The system of "industrial pluralism" set clear terms for bargaining contracts and established a common law of industrial relations whereby impartial arbitrators – labor lawyers and industrial relations specialists – would dispassionately rule on cases based on precedents and past practices. The idea was to shore-up stability. In turn, average hourly earnings for manufacturing workers increased by 81 percent between 1950 and 1965.

Business did not, however, just give away the shop, and unions still called strikes: according to Nelson Lichtenstein in *State of the Union: A Century of American Labor* (2002), from the late 1940s though the early 1970s, strike levels "stood higher than at any time, before or since." Between 1940 and 1955 alone, workers engaged in 65,000 of them. A few, such as the one in Hyden, Kentucky, where John L. Lewis and his UMWA faced off against non-union coal producers, provoked 1930s-era violence. According to the *New York Times* of September 8, 1953, UMWA had been

> waging a campaign for more than two years to bring the operatives under contract. Eight organizers have been shot, one of them died, another is completely paralyzed. Cars have been dynamited and union meeting places, members' homes and friendly merchants' stores have been blasted or fired upon. The union and local leaders have been sued, indicted, enjoined and even jailed.

Certainly this violence against union organizers fell in a long tradition of union busting. What made it stand out in the 1950s, however, was that by this time it was fairly unusual. Indeed, throughout the 1950s and into the 1960s, such outright employer violence against union drives was the exception.

No longer fought with brawn, strikes became tests of endurance over which provisions would be allowed into which contracts. Strikes for these benefits became ritualized and usually occurred at contract bargaining time. And even though they were common and expected, strikes were still important shows of unified force for power on the shop floor and quality of life improvements that management would have rather not given away. The particular provisions that lurked behind each strike differed, but in general the contests had to do with wages (could the company afford to do better by its workers) and basic workplace decision-making (management's unilateral right versus rules and past practices that unions helped to establish).

The 1959 steelworkers' strike demonstrates the character of labor strikes in this period. In July of that year, 500,000 steelworkers did not show up to work. Together they represented 1 percent of the entire US labor force, and they stayed out until the president and the Supreme Court ruled that they go back to work 116 days later. Up until the day the strike began, union leaders communicated the places where contract negotiations were falling apart through union newsletters, regional leaders, and shop-floor stewards. Hundreds of thousands of steelworkers understood what was at stake, talked with their families, and planned for the inevitable. The very moment at which Union President David J. McDonald announced to the press that steelworkers were on strike, they were. (USWA was never known for its democratic culture.) Even those workers who would rather have not been on strike never considered crossing a picket line. In the 13 years leading up to 1959, steelworkers conducted five strikes and each time witnessed significant benefits in their contracts. So even though many members had nasty things to say about McDonald, come strike time it was all for one and one for all. According to the son of a 1959 striker, "The belief in the power of collective action was so deep and strong that everybody took it for granted."

The 1959 action, and others like it, was fought in the public media, where both steel employers and unions made their case earnestly. To steel employers and business executives more generally, labor was a cost to be cut in the name of profits. If not, they would have to raise prices and unleash inflation on society. To steelworkers, however, better wages meant more spending power and opportunities to stimulate the economy. In the afterglow of New Deal government spending, this argument reverberated widely among small business owners who served working communities by selling food, cars, and beer. Both sides bought newspaper ads, put out numbers, and made their case.

In 1959, however, wages were not the only issue on the line. Instead, US Steel decided that they were through with what they called the "workplace rule of law." By this time, USWA (and other industrial unions like them) had them negotiating over all manner of workplace rules such as work schedules, seniority, vacation scheduling, and work incentives to protect workers from management's arbitrary treatment. This time US Steel had enough of these rules and committed itself to ridding themselves of them and any other provisions that protected past work practices in future contracts. To management these rules prevented the company from being as efficient as it might be if only they called the shots. They charged that the union featherbedded the factory (meaning that unions forced management to pay more workers than were necessary to get the job done), but when push came to shove and the press asked for examples of the practice, the company had none to share. The public took note. To workers, work rules protected them from massive job loss (downsizing), speedups, and dangerous work conditions. Healthy payrolls kept the workday safe and the work pace humane.

So there was really no question in many workers' minds that they would have to tighten their belts and fight. Unless they had a particularly bad hardship case, they did so without strike benefits. Fortunately, over the years, the union cultivated relationships with local communities on which they were able to rely in their time of need. After all, USWA could not afford payments for half a million people. Instead, families pitched in, cut back, and planned as best they could. Local businesses helped where they could; some kept tabs, others wiped debt off the books. Some local banks established a moratorium on mortgage payments during the strike. A few local charities helped with food and clothing. Union counselors put needy families in touch with government agencies that provided aid. Some locals used their bank accounts to establish strike kitchens, hand out food, and provide meal tickets from local restaurants. Rather than fold under the strain, steelworkers stood firm. Work rules were worth it.

President Dwight D. Eisenhower enacted the Taft-Hartley 80-day cooling off period in October 1959 and obtained a federal injunction to send steelworkers back to work, which the union fought all the way to the Supreme Court. They wanted to know how, exactly, their strike jeopardized national security. The Court simply ruled that it did, so back to work a half million steelworkers went. According to the rules of Taft-Hartley, the company then had to develop its final offer, and steelworkers would have to vote on it by referendum. On November 15 the company put forward a final offer, which included wage increases and a willingness to send the question of work rules to an arbitrator. Polling by the company and union indicated that steelworkers were not swayed. Fearing another strike and the potential of forced arbitration in the future, US Steel settled – they gave up more in wages than they originally offered and workers kept their work rules. For a half a million steelworkers from coast to coast, this was a win-win.

While most strikes after Taft-Hartley were not as large or as long as that fought by USWA in 1959, their victories were often as significant. This was especially true because – even though they did not plan for it – the results of such union victories and new benefits were not simply self-serving. Strikes of the period insured that standards won at the union bargaining table would be given to millions of non-union workers because many non-union employers wished to avoid unionization campaigns. Such firms as Sears, Kodak, and DuPont, as well as those in the banking and insurance industries, used welfare capitalism to keep ahead of the union standard as a way to prevent having to share power and lose some of their management prerogatives.

Still, there is no question that the battle for better member benefits waged in the late 1940s through the 1960s suggested that most of the labor movement had lost its larger social vision, drive, and militancy. Whereas the CIO had represented the promise of interracial unionism, shop-floor militancy, and social democratic politics, AFL unions generally represented social conservatism and business unionism. The federations' merger simply meant that the AFL's values prevailed and the CIO's earlier hopes for a socially conscious union movement died. Trade unions moved into a parochial path, and were penalized by the government for any attempts, such as secondary boycotts, to push class-wide economic tactics and social democratic visions.

Even the most socially conscious unions found themselves narrowly focusing on hammering out union contracts that made wage and welfare benefits private – no more "politicized bargaining" whereby union leaders forced labor's agenda onto the nation's political scene and into national debates. Preferring across-the-board wage and benefit awards negotiated at the bargaining table to gains won through union members' actions on the shop floor, union leaders increasingly denounced workplace militancy. Rebuffed by conservatives in their quest to extend the welfare state, unions won pensions, health insurance, and other benefits for their members – and for their members only. And while industrial unionists' local communities benefited from union members' ability to spend, their wages priming the local economy's pump, the truth is that the privatized welfare state that developed was a decidedly unequal one. The pattern established in core industries rarely made its way to service or agricultural industries dominated by women and minorities and never would become universal since not all adults worked outside the home. Pattern bargaining – where strong union contracts created a model for contracts negotiated in its wake – did not take hold in industries where unions were weak or where domestic competition was intense. "The new welfare capitalism that emerged out of the postwar labor–management accord," writes Lichtenstein, "generated islands of security, with high waters all around."

Conclusion

World War II and its immediate Cold War aftermath fundamentally recast labor relations. Following the New Deal, wartime federal power granted legitimacy to unions. The war emergency drastically increased union membership and the amount of pay war workers brought home. It also opened jobs, previously held by white men, to women and people of color, and brought waves of migrants into new communities and higher standards of living. Economically lifted out of the depths of the Depression, war workers saw improved conditions in the face of others' great wartime sacrifices.

At the same time, federal involvement increasingly muffled unions' clamor. Collective bargaining and the restrictions of the Taft-Hartley Act stifled unions from pursuing a larger, social-democratic program. Under attack from the business community and conservative Democrats and their Republican allies, unionists found less and less support for expanding workers' voices and social benefits in the postwar world. Anti-communism and anti-unionism worked hand in hand. With weakened or missing left wings, unions continued to fight, but for less expansive things.

At the same time that political forces conspired against unions, federal involvement moved struggles for civil rights forward. While the FEPC did not have the power to restructure race relations at work, it provided an important lever that local activists used in their struggles to better their conditions. Federal support of CIO unions also allowed African Americans, Mexican Americans, and women a vehicle to improve their economic standing and measure of dignity on the job. In the 1960s and 1970s, women and minorities continued the struggle to make a secure place for themselves in workplaces and communities throughout the nation.

3

Civil Rights Versus Labor Rights, 1960s–1970s

The 1960s and 1970s were tumultuous decades for working people, but generally the working-class dimension of this time of social upheaval gets lost among empassioned retellings of youth rebellion and bold new demands for African-Americans', women's, and gays' civil rights. Generally, as these stories go, the 1950s were the first modern decade during which many in the "working class" (which meant white, male workers) found they had money left to spend even after they covered the essentials. So large numbers of them moved to the suburbs, where they embraced a new identity: middle class. Enjoying their privileged lives, they continued to become even more insular and uninterested in social justice. In the 1960s and 1970s, instead of union struggles (which ostensibly vanished), the domestic conflicts that consumed newsprint and the nation involved African Americans, women, and students. The expansion of rights based on one's race or sex overshadowed class politics; and white, working-class men, and what became criticized as their out-of-touch, self-serving labor movement, began their descent into obscurity.

Working Hard for the American Dream: Workers and Their Unions, World War I to the Present, First Edition. Randi Storch.
© 2013 John Wiley & Sons, Ltd. Published 2013 by John Wiley & Sons, Ltd.

The problem is, however, that the labor movement and the struggle to expand civil rights in the United States were more intertwined than the above narrative leads anyone to believe. Throughout the 1960s and 1970s, class identity and the desire for union protection continued to motivate working people's political activity because people of color and women understood that unions paved the road to better workplace conditions for them. If unions could be broadened to extend their brotherly sentiments (and contracts) to those unorganized service and public workers (who included the sisters), then fundamental economic wrongs would be righted through collective bargaining. Even if particular unions were imperfect when it came to forging equality in their own ranks or for standing for social justice in the wider world, thousands of women and people of color agreed to live with the blemishes; contract protections meant individuals would have a foothold in their fight against daily indignities, job insecurity, and wage discrimination.

By the end of the 1950s, the idea that white, male union members and their leaders could serve as socially conscious advocates for the working class, broadly speaking, had taken a beating. Still, the promise persisted. Throughout the 1960s and 1970s, growth in health, education, correctional, emergency, hotel, restaurant, and clerical fields – job sectors where women and minorities worked – fueled dynamic union campaigns. Some workers in these labor markets understood that their economic union struggle was intimately tied to larger civil rights and feminist battles for dignity and respect. This impulse to bring democracy, safety, and dignity to the workplace was also apparent among some white industrial workers, who challenged bureaucratic union leaders and built more democratic rank-and-file movements. In other words, working-class protest, in the context of the civil rights movement and an emerging feminist movement, took on a new character; in turn, it grounded these movements in questions of class.

New calls for union rights made some of those who were already safely protected bristle. One might think that industrial unionists would have welcomed public and service workers and welfare mothers into their labor networks with open arms. After all, the New Deal's promise of full economic citizenship had benefited them so well, and weren't union rights and civil rights two sides of the same coin? Well, there were some exceptions to the general rule (especially among state-level union leaders), but overall, and in local communities, established union members did not see things this way. Instead, most AFL-CIO union members were at odds with this new surge among working people and found themselves weakened by political weapons developed to help women and minorities fight for workplace protections. Both President John F. Kennedy's executive order 10925 and Lyndon B. Johnson's executive order 11246 established "affirmative action" for federal contractors, requiring them to develop plans to discontinue historic hiring discrimination practiced against minorities. These orders packed a punch when paired with the passage of the Civil Rights Act of 1964 and its Title VII that made race and sex discrimination in employment illegal and established the Equal Employment Opportunity Commission (EEOC). With these new laws, the federal government bequeathed working-class minorities (and in 1968, women) the power to reshape their places of work. The ability to sue and file class-action suits against employers and against unions for discriminatory practices meant that minorities and women no longer had to accept their second-class economic status, and they no longer did so.

Working-class white workers were incensed by these liberalizing efforts that threatened society's traditional gender and racial hierarchies. They tended to respond to the government's attempt to widen the New Deal agenda by jumping into the arms of the right, where Nixon and social conservatives smugly received them. Female, African-American, and ethnic working and underemployed people tapped into conservative hostility and anti-unionism, which was unleashed with particular force against municipal and state governments in these decades, years before the presidency of Ronald Reagan (which is typically associated with the onset of this kind of behavior).

At the same time that some white male workers turned against fellow working-class women and minorities, the public turned its back on labor unions in general. In the context of a major fiscal crisis in the early 1970s, state and city officials reigned in public sector unions. Their successful assault and the shift in public opinion against public unionism laid the groundwork for the 1980s and Reagan's highly visible and successful offensive against unions and working America. Class, indeed, was central to these changing times.

Expanding Public and Service Sectors

From the late 1950s through the 1970s, the US economy underwent a significant shift. New technologies resulted in stunning levels of productivity in factories, mines, and farms. While the total number of workers in manufacturing remained relatively stable, employment in extractive industries – agriculture and mining – dropped sharply. At the same time, government jobs (city, state, and federal), service work, and clerical positions expanded in unprecedented numbers. Between 1947 and 1967 the number of government employees increased from 5.5 million to 11.6 million. In New York City the number of public employees increased from 347,000 in 1950 to 563,200 in 1970, leaving them the largest single group working for the city, with more employees than those in the garment, banking, and longshore industries combined. Across the country in the 1950s and 1960s the number of clerical workers, including typists and stenographers, more than doubled, from 1.6 to 3.9 million. By the mid-1970s, clerical work replaced household employment as the largest occupational category for all non-white women.

As government responsibility to care for its citizens grew through the 1960s, so did social service and such professional jobs as teaching, social work, and nursing. In New York City many public jobs were part of the city's unique social-democratic commitment: hospitals, public housing, higher education, and mass transit. By the 1970s the proportion of state workers involved in social-welfare functions increased from one half to two thirds. By 1950 half of the labor force worked in jobs outside of manufacturing. According to the census, blue-collar jobs fell to under 40 percent of the workforce in 1960, behind white-collar jobs for the first time.

Whether in the public or private sector, jobs in service, retail, and light manufacturing shared a high proportion of women and minorities and a stressful work culture. In the South, deep-seated commitments to racism meant that minority workers found little trouble securing service jobs that lacked dignity, upward mobility, and power. Regardless of geographic region, workers in these positions found their ability to make basic decisions on the job undermined by excessive quotas or tasks, too few hands to meet them, and management's watchful eye. These positions were low-paying and dead-end. Author Barbara Ehrenreich's reflections on the highly demanding and managed environment of waitressing in *Nickeled and Dimed: On (Not) Getting By in America* (2001) speaks to the challenges waitresses faced the 1960s and 1970s. She reported:

> Managers can sit – for hours at a time if they want – but it's their job to see that no one else ever does, even when there's nothing to do, and this is why, for servers, slow times can be as exhausting as rushes. You start dragging out each little chore because if the manager on duty catches you in an idle moment he will give you something far nastier to do...When, on a particularly dead afternoon, Stu finds me glancing at a *USA Today* a customer has left behind, he assigns me to vacuum the entire floor with the broken vacuum cleaner, which has a handle only two feet long, and the only way to do that without incurring orthopedic damage is to proceed from spot to spot on your knees.

At least the exhausting nature of waiting on tables could sometimes be alleviated by the ability of servers to move around the restaurant. The monotony of light assembly work, however, had no outlet. "After you have screwed a wire into its clip for about the tenth time," recounts Reg Theriault in *How to Tell When You're*

Tired: A Brief Examination of Work (1997), "the operation loses much of its fun and interest, and you still have the day to get through. And a lifetime." Even government jobs, once thought to transfer a basic level of security, felt a financial crunch in the 1960s, which worsened in the 1970s, resulting in a diminished quality of work. Trying to keep a lid on rising taxes, federal, state, and local governments slashed their budgets: school boards held down teachers' pay, city bus drivers drove failing buses, and postal workers found their workforce cut and delivery routes expanded and timed.

Public Sector Workers and Union Rights

It was the civil rights movement that proved first to African Americans and then to women and other minority groups that good jobs meant secure lives. Ending segregation and extending voting rights were essential victories, but shaking up the caste system that defined the character of work in the United States was at least as important and maybe even more so. White citizens' ability to exclude minorities and women from the best jobs reflected an uneven power structure that permeated society. Good jobs allow for home ownership, college education, and some basic creature comforts such as a radio and a reliable car. In the 1960s public and service workers still had many of these desires, but were finding them harder to achieve without basic economic rights. The rapid expansion of public and service jobs, filled with women and minorities, occurred at the same moment the civil rights and women's movements were demanding an expansion of economic citizenship. Younger workers, women, and members of minority groups were anxious to extend such economic rights as collective bargaining, available in the private sector, to those working for the public.

For many, public sector collective bargaining rights came without much of a fight. Nationally, in several states, and a small number of cities, public sector workers won collective bargaining rights from liberal, Democratic politicians. In 1962 President

133

Kennedy gave over two million federal employees bargaining rights with executive order 10988. Throughout the 1960s, 22 states gave their workers rights to collective bargaining. Such liberal, Democratic mayors as New York's Robert F. Wagner Jr. and Philadelphia's Joseph S. Clark Jr., also extended collective bargaining rights to city workers. By 1975, 36 states had granted their public employees union rights. So while industrial union workers fumed at Democratic politicians who refused to reverse the worst of Taft-Hartley's provisions that still tied their hands, public sector workers found their relationship with Democrats anything but fruitless and frustrating.

While fundamental, public sector bargaining rights were much more limited than those afforded to industrial unionists. For public workers, collective bargaining agreements covered narrow categories of them (teachers in this district but not that one, for example) and dealt with a small subset of their job-related issues. This was a far cry from the broad industry-wide contracts that set standards for industrial workers from coast to coast. State employee unions also had problems in right-to-work states because they allowed free riders (workers who refused to pay union dues even though they received all the benefits of the union's representation), which in effect encouraged union members to stop paying dues if and when conflicts over political issues, such as civil rights emerged. Unions in these states would not stand as a unified force, but instead were extremely vulnerable, and in some cases unable to function. Federal laws, at the same time, called for the immediate firing of striking government workers.

Whereas public workers certainly faced limits to their union power, they also found changing opportunities. Yes, the federal law against striking was severe, but between the mid-1950s and the 1970s, public workers generally witnessed a liberalization of labor law. Four states actually won the right for some of their public employees to strike, and a number of other states revised laws that required employers to fire striking workers. Some cities and states even increased unions' sense of security by creating "agency shops" – all workers pay union dues whether or not they sign up to be union members – since the union works for everyone in the bargaining union whether they are a member or not. At the same time that private sector labor law made conditions more difficult for unions to organize, public sector law moved, until the mid-1970s, in the opposite direction. Kennedy's executive order and state and local ordinances meant that many public employees won union rights without a battle, but this was not universally so. In the South and West, postwar racist and anti-union propaganda encouraged state legislatures and city councils to pass anti-union and right-to-work laws, if they did not already exist. In these places, unions had a notoriously difficult time building membership and waging successful drives. No wonder in these regions where right-to-work states proliferated, wages were (and are) notoriously low.

Unionists also faced off against community business leaders and politicians who equated all unions with communist outfits and used veiled racism to give legitimacy to the idea that that labor and civil rights were subversive. This was particularly true in the South, where southern Democrats aligned with Republicans to pass Taft-Hartley and Landrum-Griffin, and baldly blocked civil rights developments.

These anti-union arguments, beliefs, and actions stood in contradistinction to black workers who were open to any help they could get in their fight for dignity and personhood. In Memphis, for example, African Americans were particularly amenable to labor unions; it did not matter if city officials thought them communist-infiltrated. Racist city officials' warnings against these union organizations may have even made them more enticing. African Americans, after all, worked in service and unskilled jobs for paltry sums, which meant that about 60 percent of them lived at or below the poverty line. Led by Mayor Henry Loeb, an open supporter of segregation, the city enabled some of the worst excesses of racist living in its housing. Against these odds, a small labor community, black college students, ministers, and black professionals supported a sizable NAACP chapter in Memphis. They also successfully got together to elect three African-American men to the city council.

135

When the city's sanitation workers decided it was time for Memphis's leaders to recognize their union, they called on the city's African-American and small labor network for help. T. O. Jones, a passionate speaker and Memphis sanitation worker, tried to move his fellow city sanitation workers toward unionization as early as 1959; but it was not until 1968, after two fellow workers died because garbage trucks were unsafe and crushed them, and racial grievances began pouring in, that Jones sparked a movement. The city's sanitation workers – people who had hardly ever gained the attention of the city's white community – went on strike and stayed there for 63 days. For those 63 days, striking African-American sanitation workers were pretty much all white Memphis talked about. Some days were more dramatic than others as strikers took to the streets to march, gathered in large numbers to hold rallies, and filled churches to the brim for mass meetings. Police beatings punctuated the strike, but the most horrific violence was directed at Dr. Martin Luther King Jr., who believed that the sanitation workers' fight represented the next stage of the civil rights movement and would be an important spur to his Poor People's Movement. Dr. King was in Memphis when protesters carried signs past armed national guardsmen that declared, "I am a man," a call for manhood guaranteed by both economic citizenship and the end of white paternalism. He was also there to give support and lift workers' spirits. Unfortunately for everyone involved, he was in town when an assassin met him at the front steps of his Lorraine Motel. There Dr. King was murdered on April 4, 1968, just days before the city of Memphis agreed to negotiate a contract with the sanitation workers. In this tragic case, public employee unionism was the conduit, delivering civil rights and liberties to previously disempowered workers.

Like in Memphis, except without such national attention, other city and state workers did not let prohibitions against strikes stymie their union protests. A few skirmishes revealed creative labor strategies. In 1966 police officers in Pontiac, Michigan, held a mass sickout to protest their wages (on a coordinated day, many officers called in "sick"). Versions of the

Figure 3.1 Striking members of Memphis Local 1733 hold signs whose slogan symbolized the sanitation workers' campaign in 1968. Walter P. Reuther Library, Wayne State University. Photographer Richard L. Copley (#8886).

sickout spread to other workers: fire fighters called it "red rash"; teachers "chalk dust fever." In San Diego, county employees void of decision-making power invented "human error day": they cut off phone calls prematurely, lost paperwork, and made other office mistakes.

Others broke the law and went on strike. In 1960 public employee strikes numbered 36; by 1966 they had increased to 142, in 1970, 412, and by 1980 stood at 536. Between 1965 and 1975 the number of public sector strikes increased tenfold. New York teachers were a powerful striking force. Between 1960 and 1961, through a series of walkouts, these teachers muscled their way into a contract that limited class size, provided extra resources to struggling schools, and increased their pay. When they walked out again in 1962, New York's teachers sparked a national wave of teacher strikes. In 1970 postal workers came down with strike fever. That year a wildcat strike in defiance of federal law brought 180,000 postal workers and letter carriers off the job. Urban postal workers – about two thirds of whom were African American – demanded better pay, protested speedups in the face of new technologies and a shrinking workforce, and forced the federal government to send National Guardsmen to key cities to deliver the mail. Public union leaders, heady with their new growth, thought creatively about expanding union rights: American Federal State County and Municipal Employees (AFSCME) considered organizing state prisoners while the American Federation of Government Employees' president announced his interest in organizing members of the military.

Public employee unions also provided leadership opportunities to women and minorities. New York Hospital Workers' local 1199 blended what they called "soul power and union power" to successfully organize New York City's hospital workers and to extend their organization to professional and technical workers. In Charleston, South Carolina, black hospital workers contacted Local 1199, whose leaders sent representatives to the southern city and began strategizing with employees and black community representatives on how best to get their union recognized. Chartering Local 1199B in Charleston, the union officially called 500 hospital workers out on strike to reinstate 12 black union activists recently fired and to win union recognition. Black women hospital workers comprised the core of Charleston's new, low-wage service sector. Not surprisingly, black women were the overwhelming majority of those strikers who stayed on strike for more than four months. In other public sector unions, such as AFSCME, African Americans and women were key in moving their unions into support of the civil rights movement. A number of women and minority unionists rose to positions of power in the public sector: Eleanor Nelson, economist and daughter of a Republican senator from Maine, in 1944 became the first woman president of a CIO union, the United Federal Workers of America; Linda Chavez Thompson, a Mexican-American woman who grew up picking cotton with her parents and then translating for the Laborers' International Union, won election as a national vice president of AFSCME in 1988; and William Lucy was the highest ranking African-American union leader when he served as AFSCME's secretary-treasurer beginning in 1972. That year Lucy joined forces with American Federation of Teachers' William H. Simmons and Lillian Roberts and AFSCME's Leonard Ball to found the Coalition of Black Trade Unionists, an organization committed to advocating for black trade unionists within the AFL-CIO.

Sometimes in the push to secure newly won rights, public employee unionists and civil rights activists stood on opposite sides of an issue. Ocean Hill, Brooklyn, became the site of a great contest when African-American community activists insisted they have some control over hiring, firing, and decision-making in the community schools that their children attended. Frustrated with failed bussing efforts, community activists' sense of entitlement bumped up against AFT teachers' job security, professionalism, and dignity. In an ugly showdown, AFT President Albert Shanker turned his back on civil rights commitments and led a group of largely white and Jewish New York teachers on an extended strike in the face of diminishing support from labor's own community and the public at large. In the end, African-American community activists lost control over area schools and teachers won back their due process, but they lost in the court of public opinion.

More often, however, when it came to the public sector, economic rights and civil rights issues blended more completely. The fight to end women and minorities' second-class treatment as public workers, for example, occasionally dovetailed with anti-poverty and welfare-rights movements. In January 1964 President Johnson announced a "War on Poverty." Medicare and Medicaid, two of his most important Great Society programs, which provided healthcare to older citizens and the poor, went a long way toward extending New Deal liberal traditions. Most Great Society programs, however, did not focus on restructuring the economy or the sexist and racially discriminatory labor market. Leaders of Great Society programs assumed that the economy was just fine: poor people, however, could use some resources to help them help themselves. The heart of Johnson's anti-poverty programs centered on the Office of Economic Opportunity (OEO), charged with bringing job training and educational programs to needy people. The OEO's Community Action programs were designed to activate poor communities to help themselves.

Community mobilization was sometimes contagious. In Memphis, public hospital, school, and park employees' pay was so low that many of these employed persons lived below the poverty line. Full-time sanitation workers still collected food stamps. Together, Memphis's underpaid and underemployed workers used Johnson's programs to mobilize into what Laurie Green in *Battling the Plantation Mentality: Memphis and the Black Freedom Struggle* (2007) calls an "urban freedom movement" in which they fought for improved housing, better treatment by housing and welfare officials, training for jobs that paid decently, childcare, and increased wages. In 1967 the Memphis Welfare Rights Organization, founded by Willie Pearl Butler, a young woman welfare recipient, and Frances Hale, a welfare and tenant-rights activist, affiliated with the National Welfare Rights Organization, held weekly meetings, organized public protests, and fought against the daily indignities and forms of discrimination welfare recipients faced.

In Las Vegas, welfare mothers mobilized in much the same way. Organized in 1972 into a non-profit, community development corporation, Operation Life, welfare mothers of West Las Vegas set up shop in an abandoned hotel, planned "eat-ins" at casinos to highlight child hunger and "read-ins" at "white only" public libraries, and fought to bring basic services to their community. Ruby Duncan and the women of Operation Life pushed Nevada's officials to accept federal poverty programs and ultimately convinced the federal government to allow them to administer them. Developing a system of management for community women to run, Operation Life effectively oversaw millions in federal dollars. "Driving a beat-up old station wagon with room for ten," Annelise Orleck in *Storming Caesar's Palace: How Black Women Fought Their Own War on Poverty* (2005) describes, "Operation Life activists – welfare mothers all – scoured the Westside, picking up mothers and children who'd never had medical care and driving them to the clinic." Their federally funded medical clinic reached the highest percentage of eligible children of any other similarly funded clinic in the country.

New Laws and Workplace Challenges

When union movements reinforced the bond between economic rights and civil rights, unions made their liberal supporters cheer. In this period of the 1960s and 1970s, however, liberals did not cheer unions often. Instead of unions, the primary champions extending civil rights in the workplace were the legal system, new laws, and the people who used them. By turning to the law and suing, people of color and women made fundamental changes in the hiring and work culture of private industry and unions. The 1964 Civil Rights Act proved especially helpful since its purpose was to end segregation in all public accommodations. Title VII of the act made discrimination in hiring and employment practices based on race, national origin, and (eventually) sex illegal. It also established an agency, the EEOC, to enforce the law. Women and minority workers, bent on moving into the well-paying trades, brought cases against construction contractors and exclusionary craft-union apprenticeship practices. They also used the law to undermine traditional union seniority guarantees and promotion ladders, as they blatantly discriminated against women and minorities. In 1972 President Nixon signed the Equal Employment Opportunity Act, which further amended and strengthened the Civil Rights Act of 1964 by extending protection against job discrimination to state and local governments, small employers, and some educational institutions and giving the EEOC the power to bring cases to federal district courts. Women and minority workers found federal civil rights laws to be their allies.

At the same time, the government's labor agency, the NLRB, spent its days certifying bargaining units and elections and hearing cases of unfair management and labor practices. But its members were not in the business of undoing discriminatory union or business practices. Civil rights groups pushed to expand the Wagner Act to include a civil rights amendment that would preclude racist unions from representing only white members through closed-shop clauses, but they were defeated. The NLRB continued certifying all-white unions. Thirty-one national unions were known for their discriminatory practices. Railroad workers, electricians, plumbers and steamfitters, sheet metal workers and boilermakers were the worst offenders. And while these unions were either independent or hailed from the AFL side of the federation, industrial unions also had their share of shady practices. United Mine, Steel and Auto Workers' Unions maintained separate auxiliaries for blacks and women and gave these groups limited rights and power.

Instead of working with the NLRB, Title VII created the EEOC and legislators charged the agency with opening jobs, and therefore unions, to minority and women groups and making sure their workplace rules and union contracts did not discriminate. The question of discrimination and how it manifested itself in society became a source of controversy, and one the EEOC and the courts worked to settle through the creation of clear guidelines. But the job of quashing inequality in the labor market was complicated, and the EEOC was given weak tools: they could only investigate and ask guilty businesses and unions to comply with their rulings. Civil rights groups pushed to give the EEOC stronger powers, to no avail.

Their weak authority was quickly compounded by the fact that EEOC workers were also thoroughly overwhelmed. Officials expected a few hundred cases in their first year, but got 9,000. By 1975 the number of cases they took increased to 77,000, but there were many more that they were unable to address. Title VII specified that no more than two months should pass between the filing of a complaint and its investigation, but by the end of 1968 the EEOC was so swamped that it took 18 months to get to cases. By

1972 its backlog numbered over 53,000 cases. Over time, the limits of the EEOC's power wore thin on civil rights groups. When the NLRB faced backlogs or lacked the will to rule on behalf of labor, unionists had no recourse. Title VII, however, established rights for aggrieved parties that allowed them their day in court. This meant that women and minorities did not have to depend on their elected officials to pass social legislation that may have chafed their white, working-class constituents. Instead, women and minorities workers now had the authority (and the will) to turn to the courts as their ally in forcing open unions and workplaces to recognize them as equals. So as political officials turned authority over to judges and lawyers, civil rights and feminist activists turned to litigation as a political strategy. They found increased power in the judicial system because it provided civil rights groups increased access to judges, making it easier for individuals to uncover damaging evidence of discrimination; special masters (a judge-appointed authority) to oversee and implement court orders; and judges to determine meaningful remedies, including levying financial penalties, against those who refused to comply.

The courts also had the power of interpretation, which they used widely to close important loopholes contained within Title VII. For example, before the law was legally challenged (and therefore interpreted by a judge), it allowed unions and employers to keep their existing seniority systems as long as they did not discriminate. If individuals thought these systems did in fact discriminate, they would have to prove that the employer or union intended to discriminate. In 1968, however, the Supreme Court in *Quarles v. Philip Morris* determined that plant seniority is discriminatory when it adversely affects African Americans. Certainly, the court argued, Congress did not mean for an entire generation of African Americans to endure the negative impact of patterns established before Title VII passed.

By 1971 there were even more particulars to sue over. That year, the EEOC and the NAACP won a ruling on affirmative action. In 1971 the Supreme Court ruled in *Griggs v. Duke Power* that even if companies hired and promoted in non-discriminatory ways, their policies may still have adverse impacts on blacks and minorities. Employer and union tests, for example, that involved diplomas or written exams could have a discriminatory impact on workers. Industries and unions using such tests would therefore need to take affirmative steps to increase the employment of affected groups to stay in compliance with the law. Title VII prohibited quotas and proportional representation, but the courts agreed that numerical goals were different than quotas and that future employees had to be qualified, but not necessarily the most qualified. Title VII also called for active recruitment of future workers through African-American media outlets, the elimination of hiring tests that were unrelated to job performance, the encouragement of existing employees to seek promotion within the company, and sometimes hiring preferences for previously excluded workers.

In 1979 the court in *US Steel Workers of America v. Weber* issued its most expansive ruling on Title VII. At Kaiser Aluminum, the company and the union agreed to a training program for unskilled workers that would set aside 50 percent of the positions for African Americans. At the time, African Americans made up less than 2 percent of the company's workforce and 40 percent of those who worked in the community. Weber, a white worker, complained that he had more seniority than African-American applicants, but was not chosen. The court ruled that seniority systems could be overturned to overcome past discriminatory practices. Righting racial wrongs trumped Weber's seniority.

The EEOC investigated and pushed conciliation between parties, but Title VII, with its right to sue and bring questions before the courts, was the piece of the legislation that most directly led to success in grassroots struggles for jobs and justice. Individuals and civil rights lawyers brought 350 cases involving Title VII to federal court in 1970, 1,500 by 1975, and 9,000 by 1983.

The law's effect on the southern textile industry was particularly dramatic. Unwilling to comply with the Civil Rights Act, mill owners insisted that they did not discriminate: blacks were simply unqualified. Courts required seniority systems be revised and made plant-wide rather than department-by-department, to give minorities the chance to move into better-paying positions. They also required mills to set racial hiring goals to ensure equality. Mill executives argued that all this was "reverse discrimination" and ignored the order. In response, the NAACP's legal counsel and the NAACP Legal Defense and Education Fund (an independent organization) filed over 1,200 class-action lawsuits between 1965 and 1971. By 1970, 15 percent of the textile labor force in the Carolinas was African American and almost half of African-American textile workers were women. The southern textile industry as a whole saw black employment increase from 6 percent to more than 25 percent in a little more than a decade.

Class-action suits were often successful but also potentially dangerous to those workers who screwed up their courage and came forward and sued. A. C. Sherrill, an African-American worker at J. P. Stevens, a southern textile manufacturer, agreed to be the lead plaintiff in a class-action suit against his employer. Once he asked about promotion policy, attacks against him began. Sherrill endured trash placed in his car, a knife put to him by white co-workers, and other threats of violence. In the end, Sherrill won (for himself and fellow plaintiffs) promotion, back pay, and court oversight of company compliance. Class-action suits were threatening to white southerners because they fought to remove fundamental barriers to economic security and power: separate seniority lists, discriminatory hiring and promotion procedures, racist recruitment, segregated locals in union plants, discriminatory pay, and tests unrelated to job performance.

The suits also had the power to bring around the Textile Workers Union (later ACTWU and now Unite Here) on the question of race. Before Title VII, even anti-racist unionists were unsure how far to push white workers on the question of racial equality. But after Title VII, TWU leaders quickly backed black workers who in turn were backed by the federal government. In one case, courts required Cannon Mills to pay $1.65 million in back wages to 3,700 black workers to compensate for discrimination, giving a huge boost to union drives in the region. It was black workers, after all, who would prove to be the union's strongest supporters, even when they criticized unions for racial discrimination. Black workers recognized that unions, regardless how flawed, were workers' last stand against workplace indignities. Many calculated that it was worthwhile to reform them from within, where at least they had some protections, rather than cast stones from the outside, where their voices would go unheard.

Whereas court cases connected to the tobacco, steel, and textile industries dealt largely with company hiring practices, demands for inclusive hiring on construction sites focused on the discriminatory actions of craft unions. Construction co-workers bonded at work through their technical skill and over their physical strength. Whiteness and manhood blended into their notions of skill and informed their definitions of labor militancy. At the same time, their work was seasonal, forcing their reliance on hiring halls, insider status, and union loyalty. As Josh Freeman argues in *Working Class New York: Life and Labor Since World War II* (2001), union control of access to jobs served as a "kind of social capital" that was passed on to family and close relations. White workers lacking other resources viewed ethnic and family control over union hiring as a sign of their security, one not willingly given up. Some locals guarded against a multicultural membership with zeal: one asbestos local required potential apprentices to have letters of recommendation from three of the local's members, a majority membership vote of approval by secret ballot, and four years' helper experience. Local 28 of the Sheet Metal Workers Union never had a non-white member and gave positions to family members before others on apprenticeship waiting lists.

The tight, closed nature of the construction industry gave civil rights groups a good reason to focus on it. But more than simply access to and entry into construction trades would redefine the status of black men in the United States. Testifying before a congressional subcommittee, Herbert Hill, NAACP leader and one of the prickliest thorns lodged in the AFL-CIO's side, summed up this sentiment: "Jobs in the building trades are for men." White men in the construction trades took home more pay than workers in any other blue-collar position, and many of them earned those wages on publicly funded projects in the heart of black communities. Skill, good pay, and personal dignity were all at stake.

The construction industry, however, was enormous and diffuse, proving extremely difficult for minorities to penetrate. Over 900,000 contractors worked with 10,000 local unions who oversaw 30,000 separate labor agreements. Civil rights activists focused on state-funded construction projects where they at least would have public leverage, but even then lines of authority were unclear. In 1963 NAACP activists in Philadelphia, Cleveland, Newark, New York, and Pittsburgh organized against discriminatory construction sites and demanded that construction unions hire African-American and Puerto Rican workers. That summer a Joint Committee for Equal Employment Opportunity, with members from the NAACP, the Negro American Labor Alliance, the Workers' Defense League, the Urban League, and the Association of Catholic Trade Unionists, targeted a Harlem hospital annex building site with picket lines. The city stopped the project, afraid of potential unrest, and charged a committee to investigate discrimination in the building trades. The city's central labor council agreed to open a discussion about discrimination in the trades, but when little follow-up occurred, the Joint Committee took their protest to Mayor Robert Wagner's office, where they conducted a sit-in. They then moved their demonstration to a Lower East Side housing construction site, where they set up pickets, and then to Governor Nelson Rockefeller's city office, where they attracted public attention. Finally, they demonstrated in Bedford-Stuyvesant, where the State University was building a medical center with public dollars.

In 1965 President Johnson issued executive order 11246 that required federal contractors to take affirmative action to insure equal employment opportunities. Contractors needed to file reports describing their employment practices and advertise their commitment not to discriminate and show good-faith efforts to meet hiring goals in each construction trade. The Office of Federal Contract Compliance (OFCC) in the Department of Labor was charged with insuring compliance, but like the EEOC the OFCC was understaffed and lacked funding. Construction union officials encouraged that the office take a hands-off approach to their hiring systems, and they did.

147

Whereas construction trades had a long tradition of racial and gender exclusion, the discriminatory practices of AFL-CIO affiliates with industrial traditions was particularly troubling. Unlike construction jobs that were brokered through unions whose members kept their entry door tightly shut, employers handed out industrial jobs. Industrial unions, with a pubic commitment to organizing all manner of worker within an industry, cast their membership net widely. They just did not treat their members equitably. Questions of job security and promotion within industrial unions depended on how contracts defined seniority. Would seniority be earned only within certain departments or along particular skill lines or would it carry throughout the entire plant? One model insured white, male, skilled workers more security than the other. Before Title VII, the practices of defining seniority narrowly, maintaining segregated locals and auxiliaries, and refusing to integrate departments prevailed, which increased the vulnerability of non-white and female workers and prevented their ability to move up within plants.

Two industrial unions with the most militant and democratic traditions, the ILGWU and the UAW, came under particular scrutiny. In 1962 Herbert Hill charged the ILGWU with racism. Ernest Holmes, an African-American garment worker, joined Hill and filed charges with the New York State Commission for Human Rights, charging that Local 10 of the ILGWU, an all-white union of fabric cutters, would not admit Holmes because he was black. At one time the ILGWU represented the best in social-democratic union traditions, but by the 1960s and 1970s Jewish and Italian union leaders ruled the union with an iron fist and discriminated against their own African-American and Puerto Rican members. Skilled jobs – and the locals that organized them – excluded blacks and Puerto Ricans. Union rules, restrictive to newcomers, prevented members of these groups from taking union office and fighting from within. In response to Hill's and Holmes' charges, Congressman Adam Clayton Powell Jr. convened hearings in the House Committee on Education and Labor on ILGWU's alleged discrimination. With the liberal press covering the case, industrial unionism took a hit.

Even worse was the turmoil surrounding the UAW. There was no question that the big union was at the forefront of liberal unionism: its leaders took public positions in support of tax reform, national health insurance, and civil rights legislation. Within its own house, UAW leaders stood behind their constitution and its anti-segregation provisions. When locals dragged their feet on this matter, UAW leadership revoked charters, put local members under their direct control, and forced their compliance. But in 1960 the UAW's executive board lacked black representation; and its black members remained clustered in the lowest-skilled and lowest-paying positions. By the late 1960s black workers made up the majority of the workforce in Detroit's inner-city plants. Dodge Main's enormous complex of 30,000 workers was at least half African American. African Americans laboring in Chrysler's Eldon Avenue gear and axle plant made up about 80 percent of the workforce. These workers were young: in 1968, for example, more than a third of the UAW's Chrysler's membership was under 30 and more than half had less than five years' seniority.

Emboldened by a militant racial consciousness, these workers challenged poor work conditions, hostile employers, and UAW leaders. David Lewis Coleman in *Race Against Liberalism: Black Workers and the UAW in Detroit* (2008) finds the origins of radical African-American protest groups in black "victory committees" that formed during World War II. Linking workplace politics with community based struggles over housing, education, and electoral politics, groups of black workers organized workplace councils, articulated anti-imperialist, Marxist messages, and staged wildcat strikes over shop-floor issues. The group in the Dodge Main plant called itself the Dodge Revolutionary Union Movement (DRUM); Ford's black worker council was called the Ford Revolutionary Union Movement (FRUM). Such sympathetic UAW leaders as Douglas Fraser did not like the groups' extremism, but agreed that they raised legitimate issues. Others were less convinced, characterizing these protesters as a bunch of "fanatics." In the end, this radical style of rank-and-file protest won changes in the union. A number of locals in Detroit elected black officers and the international union increased its number of black staff

149

members. Small improvements also occurred in the plants: UAW contracts pushed harder against companies and to get minorities into skilled jobs.

Whether unions were sympathetic or not, individuals found they had a powerful weapon in the form of the courts. Overall, the EEOC opened 658 investigations against the AFL-CIO before June 1967; eleven years later the number was 2,617. Between 1964 and 1985, 296 local affiliates faced federal court charges, with the International Brotherhood of Electrical Workers (IBEW) alone implicated in 44 cases of discrimination. The IBEW's legal fees quadrupled between 1965 and 1975, and the Sheet Metal Workers Union's increased six times in the 1970s. The United Steel Workers signed a national decree to defend their locals against potential bankruptcy. The costs of litigation were huge: courts ordered back pay and attorney's fees, and forced financial sanctions. They also brokered consent decrees whereby unions paid millions in initial settlements and then agreed to change their practices. Judges readily recognized the power of the pocketbook in enforcing change.

They were right. In 1972 a class-action suit against the Teamsters Union resulted in the integration of previously segregated locals in Boston, Buffalo, and Washington, DC. Minority membership increased in these places by 1975 from 0 percent to 13 percent. In Seattle a federal court ordered ironworkers, sheet metal workers, electricians, and plumbers and pipefitters to participate in an affirmative action apprenticeship program. When unions waffled on committing to compliance and civil rights groups turned up the pressure, a federal judge took the initial ruling even further, including a rewriting of the unions' collective bargaining agreements and appointing a special master to participate daily in overseeing the unions' implementation. The improvement was not dramatic, but within three years, three of the unions were within 50–70 percent of mandated goals. The electricians were the only ones to meet them. In Washington, DC, seven craft unions targeted by class-action suits improved their practices, the sheet metal workers increasing from 8.5 percent minority workers to 21.8 percent.

Women and Workplace Rights

The EEOC assumed that their cases would largely come from male workers, but they were wrong. Women's groups were inspired by the way civil rights activists and individuals used Title VII to extend economic citizenship in the wider world of work. In the summer of 1965, 2,432 women filed complaints about discrimination at work. They questioned companies' hiring practices, unequal wages, sex-segregated seniority lists, unequal benefits, and discriminatory promotion and recruitment. With assistance from the National Organization for Women Legal Defense and Education Fund, women workers at Bell Telephone filed a landmark class-action suit in 1971 that outlined the company's systematic gender, race, and national-origin discrimination.

Such active women as these continued the tradition of labor feminism into a new generation. By the 1950s, labor feminists hailed from CIO unions that had purged the left and embraced liberal and anticommunist commitments, such as the UAW, the International Union of Electrical Workers (IUE), the Amalgamated Clothing Workers of America (ACWA), and the Communications Workers of America (CWA). They were also active in those unions still influenced by left elements, such as the United Packinghouse Workers of America (UPWA) and the United Electrical, Radio and Machine Workers (UE), as well as in AFL affiliates such as the Hotel Employees and Restaurant Employees Union (HERE). These rank-and-file women workers were joined in their political commitment to improve women's position in unions and within the world of work by college-educated women who often took union staff positions: in 1953 women headed eleven research departments. The federal Women's Bureau and its Labor Advisory Committee served as an important support system, helping to channel the voices of labor's women down corridors of power.

In the 1960s the generation of women activists who hailed from the period of World War II found common cause with a younger generation of feminists and women workers. Labor feminists ignited second-wave feminism (the women's movement that emerged in the postwar period) and helped direct feminist concerns toward the world of work. In 1966 the National Organization for Women (NOW) came into existence and called immediately for women's equal treatment in the economy and for President Johnson to add a sex provision to his executive order 11246 that prohibited race discrimination among federal contractors. Several labor women took positions in NOW, and the UAW, under pressure from its women leaders, offered them office space and administrative support. WAGE (Women's Alliance to Gain Equality), an organization of female unionists in California, formed in 1971 in hopes of extending protective labor laws to men; and beginning in 1974 the Coalition of Labor Union Women (CLUW), a national organization, represented a growing power within the labor movement. Once in motion, however, labor union women quickly learned that not all of them saw issues in the same way. Title VII helped to crystalize their differences.

Figure 3.2 Participants at the CLUW founding conference at Rich Congress Hotel, Chicago, Illinois. Walter P. Reuther Library, Wayne State University (#28345).

Perhaps the biggest issue dividing them was the question of protective legislation – laws that "protected" one group of people, in this case women. As early as 1908 the United States Supreme Court established in *Muller v. Oregon* that it was legal to limit the number of hours women could work. The majority ruled, based on the famous Brandeis brief that was prepared by progressive labor reformers, that since women were biologically weaker and the bearers of society's future children, some sex-based laws and discrimination were legal. Progressive labor reformers hoped that these protections would be extended to all workers eventually, but until that time they were willing to let women stand on an unequal footing.

By the mid-1960s the new generation of labor feminists questioned whether women should be treated differently than men. At first they were rebuffed by the EEOC, whose members advised employers that they would be in compliance with Title VII even if they refused to hire a woman because of her sex. But then EEOC members changed their mind and began to hear cases dealing with state violations of the federal law. Under pressure from NOW, the EEOC issued administrative guidelines clearly stating that state laws prohibiting opportunities for women violated Title VII. NOW members felt the thrill of victory when ensuing federal court decisions agreed. WAGE, on the other hand, hoped to extend the beneficial protections of such legislation as hours laws to all workers instead of getting rid of them altogether. In the end, a few states extended their protections regarding working hours to men as well as women, but most simply repealed the old directive.

The new generation's sensibilities also pushed women to ask questions about the legitimacy of employers' pregnancy and childbearing-age policies. If women could be excluded from jobs because of pregnancy or being of childbearing age, then economic discrimination against women would be allowed to continue. In early 1972 NOW pushed the EEOC to develop guidelines treating pregnancy as any other temporary disability, with women having the right to leaves of absence as well as the right to keep seniority. The IUE filed a class lawsuit against General Electric, Westinghouse, and General Motors because these companies barred pregnant women from using their sick leave as maternity leave. A CWA class-action suit against AT&T focused on the fact that its temporary disability policy excluded pregnancy. The courts initially sided with the union women, but when the Supreme Court ruled in 1976 that employer plans could make distinctions between the pregnant and non-pregnant, women pushed for federal legislation. And they got it. The 1978 Pregnancy Discrimination Act amended the Civil Rights Act to protect pregnant women from unfair treatment, including lesser benefits.

Issues dealing with pregnancy sometimes divided women who worked. Some women insisted that pregnancy be treated like any other disability when it came to benefits, while others drafted state statutes that emphasized pregnant women's difference from other disabled workers. California was one of the states where labor women secured such a benefit; its pregnant workers could be treated differently than other disabled workers. In 1982 a receptionist at the California Federal Savings and Loan Association, Lillian Garland, tried to come back to work after a pregnancy leave, but the bank refused her return because it had filled her job. Garland turned to California's Department of Fair Employment and Housing and found their lawyers willing to charge the savings of loan with violating California law. Her employer found support from the Chamber of Commerce and employer groups, who argued that the state law discriminated against men and women with disabilities unrelated to pregnancy and should be overturned. The labor-women's community divided over the case. NOW and the Women's Rights Project of the American Civil Liberties Union (ACLU) agreed with the bank while 9to5 and other labor groups supported state law. In the end the Supreme Court sided with the state against the bank and ruled that states may require employers to grant job protections to pregnant employees even if they do not do so for workers with other disabilities.

However divisive questions of difference and job security were, labor women united their forces in the call for comprehensive childcare. In 1971 President Nixon vetoed a comprehensive childcare bill, which channeled labor-women's energies back to their unions and their contracts. They wanted federally funded and union-negotiated plans. In 1972 ACWA pressured the AFL-CIO to hold its first conference on daycare in Chicago and CLUW and the AFL-CIO pushed throughout the 1970s for universally available and federally funded, affordable childcare programs. Tax credits for childcare did expand in 1976 and 1978, but conservative opposition to government subsidies doomed unionists' larger agenda. In many ways the 1993 Family Medical Leave Act, which allows for up to 12 weeks of unpaid protected leave so workers can have time to tend to childbirth, adoption, and family members' illnesses, is a product of their efforts.

Women workers also used Title VII to fight against sexual objectification at work. Kathleen Barry in *Femininity in Flight: A History of Flight Attendants* (2007) shows how flight attendants challenged the "wages of glamour" that suggested that these women did not really work. Restrictive marriage, weight, pregnancy, and age rules combined with provocative uniforms and the "fly me" message to give flight attendants all the ammunition they needed in their court battle against the airlines. Women unionists fought from within the Transport Workers and Pilots unions to get their fellow members to take their issues seriously; individual women also filed complaints with the New York Human Rights Commission and the EEOC. With the TWU convinced of their women members' cause, their leaders testified before Congress in 1965 and 1967 and won the Age Discrimination Act of 1967. The problem, however, was that the law only covered workers over the age of 40. The airlines forced women to retire sooner than that. American Airlines argued that older women were less perky, and after age 38, physically and emotionally unfit to do their jobs. Union and EEOC pressure forced airlines to change their policies. Flight attendants then brought their frustration with marriage and motherhood restrictions to the bargaining table and the courtroom: again, their voices were heard. A 1967 EEOC ruling against marriage restrictions gave women and unions grounds to sue against non-compliant employers. A 1971 United States Court of Appeals decision struck down "female only" hiring in the airlines, opening the flight attendant job to men.

By the early 1970s the focus of female flight attendants shifted from discriminatory hiring policies to the right to control their own sexuality. Whereas flight attendants generally took pride in their appearance, airlines' selling of flight attendants' femininity and sexuality in ads, suggesting, for example, that they would make passengers "feel good all over," diminished their profession and encouraged unwanted advances by male passengers, argued many flight attendants. Facing a union that was less sensitive than were they to these issues, stewardesses launched the first women's national organization of flight attendants, Stewardesses for Women's Rights. Calling out their union for caring more about economics than women's personhood, they allied themselves with middle-class women, picketed outside theaters that showed films depicting flight attendants as sex objects, filed lawsuits, and launched a media campaign complete with "Go Fly yourself" buttons and "National [airlines], Your Fly is Open" bumper stickers. Arguing against "sexploitation," these women redefined the flight attendant's role from one of servant to one of safety professional. Eventually joined by female-led flight attendant unions, these women successfully changed company policies regarding uniforms, grooming, and weight requirements.

Like flight attendants, clerical workers in the private sector increasingly resented the demeaning aspects of their jobs. Largely ignored by labor unions because they were thought to be incapable of being organized and too loyal to their employers, clerical workers surprised many when in the early 1970s they stood up in creative and militant ways. In 1973, 9to5 grew out of Harvard University secretaries' lunchtime discussions and grew into a community organization of hundreds led by Karen Nussbaum and Ellen Cassedy. By the end of the 1970s the National Association of Working Women united local groups from around the country into a national organization representing 10,000 women. Using lawsuits, pickets, and demonstrations, clerical workers brought attention to their workplace culture and bosses' expectations. Successfully changing society's expectations of clerical duties, the movement was most effective among workers in small offices. Those in larger offices, responsible for typing, filing, and processing paperwork, reaped fewer of the benefits until Nussbaum worked out an agreement with the Service Employees International Union (SEIU) and began unionizing. Such unions as SEIU and AFSCME organized among low-wage public sector and service workers, and by the late 1970s turned their attention to women workers and their specific issues.

Whereas flight attendants and clerical workers represented large groups of white women, the 1965 National Committee of Household Employees grew out of local communities composed largely of African-American female domestic workers. Inspired by civil rights organizations, these groups mobilized for respect, better pay, and federal protections. Labor women in the Women's Bureau aided their mobilization. All eyes focused on extending the Fair Labor Standards Act (FLSA) to domestic workers. In 1974 they succeeded and domestic workers gained the minimum wage, unemployment insurance, and workers' compensation coverage.

The Push and Pull of Changing Times: New Unionists, Rank-and-File Movements, AFL-CIO Leaders, and Nixon

Over the long run, the ferment that swirled around civil rights and feminist movements in the public and private sectors served to awaken some in the otherwise stagnating labor movement. The labor and civil rights activists Cesar Chavez and Dolores Huerta and what became the United Farm Workers (UFW) provide a good example of this. As late as the 1960s, the AFL-CIO's half-hearted attempt to organize farm workers was faltering. Larry Itliong, a Filipino grape worker, led one of its only viable locals in Delano, California, but California agricultural interests had deep pockets to influence state policy and most farm workers were too poor and too vulnerable to challenge their pathetic pay, inhumane living conditions, and toxic, chemically laden work conditions. In part that is why everyone was so surprised when, under Itliong's leadership, grape workers sat down in their farm labor camps and refused to work for less than $1.40 an hour and

157

Figure 3.3   AFL-CIO members support striking farm workers during the Delano strike, *ca.* 1965–1966. Larry Itliong (left), Walter Reuther (center), and Cesar Chavez (far right) are shown carrying signs. Walter P. Reuther Library, Wayne State University (#362).

25 cents a box. This simple act ignited a movement, but the work of Chavez and Huerta was key to its success. First they organized a small number of farm workers into a National Farm Workers Association to support the grape workers' strike, and then they reached outside the San Joaquin Valley community for help. In came members of the California Migrant Ministry (an agency of the Southern and Northern California Councils of Churches), who walked picket lines and went to jail, all the while calling for basic labor and civil rights for farm workers. Then came the Reuther brothers – Roy and Walter – with a $5,000 check from the UAW and another that size from the AFL-CIO and promises for the same amount for each month the strike continued. Bill Kircher, the AFL-CIO's chief organizer, commuted back and forth between Delano and Washington, DC, to help the strike.

National attention kept building. In 1966 Democratic Senator Harrison Williams from New Jersey brought a migrant labor subcommittee to Delano High School's auditorium and listened as migrant farm workers introduced the nation to their plight. Their words caught the ear of Robert Kennedy, who became an important national ally to what became widely known as *la causa*. They also gained the backing of Bishop Hugh Donohoe, who reiterated the Catholic Church's commitment to working people's right to organize. Unimpressed, growers trucked in scabs from Texas and Mexico, right past the pickets. With the new pickers on the job, the growers could afford to ignore Chavez, Huerta, and their ilk.

But then Chavez called for a boycott of table grapes and Huerta helped direct it. First they called the boycott against the produce of the 11,000-acre Giumarra vineyard, and eventually against all California-grown grapes. The federal government excluded farm workers from the National Labor Relations Act, Taft-Hartley, and Landrum-Griffin, which stung at first, but actually came in handy in this struggle, for this meant that there were no restrictions on a boycott. Chavez admitted, "The boycott is our only economic weapon; without it we are dead." Farm workers and their supporters fanned out to cities across the nation and shared their co-workers' plight. As a direct result of their efforts, among Americans living in big cities and suburbs across the nation, boycotting non-union grapes became a convenient, painless, and direct way to support civil rights, unionism, and anti-poverty movements in one act. Grapes shipped with the iconic farm worker union's red-and-black Aztec-styled Eagle, which morally conscious consumers could eat guilt free, turned up at grocery stores across the country, in high demand and fetching a pretty penny. To further draw attention to the migrant farm workers' non-violent struggle, Chavez went on a highly publicized water-only 25-day fast. Huerta, meanwhile, lobbied in Sacramento, California, and Washington, DC, and spoke out against the danger that pesticides posed to workers, consumers, and the environment.

In the end the boycott succeeded. In 1969, under economic pressure, growers succumbed to the calls of a group of bishops to begin talks with the farm workers. Slowly, one-by-one, the growers broke ranks, and when 30 percent of the industry signed formal labor contracts, the farm workers got their biggest victory in their struggle: Delano growers gave in. After five years on strike, Chavez, Huerta, and Itliong merged their groups into what became the United Farm Workers (UFW) and pushed for (and ultimately won) state-specific laws that allowed farm workers the right to union protection. All was not, however, smooth riding. The Teamsters signed labor contracts with lettuce growers behind their backs, keeping the UFW out of the lettuce business. At the same time, UFW organizers were unable to gain a foothold on the East Coast, where sugar and fruit growers succeeded in manipulating guest worker programs to their advantage: they even had the authority to deport workers who questioned their squalid living or dangerous working conditions. With the threat of deportation before them, most guest workers in this part of the nation gave UFW organizers the cold shoulder. But in California, at least, farm workers were finding union protections. By 1970, 85 percent of table grape growers in California signed union contracts, as did a number of strawberry and lettuce growers.

These civil rights movements that equated the benefits of union membership with democratic principles and just workplace practices also inspired rank-and-file activism among those already unionized in the private sector, but, sadly, in unions that disregarded democratic principles. Throughout AFL-CIO affiliates, movements of rank-and-file workers burst onto the scene in the 1960s and 1970s and challenged contracts their leaders negotiated, union corruption, degrading work conditions, authoritarian management tactics, and a general lack of internal union democracy. In the United Steel Workers of America agitators called themselves Steelworkers Fight Back; in the United Auto Workers, they were New Directions; in the United Mine Workers of America, they were the Miners for Democracy. Teamsters for a Democratic Union resulted from a 1979 merger between a reform group by the same name and the Professional Drivers' Council. By the 1960s, a younger generation that was beginning to question authority and tradition had entered these core industries; and they were not as easily intimidated. They shared the anti-authoritarian values of their college-educated peers; and even though they valued their union, they were not necessarily loyal to their union leadership, which included older persons with different values.

It was out of these rank-and-file movements that ordinary union members created intra-movements to safeguard health and safety standards on the job. Coal miners led the way in 1969 when hundreds of them, members of the protest Black Lung Association, marched on West Virginia's state capitol demanding compensation for black lung disease, a debilitating condition caused on-the-job from prolonged breathing of coal dust. Initiating a strike for a black lung law, the powerful demonstration inspired fellow workers to shut down mines throughout the state-this in the face of UMW leaders' disapproval. When a West Virginia mine exploded killing 78 workers that same year, UMW leaders finally negotiated a federal coal mine health and safety act. The new law included black lung compensation, but roadblocks made it difficult for those miners actually suffering to get their hands on the money.

Still, having won federal legislation, rank-and-file miners decided the time was ripe to oust their corrupt leader, Tony Boyle. This would not be easy. Boyle ran a tight and conservative ship, one that he was not willing to abandon. To prove it, he gave the order to have the Black Lung Association-backed candidate Jock Yablonski and his family murdered on New Year' Eve of 1969. That day three hired assassins broke into the Yablonski home in south-western Pennsylvania and shot Yablonski's 25-year-old daughter and his wife. One of the killers then filled Jock with a half a dozen bullets. With pressure from Miners for Democracy, an organization started by Yablonski's surviving sons and union reformers, the Department of Labor called for a new election, which reformer Arnold Miller, with the support of the Black Lung Association, won. Tony Boyle was charged and convicted of conspiracy and went to prison, where he died in 1985.

On the heels of the coal miners' new crusade for health and safety, President Richard Nixon signed the Occupational Safety and Health Act (OSHA), legislation that sparked health and safety movements among rank-and-file union groups in various industrial cities. Traditional dangers faced by coal miners and steel workers became terms of the debate, as did new job responsibilities managers increasingly put on office workers and restrictions they put on pregnant women and women of childbearing age. The Oil, Chemical and Atomic Workers Union struck against Shell Oil in 1973 because of safety concerns. They also supported Karen Silkwood, a union activist and nuclear plant technician who was murdered on her way to reveal to reporters the ways in which Kerr McGee's nuclear energy plant near Oklahoma City violated safety standards. The company was later found guilty of purposely contaminating her apartment and the case established corporate liability for nuclear radiation contamination. The 1983 film *Silkwood* chronicles her story.

At the same time that civil rights and feminist struggles infused the rank-and-file movements with new energy, court cases mounted against the AFL-CIO and its affiliates, and unions continued to struggle with their relationship to the larger movements around them. Not all union leaders were of Tony Boyle's ilk. Some were genuinely committed to economic justice for all and saw their union interests as closely aligned with civil rights struggles for equality. Still, even if they wanted to be, union leaders could only be as strong as their membership permitted.

Nowhere was this tension more palpable than in the South, where whiteness was tightly tied to workplace privileges; it was not unusual for union members in this region of the country to hold membership in the Klan or the White Citizen's Council. Throughout the land of Dixie, Jim Crow was still a way of life and white workers, in general, were committed to defending it. Since all southern states, with the exception of Louisiana, were right-to-work states, national or state AFL-CIO leaders had to balance their commitment to civil rights with their responsibility to protect their members. If they took too strong a stance in support of civil rights and their white members stopped paying dues, it would weaken their ability to function, threatening the very existence of unions in certain locales. This is exactly the kind of thing that happened in Virginia and Arkansas after the Supreme Court ruled in *Brown v. Board of Education of Topeka, Kansas* that segregation in public schools was illegal, as legislators in these states closed their schools rather than see them integrated. Trying to redirect the issue from segregation (a sentiment they knew their members supported), Virginia's and Arkansas's AFL-CIO leaders touted the importance of a free public education. Schools should stay open in the name of free public schools; the fury against integrated schools, these union leaders insisted, missed the larger point. That they did not directly challenge racism should not be surprising given their members' commitment to Jim Crow. Still, even having been careful to hedge on the issue, the state federations lost members. In 1955 there were 26 carpenters' locals in Arkansas, but by 1960 there were only seven. The plumbers went from five locals in 1955 to one in 1960. Most of the losses were among workers in the trades, a traditionally conservative enclave within the labor movement. Their abdication sent their state federation into the red and forced the national AFL-CIO to redirect its monies from organizing campaigns to stabilizing state federations.

In spite of southern unionists' support for school segregation, the national AFL-CIO openly took official positions in support of civil rights writ large. As early as the AFL-CIO merger in 1955, the federation called for fair employment practices laws, non-discrimination clauses in union contracts, integrated public facilities, and no barriers to African Americans' full political participation. In 1955 AFL-CIO President George Meany encouraged federation lobbyists to work in the District of Columbia with those pushing the civil rights agenda. Both the Student Nonviolent Coordinating Committee (SNCC) and the Congress of Racial Equality (CORE) received resources and support from trade unions. Southern labor activists worked to register African Americans to vote. Peter Levy's *The New Left and Labor in the 1960s* (1994) documents the collaboration that existed in the early 1960s between the labor movement and student groups in their effort to organize the poor through the Economic Research and Action Project. According to Levy, the early 1960s was a period when new left students, civil rights activists, and progressive trade unionists shared a similar goal of realigning the Democratic Party on behalf of civil rights and economic equality. By the early 1960s the labor movement had desegregated its state-wide union conventions so, for example, when West Virginia's delegates met at the Daniel Boone Hotel in Charleston, West Virginia, in 1959 they were the first in the state to breach the color line.

With the 1963 March on Washington, however, cracks in the labor movement began to show. Most of the industrial unions from the CIO's side of the house supported the march, as did several state federations. In addition to the liberal unions that would be expected to support this kind of event, even a few white locals from unions with their own patterns of discrimination – the IBEW, the ILGWU, and the longshoremen – jumped on board. For them, it was easier to support the dream of equality than to live it as a daily workplace practice; and they went through the motions of showing support. But former plumber and postwar Cold Warrior Meany refused to do that because mass mobilizations threatened him, and he was not sure that they would be effective. And while he did not back the march, he did support civil rights legislation, including Title VII. It is beyond dispute that union members' electoral influence and lobbying activity in Congress and in the White House helped win passage of the Civil Rights Acts of 1964, 1965, and 1972.

And yet Meany's refusal to support the 1963 march for jobs and freedom hinted at a larger ambivalence that a number of white, liberal, national labor leaders showed toward questions of race and gender equality. Men like Meany, Reuther, David McDonald of the Steelworkers, and David Dubinsky of the Ladies Garment Workers did not grasp the urgency or desperation that moved working-class women and minorities to act. These leaders' sense of self, their institutional power, and overall respect they commanded came from the battles they fought in the 1930s and 1940s to establish their unions and bring security to groups of working people, and from victories in the 1940s against communists and in the name of America. Yet despite the fact that in the early 1960s African Americans constituted about one quarter of the AFL-CIO's membership, only one African American, A. Philip Randolph, from the Brotherhood of Sleeping Car Porters, sat on the federation's leading council. White leaders' inflexibility on these matters would ultimately cost them and their unions public respect-as well as lots of money settling legal challenges.

Interestingly, the most determined and courageous support for racial equality within the AFL-CIO came not from the North, but from down in Dixie. Down south, commitment to racial equality required fearlessness from union leaders because the people they represented generally opposed social change and preferred to disaffiliate from the AFL-CIO rather than suffer its liberal stands on race or gender. From where southern-state AFL-CIO leaders sat, though, the one-party Democratic South was much more of a burden than a benefit. They understood that if black Americans could win the right to vote, labor would have an ally in the South and together the black–labor alliance would rid the region of those politicians who insisted on anti-labor and racist laws (the two agendas often worked hand in hand). With white conservative Democrats out of office, the war against the South would finally be won. On September 10, 1966, *The AFL-CIO News* printed the words of white Mississippian Claude Ramsay, who led the state's AFL-CIO and understood the urgency of a labor–black political coalition: "Twenty-six counties in Mississippi have a Negro popular majority. Many of labor's worst enemies in the Mississippi state legislature live in these counties: If these people are to be removed from office it will have to be with the Negro vote. To a large degree our legislative program is dependent on our ability to form alliances with these people and this we are trying to do." To that end, southern state council officers opposed segregation in public facilities, schools, and at their own conventions, openly defended the national Democratic Party, and supported civil rights voter registration drives.

Their actions put them in harm's way. Victor Bussie, Louisiana's state president of the AFL-CIO, came home one night to find a cross burning on his front lawn. In another incident his car was firebombed. Mississippi's Claude Ramsay carried a gun wherever he went; he just received too many death threats not to be cautious. No wonder these state council leaders were unable to turn their state federations around on questions of race, and that in some cases they felt forced to take positions on civil rights that skirted the issue. Still, as Alan Draper in *Conflict of Interests: Organized Labor and the Civil Rights Movement in the South, 1954–1968* (1994) argues, "Southern state council officers provided courageous leadership in the face of a resistant membership and antagonistic political culture."

To a person, these southern AFL-CIO state officers belie stereotypes. According to Draper, "no southern state council president came from the liberal, industrial wing of the labor movement; almost all of them began their careers in segregated union locals." They hailed from the firefighters, typographers, papermakers, electrical workers, plumbers, and teachers, and represented workers in Alabama, Mississippi, South Carolina, Texas, and Arkansas. In this case, union principles helped them overcome a larger culture of racism.

As the union movement pushed and pulled against civil rights imperatives, the costs of Title VII litigation weakened it to a large degree. The Sheet Metal Workers Local 28 in New York City, for example, faced continual litigation in the 1970s and 1980s. The union failed to meet court-ordered quotas of 29 percent racial minorities, only reaching 10 percent by 1982. By the end of the 1980s they succeeded in reaching 20 percent minority membership, but went bankrupt: the courts required them to pay more than $12 million in wages. United States Supreme Court Justice Thurgood Marshall was more sensitive than other judges when it came to penalizing unions with punitive damage awards. After all, what good would weakened unions be for African Americans, women, and minority groups?

Unlike Marshall, who respected the role of unions in American society, President Nixon only hoped to use them when he thought they could shore-up his own political position. Racial tensions within the movement and among working people more generally encouraged him to act in a divisive way. His first attempt to put a wedge between working people came in the form of the Philadelphia Plan, a blueprint for integrating the trades. It promised city jobs to non-union minority men, the abolition of union-run, racially exclusive apprenticeship programs, and numerical hiring goals and timetables for hiring black workers in each craft. Nixon and his staff were joyful in the knowledge that they had crafted a civil rights initiative that made labor and liberals uncomfortable. And while the president took pleasure in fracturing the Democratic–liberal coalition, his political commitments were never with black workers or the civil rights movement, and few missed his hypocrisy. It was Nixon's administration, after all, that fought EEOC funding tooth and nail and worked to diminish the authority of both the EEOC and the OFCC. It was also Nixon's administration that announced a 75 percent cutback in federal spending on construction. Nixon's plan enticed black workers into an industry at the same time that jobs were leaving and white workers were growing desperate. In the end, the administration backed off the plan and agreed to voluntary efforts in the industry.

This was not where Nixon was going to draw the line. In relation to working people, he would court white working-class men and reshape class politics. The plan, it turns out, was a distraction to Nixon's developing "blue-collar strategy" of co-opting blue-collar workers for the Republican Party. Whereas the "Southern Strategy" focused Republican efforts on segregationists and their frustration with civil rights legislation in the South, Nixon's blue-collar strategy would make these race-based politics a national strategy, with the forgotten white, virile, patriotic worker at the center. The political right won the hearts and minds of much of white, male, working-class America on cultural grounds at the same time that liberalism was drained of much of its class-based appeal.

Nixon sensed he was on the right track in the wake of the May 1970 construction-worker attack on antiwar protesters. In the incident, 200 construction workers shoved their way through New York City's financial district in hot pursuit of peaceful demonstrators out to protest the Kent State killings and the extension of the Vietnam War into Cambodia. In their fury, the construction workers caught up to and roughed up 70 of the hated "hippies," shedding blood. Later that month, 100,000 war supporters turned out for a Building and Construction Trades Council of Greater New York rally, waving American flags.

The president put his Special Counsel, Charles Colson, on the job to shore-up relations with conservative union leaders and, over time, with the rank and file in more liberal unions. Some union leaders did not require much courting. The head of the New York Building Trades Council presented Nixon with a hard hat labeled "Commander in Chief," which Nixon attempted to

167

use to his symbolic advantage. He, in turn, invited AFL-CIO officials to a Labor Day dinner at the White House. His administration's analysis of the 1970 election returns revealed to Nixon that
the blue-collar vote was up for grabs. And while he and Meany
did not see eye to eye on economic policy, they bonded tightly
over foreign policy and US commitments in Vietnam.

The extension of Cold War policy into Vietnam divided working
people and split once solid liberal–left coalitions. As student, civil
rights, and new left groups allied into antiwar coalitions, the AFL-
CIO's leaders stood firmly behind Johnson and then Nixon in
support of an increasingly unpopular war, continuing their postwar
commitment to US foreign policy and victory in the Cold War.
Between 1960 and 1968 the AFL-CIO funneled $20 million sup-
plied by the Department of State's Agency for International Development to Vietnam to help build non-communist unions. A 1967
AFL-CIO convention antiwar resolution was defeated 2,000 to 6.

Meany and federation leaders stood tough for US foreign policy
even when it meant backing military dictators and corruption, but
by the late 1960s individuals within the house of labor showed
they felt differently. Jerry Wurf from AFSCME publicly attacked
Meany, Nixon, and Vietnam policy and won the honor of being
placed on Nixon's temporarily secret "enemies list." Anger over
Vietnam also pushed the UAW out of the AFL-CIO federation. The
federation's pro-war position meant that antiwar Democratic presidential candidate George McGovern ran for president in 1972
without the AFL-CIO's official endorsement; state and local labor
supporters went out on their own in a futile effort to raise money,
knock on doors, and bring home a McGovern victory.

The fact that the federation refused to back pro-union and
antiwar McGovern, and 57 percent of the manual worker vote
and 54 percent of the union vote went to Nixon (a 25 percentage-
point gain over 1968), suggests to some scholars that Nixon's
strategy paid off. Of course, white working-class reaction to
liberal government policy grew in the face of bussing and school
integration, public housing conflicts, and "white flight" to the
suburbs. A growing right, in many respects a backlash to the
student and anti-Vietnam War movements, believed in individu-

alism, untouchable property rights, small government, and the power of the free market to reward the worthy. Postwar ideals of economic security in one's job and one's neighborhood meant different things to different groups of people, resulting in ugly conflict, hostility, and even violence.

Nixon was able to fan the flames of anger and racial discontent, but his own fear of inflation and recession exposed his inability to be a true ally of working people. Just as his lack of sincerity came through in his giving of the Philadelphia Plan and then taking away construction jobs, Nixon was unwilling to rethink his economic assumptions in regard to his new blue-collar supporters. Construction wages, he believed, drove inflation and their rise needed to slow, maybe stop. The Davis-Bacon Act of 1931 required federal contractors to pay the highest prevailing wages to their workers, which were usually union wages. Many believed this was the cause of artificially inflated construction costs. In February 1971 Nixon suspended the act when unions refused to change course and then put it back in place a little over a month later once he got unions to agree to control wage increases. Wage and benefit increases negotiated after Nixon's tough stand decreased from 19 percent to 11 percent. Later that year Nixon announced his New Economic Policy, which included wage and price freezes that undermined unions' basic right of negotiation. Many UAW leaders and AFL-CIO officials fumed over Nixon's betrayal of labor rights, but the larger public loved it. As labor leaders and unionists were quickly learning, their cause was falling out of favor.

Unionists Divided and Under Siege

Public employee unionism hit its stride in the early 1970s, but like federation leaders and workers in the trades, it quickly faced the harsh reality that its successes were largely dependent on public opinion and the larger economic and political context. Beginning in the early 1970s, none of these forces were moving its way.

Between 1973 and 1975 an economic recession exposed the US economy's vulnerability. In the 1970s the average annual rate of inflation was 7.1 percent, up from 2.3 percent in the 1960s. Unemployment reached 8.5 percent in 1975 – 40 percent among black youth. Inflation and unemployment rates pushed budget deficits to new heights. State and local government finances were a mess. Public employers issued hiring freezes, played hardball during contract negotiations, and laid off many employees. In 1975 Pittsburgh's mayor cut his city's payroll by one third, California's governor slashed planned wage increases for state workers, and New York's mayor laid off 19,000 city workers. New York City was in particularly desperate straits because investment banks refused to underwrite city bonds. The state's governor and legislature turned to the Municipal Assistance Corporation, which refinanced the city but at a huge cost to public workers.

In the face of layoffs, wage freezes, and wage reductions, public employees broke the law and went on strike, unwittingly playing into the hands of increasingly vocal anti-union forces. In 1975 there was a 24 percent increase in public sector strikes, which included 446 walkouts in state and local governments. In New York City sanitation workers left garbage on the streets while laid-off police officers marched on city hall. In Seattle firefighters encouraged a recall election to oust the mayor and his draconian budget cuts. A second wave of strikes peaked in 1978 when schoolteachers walked out in 75 different school districts. That year police walked off the job in Memphis and Cleveland, and firefighters did the same in Chattanooga, Tennessee, and Manchester, New Hampshire. In many of these conflicts, workers won their demands, but at a great cost.

Public worker militancy tapped latent tensions in society and enlivened an anti-union backlash. Some public grumbling was apparent in the late 1960s when public sector unions were establishing themselves, but the 1970s fiscal crisis whipped 1960s whispers of discontent into a public outcry that manifested itself in an anti-tax revolt. Unorganized working people joined forces with such anti-union groups as the Chamber of Commerce. Anti-tax workers and business conservatives blamed labor for soaring inflation rates and property taxes and won in the court of popular opinion. Former Democratic Party allies sensed the shifts in the wind. Working desperately to close their budget deficits and prove that labor did not control them, they clung to the mantle of fiscal responsibility and lashed out against the greed of public workers. Higher taxes, rising inflation, and unemployment also pitted private sector workers in the core industries against women and minorities in the public sector. Union wages, while higher than those for non-unionized workers, failed to keep pace with the increased cost of living imposed by taxes and inflation. Union brotherhood and sisterhood aside, unionized private sector workers joined the chorus against public unions.

Wrapped in the rhetoric of smaller government and lower taxes, public employers increasingly used their power to permanently replace striking public workers. Joseph McCartin in "'Fire the Hell Out of Them': Sanitation Workers and the Normalization of the Striker Replacement Strategy in the 1970s" highlights this 1970s shift by focusing on the increasing public backlash against sanitation workers. Between 1967 and 1973 cities increased their expenditures by over 60 percent for sanitation services. In light of the fiscal crisis, this line item looked ripe for pruning. Some turned to new technologies that would lessen the number of workers per truck, and others outsourced garbage pick-up to private contractors. When municipal sanitation workers struck after 1973, mayors also reversed their previous practice of negotiating with these workers even though it was not legal for them to strike. This time they fired them for good and hired permanent strike replacements. President Reagan would not be the first to use the permanent replacement tactic, as he did against the Professional Air Traffic Controllers Organization (PATCO) workers in 1981; municipal and private employers had paved the way in the 1970s.

The public reaction also undermined a larger labor movement push for federal legislation that would encompass all government workers and allow collective bargaining. Between 1970 and 1976 AFSCME led the way in the fight to extend collective bargaining rights to all state and local government workers along the liberal Wagner model, complete with a National Public Employee Labor

Relations Board. But the public backlash against pubic employee strikes and unions in light of the fiscal crisis made this goal elusive. As a result, public sector unions were never freed from state and local laws that limited government workers' rights. Government employees' public influence, moreover, was weak and regionally concentrated, which meant that any national drives for labor reform requiring southern congressional support would be difficult. By 2000 only 37 percent of the people working in the public sector had union recognition.

The weakening of public employee unionism and heightened divisions between working people gave a green light to employers to accelerate their aggressive anti-union culture and tactics. Business leaders and government advisors worked closely with law firms, the National Right to Work Committee, and the Business Roundtable to defeat unions and labor law reform. Goodwill between employers and unions, which began to erode in the 1960s, had all but vanished by the end of the 1970s and would only worsen in the decades to come.

Conclusion

The decades of the 1960s and 1970s represent important turning points for working people and their unions. Women and minorities represented the new character of the working-class demographic. The timing of their entrance into higher-paying and more respectable workplaces, however, was unfortunate. Just as these groups sued and fought their way into government and manufacturing jobs, the United States headed into a recession. New technologies and international trade made a bad job market worse. Upon their arrival, labor's newest members became competitors for shrinking jobs, stoking the flames of racism and sexism.

Rights consciousness – the awareness of race and gender inequalities and the movement to make change – led to hard fights that fundamentally reshaped US law, culture, and the way that scholars think and write about working America. But labor historians caution that rights-based movements were problematic in several ways. For one, the fight for racial access and equality too often occurred without larger economic goals and demands. What good were steel jobs to African-American men when the steel plants shut their doors and moved overseas? New work rights based on race and gender were problematic in other ways. They were individualistic and represented the twilight years for a US liberalism that valued social solidarity and democratization of corporate workplaces. As racial divisions won more attention and sympathy from society, class divisions were increasingly viewed in the public as threatening. In the end, work to bring racial and gender equality to workers in the private industrial sector did not occur on the labor model but was fought in courts by civil rights lawyers. As labor lost ground, workers everywhere were more vulnerable.

4

Working More for Less and Other Troubles for Workers in the Late Twentieth Century

By 1978 the bottom had fallen out of New York City's economy. Rising prices and unemployment meant widespread hardship. My dad, an International Brotherhood of Electrical Workers (IBEW) Local 3 electrician, faced these hardships head on. Eighteen years prior, family connections won him an electrician's apprenticeship with IBEW Local 3. These kinds of "ins" were part of a larger, corrupt union culture. And while the union was not democratic or diverse, my dad made a good living for eighteen years as a Jew in an overwhelmingly non-Jewish trade. From the beginning of his tenure in the trade, he learned that IBEW's leaders (at least the ones who ran the hiring hall) did not call electricians to jobs based on merit or what was fair. You needed pull. Somehow he managed to have just enough of it to get the bills paid.

In 1978, however, this way of life was about to come to a crashing end. Work in the city had slowed to the point that too many electricians did not have jobs. Union leaders decided that members would "share the work." In other words, they would take turns being unemployed. For six months, union members

Working Hard for the American Dream: Workers and Their Unions, World War I to the Present, First Edition. Randi Storch.
© 2013 John Wiley & Sons, Ltd. Published 2013 by John Wiley & Sons, Ltd.

stayed home, collected whatever government unemployment benefits they were eligible for, and waited for time to pass. When my dad's six-month period came to an end, he got the word that work had not picked up yet and that he'd need to sit out for another stint. Clearly whatever pull he once had was no more. Out of government benefits and without union wages, what was a person to do? Unfortunately for working people – men and women, industrial and service, union and non – this story of economic hard times leading to an uncertain future was not uncommon in the last quarter of the twentieth century.

Between 1973 and 2000, by almost every measure, working people throughout all sectors of society lost economic ground and power at work and in society. A period of de-industrialization ensued when manufacturers increasingly shut their doors, laid off their workers, and left communities to cope with the fall out. Global competition sent US manufacturing jobs and investment dollars abroad, and brought waves of vulnerable immigrants to low-paying and dangerous jobs in the United States. Meanwhile, a rise in public sector union organizing masked the hemorrhaging experienced in private sector unionism, where labor's power and political influence took a beating. How did this happen, and how did working people and their unions respond? My dad left everything he knew behind him and headed south based on a tip from a cousin and a family friend. Not everyone, however, had mobility – and a leap into the unknown – as an option.

Corporate America's drive for increasing profits inspired business leaders to try cost-saving measures that fundamentally changed work in the United States and around the world, making it increasingly difficult – and in many communities impossible – to live a fulfilling life while working a non-salaried job. Plant relocations, concession demands, efforts to maximize workplace efficiency (referred to as lean manufacturing), contracting out business functions that were done previously in-house (also known as outsourcing), and the use of part-time, vulnerable workers (also known as contingent labor) were elements of the pain capital caused working people. But if the only changes of the period had been economic, working people's hardships would have been less dire. Instead, political and ideological forces exacerbated these economic changes and undermined unions and working people in industries that were mobile as well as place-bound – including construction, trucking, healthcare, custodial services, and office work.

Throughout the period between 1970 and 1995, the AFL-CIO and its member unions largely played defense, at a loss over how to reverse workers' rapidly declining standard of living and their unions' falling numbers. Actions and organizations emerging from the grassroots of the labor movement as well as outside groups pushed the federation to rethink its mission and consider the larger world of the laborer. By the mid-1990s, new leadership at the top of the AFL-CIO promised to commit themselves to the broad diversity of America's workers and develop new approaches to the country's changing political and economic environment. Some labor activists believed turnover in the AFL-CIO's leadership held promise for workers and their unions, but at century's end many others were not so sure. One thing was clear: at the conclusion of the twentieth century the US labor movement was at a crossroads: one path leading to its further decline and irrelevance; the other to a renewed vigor, significance, and period of growth.

Profit Making in a Global World

As early as the 1950s manufacturers became obsessed with their declining rates of profit. US companies still made more than ever before, simply not at the stellar level that had attracted the kind of capital investment to which they had become accustomed during the war and early Cold War years. To business leaders whose job it was to turn ever-growing profits, this was an unsustainable situation so they drastically changed course, a move that would undermine the economic livelihood of millions of working Americans.

For many manufacturers, international competition lay at the root of their troubles. In the case of steel, large integrated producers (steel companies with the ability to convert ore to liquid iron and pig iron to liquid steel, and also solidify liquid steel and roll

176

it) lost their competitive edge in the years following World War II. In this period, Asian and European steel manufacturers rebuilt their war-torn plants with the newest technology and under protectionist national policies. In the 1950s the Japanese government footed almost half of the bill to modernize its country's steel industry through loans. The Japanese government then enacted tight restrictions on imported steel and in times of recession permitted steel companies to plan lower production levels while maintaining high prices. To compensate for their overcapacity and pay back the loans, Japanese steel producers entered foreign markets by selling their steel at artificially low prices. Japan's share in the US steel market was on the rise, but less than 1 percent of its own consumption came from imports. Asian, South American, and Western European industrialists and governments took note and followed the model Japan had created. By 1982, cheap foreign steel flooded US markets, making a bad situation for the national steel industry worse.

Auto manufacturers also faced new challenges – this time starting in the aftermath of the Korean War – as Japanese manufacturers built new factories with the latest technologies. During this rapid period of growth, Japanese auto makers bought technical information from US and European manufacturers, but also benefited from homegrown expertise. With increasingly robotic and mechanized production facilities, Japanese research into auto making was one of the most robust technological sectors of that nation's economy.

Until the early 1970s, US auto manufacturers withstood Japanese competition and continued to produce large, gas-guzzling cars, but a decision by the Organization of Petroleum Exporting Countries' (OPEC) in 1973 to use the price of oil as a tool for political leverage against nations supporting Israel pulled the rug out from under US auto manufacturers and pushed them into a harsh new reality of having to compete with more efficient, smaller, foreign imported autos. Exacerbating their troubles, Japanese companies, beginning in the 1980s, established non-union factories right in the United States. US auto manufacturers' share of the domestic auto market fell to 71 percent by 1981 and to 37 percent of the world market by 1980. For the first time in sixty years, foreign competition and economic worries pushed US auto makers to fundamentally rethink their car designs, business models, and labor relations.

Lower-priced imports also needled US manufacturers in industries related to clothing and hurt their net income as well. In the 1960s, apparel imports represented only 2.5 percent of the US domestic market, but by 1976, they represented one third and by 1987 more than one half. Between 1980 and 1985, imports of fabric, garments, and yarn grew at a combined rate of 17 percent per year. At the same time, apparel and textile imports amounted to $2 billion.

In one industry after another, then, international competition affected US manufacturers' rate of profit. Kim Moody in *Workers in a Lean World: Unions in the International Economy* (1997) explains: "The irony is that the amount of profits can grow and the size of the capital…become massive and the capitalists still face a falling rate of return." At the end of 1971, for example, when General Motors made an after-tax profit of $1.9 billion, GM's chairman James Roche declared profits not "as good as I would like to have seen them." US steel producers made 6.7 percent profit between 1968 and 1977, which was head and shoulders above the meager 1.7 percent profits of Japanese and the even smaller profits of European producers. The problem, however, was that 6.7 percent was not a high enough rate of profit to convince investors to put their money into US steel. As a whole, non-financial corporations' after-tax rate of return fell from 13.7 percent in 1966 to 7.6 percent in 1979.

With their rate of profit plummeting, US investors looked for new ways to improve the rate of return on their investments; and in one industry after another, corporate leaders made business decisions that devastated the people who worked for them, the communities where they were located, and the unions representing their workforce. US Steel's Chairman David Roderick supported his company's diversified investments in non-steel businesses. In December 1981, US Steel purchased Marathon Oil for $6.4 billion and then in 1986 Texas Oil for $3 billion, money that might have been used to update steel manufacturing technology. Between 1975 and 1980 the number of integrated steel companies in the United States fell from 20 to 14 and their combined domestic capacity fell by 25 percent. Jumping out of steel and into the energy sector, Roderick clarified what might have otherwise appeared to be a hasty business decision: "US Steel is in business to make profits, not to make steel."

Steel magnates were not alone. Corporate leaders shut US auto, textile, and electronics factories as well and invested their manufacturing dollars in healthcare, real estate, and insurance sectors, where profits came easier, labor costs were lower, and labor unions were not as strong. In 1978, Uniroyal shut its profit-making tire plant in Indianapolis to make even more profit by investing in chemical products. Through redirection of profits, reallocation of capital, the physical relocation of equipment or complete closure, scholars estimate that US industry lost 32–38 million manufacturing jobs in the 1970s.

Plant closings had painful effects on the communities of laid-off workers and families left in their wakes. When a Ford plant in New Jersey shut in 1980, nearly half of the affected workers were still unemployed two years later. As time passed, they depleted their family savings, some experienced psychological problems and all of them suffered as they watched their community crumble around them. In the mid-1980s GM offered a buyout to production workers in Linden, New Jersey, who agreed to give up their jobs while the company restructured the plant, added new technology, and downsized its workforce. Some found new employment in the region's diverse economy. But in the Linden case, African-American workers did not fare as well as their white counterparts, and workers from more de-industrialized regions such as Youngstown, Ohio, or Flint, Michigan, more often faced economic, personal, and social crises. High levels of unemployment in Youngstown negatively affected the public's memory and how they represented their community's steel workers, their collective struggles, and their unions. By the 1990s Youngstown's once thriving working-class communities became sites of abandonment, charred buildings and empty lots, and a new, privately financed, prison – that is until 2001 when its prison guards organized and affiliated themselves with the Teamsters, causing Corrections Corporation of America to close this Youngstown facility.

Having left devastated communities in their wake, mobile industry leaders searched out new, low-wage communities, often in such non-union, "right-to-work" regions of the United States as the South and parts of the West and Midwest, to try out cost-saving and profit-maximizing management styles, new technologies, and restructuring schemes. Until the 1950s in the regional meatpacking market controlled by Swift, Cudahy, and Armour, the United Packing House Workers of America negotiated strong contracts through pattern bargaining and developed strong communities through social activism. By the 1980s their work was decimated. The Iowa Beef Processors (IBP) "revolution," which began in the mid-to-late 1950s, resulted in a reorganized and relocated industry. Technology streamlined the "kill-and-cut" process, reducing the number of skilled workers needed and easing the industry's mobility into the rural Midwestern countryside. In the 1980s global grain-marketing firms such as Cargill and Conagra joined IBP to take over the industry and aggressively undermine patterns set in bargaining to squeeze out new levels of profit. Here, global firms took advantage of tax subsidies and such state-sponsored programs as the Iowa New Jobs Training Program and the Iowa Bureau of Refugee Services to lure vulnerable workers from Somalia, Mexico, and Laos to the Midwest, where they faced unreliable work and inadequate social services. By 1991, even a company as place-bound as Camden, New Jersey's Campbell Soup's Plant Number 1 shut down in order for the company to reap higher rates of profit in the low-wage South.

Other manufacturers, in electronics and apparel for example, did not waste time relocating within the United States. Instead they reorganized their companies to manufacture products from outside the country, where unions were weak or non-existent, workers' wages were depressed, and higher rates of profit, even if only marginally so. Encouraged, the forces of globalization only grew stronger. Between 1965 and 1980, corporate profits from foreign investments tripled.

Jefferson Cowie's study of the Radio Corporation of America (RCA), *Capital Moves: RCA's Seventy Year Quest for Cheap Labor* (1999) shows the historic race of this electronics manufacturer away from unionized, high-wage environments – starting in Camden, New Jersey – to low-wage, non-unionized facilities, ultimately in Mexico. Such states as Indiana served the manufacturer well until its workers organized a union and made demands. In response, RCA closed shop and opened a factory in Memphis, which it then closed in 1971 only to ship operations to a Mexican industrial park in Ciudad Juarez. By 1974, approximately 500 *maquiladoras* (foreign-owned factories whose workers are involved in a part of the manufacturing process that will then be exported) were operating just south of the US border, employing 80,000 workers. As manufacturers relocated abroad, reorganized production methods, and watched their rate of profit grow, hundreds of thousands of workers in the United States lost their livelihoods and scoured help-wanted ads. Rent and mortgage payments were still due.

As jobs fled the United States and as US corporations propped up international profit-making ventures, these same globalizing US manufacturers engaged in a wicked act of deception against US workers: they whipped up nationalist fervor and initiated a series of "Buy American" campaigns. US manufacturers promised consumers that by spending their dollars on the products of their companies, as opposed to foreign-based ones, US jobs and the nation's economic future would be revived, even secured. Their campaign pitted US manufacturers and their workers against foreign, usually Asian, nations. North American trade unionists quickly got on board, turning their backs on workers in other nations. Newspaper accounts reported on cases wherein US workers took sledgehammers to Toyotas, hyper-nationalist zeal tragically led to a US worker killing an Asian man, and anti-Asian threats routinely animated workers' exchanges with one another. In the meantime, their "patriotic" employers announced dramatic reductions in domestic production allegedly forced by foreign competition. With no public fanfare, however, by the end of the 1980s, the big three automakers (GM, Ford, and Chrysler) had heavily invested in foreign companies: Ford owned 25 percent of Mazda; Chrysler owned 24 percent of Mitsubishi; and between 1982 and 1987, GM garnered one quarter of all of its profits from its overseas investments.

Capital flight took its toll on certain workers, economic sectors, and communities. Meanwhile, "Buy American" campaigns generally succeeded in pitting US workers, afraid of globalization, against low-wage workers around the world, people who could have benefited from US unionists' support. But, as Kim Moody argues in *Workers in a Lean World: Unions in the International Economy* (1997), it is "globalony" to believe that capital can relocate anyplace in the world where low wages exist. In fact, he asserts that the majority of world trade (about 80 percent) takes place between highly industrialized nations. Moody and others believe the most significant impact on working people in this period was not the fact that some capital was mobile, but instead that capitalists accelerated and directed an attack on the organization of work, workers' lives, and their unions. And on these points, the evidence was – and is – overwhelmingly clear.

The Human Price of Modern Capitalism

Workers in the auto industry were some of the first to bear the brunt of this homegrown assault, but its effects reached beyond auto to working people in other industrial and service industries. In the fall of 1979, Chrysler turned to the US government for a bailout. The parties agreed to an arrangement whereby banks would give the automaker $750 million in loans that Congress underwrote while the United Auto Workers (UAW) gave back negotiated benefits for the workers it represented. Adding up to a billion dollars in forfeited paid holidays, work hours, cost-of-living increases, pension contributions, and already negotiated raises, the UAW's giveback opened the union to demands from Ford and GM that they also get similar concessions. Then, this "reverse-pattern" bargaining became trendy in other manufacturing industries and then even in companies in sectors of the economy outside of manufacturing, including Texaco, UPS,

Kroger, and Greyhound. In 1982, 19 percent of corporate executives surveyed by the magazine *Business Week* agreed to the statement, "Although we don't need concessions, we are taking advantage of the bargaining climate to ask for them."

Concessions, however, undermined the ideological basis for unions in this period. Not only did concessions provide a powerful model whereby unions would, ironically, serve as the catalyst to give back wages and benefits to employers, but they also shifted the entire understanding of unionism. Rather than identify with fellow workers in opposition to their employers' goal of getting as much work out of each worker for as little pay as possible, concession bargaining encouraged workers to identify with their employers and the fate of their firms to succeed at all costs.

All the while, workers' productivity was increasing, even as their wages were declining. On the defensive and increasingly without union representation, workers were unable to turn productivity gains into wage gains. If the 1968 minimum wage were adjusted over time for productivity increases and inflation, the 2000 minimum wage would have been $13.80, but, at $5.15 an hour, it was not even close. If minimum wage kept pace proportionally with CEO pay, which increased by 571 percent in the period from 1990 to 2001, minimum wage workers would have earned $25.50 an hour. But, instead, in 2001 the minimum wage remained only $5.15 an hour. The fruits of workers' labor increasingly landed in the pockets of the richest people in the United States.

While explaining to their employees that they had their best interests at heart, employers established new work rules and job cultures that undermined a person's dignity at work. Quality-of-Work-Life (QWL) programs had appeared as early as the 1970s in response to employers' "discovery" of workers' alienation on the assembly line. Such attention was particularly sharpened in 1972. That year workers at a General Motor's plant in Lordstown, Ohio, engaged in a three-week strike in response to GM's unilateral decision to speed the assembly line to 100 Chevrolet Vegas per hour and crack down on anyone who stood in the way. In Lordstown, Ohio, a young multiracial workforce, which included Vietnam veterans and other twenty-somethings who were raised in a protest-willing generation, did not ask for more money. Instead they asked for their work to be more fulfilling, their management to treat them with more dignity, and their work pace slowed to a more humane level. Through the UAW they beat back GM's breakneck productivity rate to the one they had worked under in 1970 and got 1,400 laid-off workers returned to the line. But in the end, life on the line was no more humane or fulfilling.

The great "discovery" that factory work dehumanized line workers and that management treated them merely as extensions of the machines on which they worked was exactly what QWL programs sought to address. Their focus was on improving life at work for workers: profits were a secondary focus. Early supporters of QWL hoped that this management initiative would increase workers' sense of worth and job satisfaction. In the auto industry, workers found their workplaces restructured and their employers turning to a new vocabulary, littered with such phrases as "lean operations," "team management," and "flexibility." The understanding was that the company's main problem lay with its inability to compete effectively and that its own workers held the key to turning the problem around. The steel industry called its team concept "labor–management participation teams," Xerox called it "commodity study teams." As late as 1994, after two decades of assault on unions and their members, the AFL-CIO committee on the Evolution of Work urged labor–management cooperation. According to one study, the percentage of Fortune 1000 companies with at least one employee-involvement practice rose from 70 percent in 1987 to 85 percent in 1990.

The teamwork model supported by the AFL-CIO, corporate employers, and even presidential administrations has been at the core of much debate among labor scholars and activists who differ on the program's value to working people. Ruth Milkman in *Farewell to the Factory: Auto Workers in the Late Twentieth Century* (1997) finds that workers are "attracted to participation" and argues "successful participation can strengthen unionism." Joel Rogers and Richard Freeman's survey of workers convinced them as well: their findings helped President Bill Clinton's Secretary of Labor, Robert Reich, to join the "team" bandwagon with particular vigor.

Other scholars, however, could not disagree more, arguing that such logic was incorrect and that the resulting policies led to a loss of solidarity among workers and increased overall employee exploitation. According to one worker quoted in Mike Parker and Jane Slaughter's edited collection, *Work Smart: A Union Guide to Participation Programs and Reengineering/With Union Strategy Guide* (1997), "We all had to take responsibility for productivity increases, and apply peer pressure if our co-workers were not pulling their load." Such insights suggest that these programs caused co-workers to turn against one another in the name of efficiency and corporate profit. In addition, these new systems of participation programs became gateways to what management calls "lean production" but what Parker and Slaughter more rightly describe as "management by stress," which includes eliminating job classifications to allow for more interchangeability among workers, continuous speedup, and just-in-time delivery, which means, among other things, that companies build up less inventory and cut warehouse and delivery costs. Such changing workplace systems appeared in the 1980s in places as diverse as manufacturers GM and GE, as well as service providers, including hospitals and the federal government. In the end, QWL programs supported a culture of concessions (how much can you give your employer); by the end of the decade, the once-lauded team concept more fully developed into a heavy-handed excuse for employers to push workers (and workers to push one another) to help their firms better compete – quality of life at work be damned.

In addition to labor–management team models and the restructuring that accompanied them, new technologies, including computers, helped to diminish workers' power and deskill work. In the early 1980s some scholars argued that technology and flexibility would not necessarily undermine workers' power on the job. New technology, the argument went, would require a highly educated workforce that could quickly adapt to changes in production technology and serve specialized markets. Higher-tech workplaces and workers, according to some, would also lead to more democratic workplaces. These scholars argued that technology had the potential to increase workers' skills and put oppressive managerial practices to rest.

Experience, however, revealed that management often used new technology in ways that negatively affected workers. Even though GM spent $300 million modernizing plants to make them efficient, the division between workers in skilled trades and unskilled production work remained; this was in no way a democratizing trend. Fewer production workers and more skilled workers resulted, but production workers still faced routine, deskilled work and found new technology to be controlling and dehumanizing. Technology itself, of course, is not to blame: management was unwilling to abandon its authoritarian ways and the UAW was not able to maximize the benefits of technology for its workers.

Essentially, however, computerization and technology became a means for management to appropriate workers' knowledge and increase corporate control. Such developments characterized the way that technology enabled GTE, the third largest telephone company in the early 1980s, to "reengineer" its workplace at the price of workers' jobs. There, management reengineered its telephone operations, moving phone-testing equipment from one group of its workforce and giving that job to repair clerks and training those clerks how to use it while customers were on the phone. They then invested in new software so that an operator could also handle sales, billing, and repair: now one person could do the job of three. As *Fortune* magazine explained, the process was controversial. In the face of resistance, management offered a heavy, masculine, and violent hand: "The way that you have to deal with this resistance is a combination of relentless communication, support incentives, and a bloody ax." Such reengineering systems require companies to free themselves of anything that might get in the way of turning a profit, which might mean the elimination of factories, machines, and entire job classifications-along with all of the people doing them.

Reengineering and restructuring often hurt workers and their unions by opening the door to corporate outsourcing of union jobs to non-union plants. Producing "in-house" allows firms to control quality, but buying parts from non-union outside suppliers allows companies to save on their bottom line. In the auto industry, complete car interiors and brake systems began being outsourced to non-union plants. By the 1980s, established, unionized workforces in consumer durables (such products as automobiles and washing machines that have a multi-year life), aircraft parts, and industrial and agricultural equipment lost jobs to this new profit-making venture. By the 1990s, with cheaper labor costs abroad and new technologies at employers' disposal, a new surge of outsourcing occurred. This time it affected firms' distribution, finance, information technology, and customer service departments. According to the Outsourcing Institute in New York, spending on outsourcing grew fivefold in the 1990s and was expected to exceed $100 billion in 1996 alone.

Tom Juravich's *Chaos on the Shop Floor: A Worker's View of Quality, Productivity and Management* (1998) offers an insider's view of the daily problems workers face in a non-union subcontractor's shop. Working as a participant observer at National Wire and Cable Company, Juravich found an irrational, confusing work environment characterized by regularly breaking machines, blurred managerial hierarchies, short-term planning, and high turnover. As a result, workers' frustration levels were as high as the structural barriers the firm put in place, and that undermined the quality of the products.

Still, the cost savings to corporations meant that the practice of outsourcing quickly spread out from manufacturing firms to the healthcare industry, government agencies, and universities. The use of outsourcing left hundreds of thousands of workers displaced, many others disempowered, and unions reeling from membership losses. Among airlines, companies began outsourcing maintenance of planes to foreign facilities, decimating their mechanics' union. In the 1990s, hospitals began outsourcing the transcription of medical records, creating a new $4.6 billion industry. To compete in the two-day service market, the United States Postal Service outsourced its operations to Emery Worldwide Airlines, where a separate stream of mail flowed through ten East Coast hubs peopled with non-union workers. Even Yale University announced, in 1996, its plan to subcontract clerical, food, and maintenance work. Despite the fact that the university was sitting on a nearly $4 billion endowment, non-union labor would mean less meddling from Locals 34 and 35 of the Federation of University Employees.

As they outsourced work to separate non-union companies, employers gutted their full-time workforce and turned to a new, temporary, and vulnerable standard. When hiring workers on a temporary basis, employers had no responsibility for workers' unemployment or health insurance and could easily save 20–40 percent per worker. According to the *Independent* (March 27, 1993), between 1987 and 1993, the number of temporary workers increased ten times as fast as the number of full-time employees. In 1993, one in four Americans was "self-employed" as employers restructured, outsourced, and hired out work to consultants, free-lancers, and subcontractors. Perhaps it was no surprise then that in 1993 *Time Magazine* found that the country's largest employer was not a Fortune 500 company. Manpower Inc. earned that distinction by offering employers temporary workers.

Even in the university, where academic integrity and freedom are thought to be a mainstay of full-time, tenure-track appointment, numbers of contingent faculty soared and exposed the vulnerability of full-time, professional employment in higher education. Part-time, contingent, and non-tenure track instructors generally do not have offices or benefits; are paid miserably; can be fired at will; and have no voice in university or department governance. According to the American Association of University Professors (AAUP), contingent faculty percentages increased from 22 percent in 1970 to 32 percent in 1980. In 2001, the American Federation of Teachers (AFT) estimated that contingent faculty represented more than one half of all faculty appointments in higher education in the United States.

Combining the benefits of outsourcing and contingent labor, other employers turned away from full-time factory workers and gave new interest to home workers. In a process oddly reminiscent of the putting-out system of pre-industrial England and America, women in rural communities answered the call of transnational firms, from automobile part makers to coil manufacturers, whose hiring managers scoured the countryside in search of cheap and docile labor. Reemerging as a politically charged issue in the conservative political climate of the 1980s, the political Right wanted all prohibitions against work at home removed while the Left wanted no such work allowed. The 1938 Fair Labor Standards Act contained regulations against knit and garment industries' use of home workers and provisions relating to wages, hours, child labor, and record keeping in all other industries that use home workers. But monitoring compliance was difficult and, in the rapidly changing economic and political climate of the 1970s and 1980s, more companies turned to women to do paid work in their homes. For many of these women, homework allowed them to combine family responsibilities with money making. Studies of Puerto Rican women in New York City show that these women chose home work over factory work or domestic work in others' homes as a way of upholding "La Familia." They do so without the protections that labor law provides to factory workers because labor law conceptualizes all employees as factory workers. So these women, who are often caregivers, juggle responsibilities of family, community, and work without federal benefits or protections as workers.

The Political Shaping of the Economy

Clearly, corporate leaders' economic responses to falling rates of profit negatively impacted manufacturing, service, and professional workers. But corporate economic decision-making was not the only culprit in this late-twentieth-century crisis. Workers' problems sat squarely on the shoulders of government policy.

When the US government encouraged overseas investment by deferring taxes on foreign earnings, it exacerbated workers' problems. Instead of paying taxes on their overseas profits, US companies were able to reinvest them abroad. According to Judith Stein in *Running Steel, Running America: Race, Economic Policy and the Decline of Liberalism* (1998), "taxes paid to foreign governments were not simply deductions against income, but credits against American obligations. A dollar earned abroad was taxed less than one earned at home." With their rates of profit

189

shaping investment strategies, corporations took advantage of what the US government was offering.

In the apparel industry, new tax codes put in place as early as 1963 sent US manufacturers abroad in search of cheap non-unionized workers. Item 807 of the United States Tariff Code allowed US apparel companies to cut garments in the United States, sew them in Mexico or the Caribbean, and then re-import them into the United States, only having to pay a tax on the workers' cheap wages – the value added to the garment overseas. Between 1983 and 1987, garment imports under this program increased from 416 million to 1.12 billion. By 1987, workers in 70 apparel plants in Jamaica alone sewed for Jockey, Levi Strauss, Ocean Pacific, and Hanes. Manufacturers who enjoyed profits generated by the new US tax code soon found further incentives for subcontracting to production firms in Asia. Just as they were getting comfortable, however, these older and established companies were outflanked by a new group of competitors – Target and Wal-Mart, for example – who drew up contracts with foreign producers, skipping US manufacturers all together.

US leadership in global financial institutions – the International Monetary Fund (IMF) and the World Bank, for example – furthered free-market capitalist principles around the world at the expense of nationalized, humanitarian ones. The result was that nations getting assistance from these organizations jeopardized national programs that often worked in the interests of the public – education, health, and security, for example. If nations wanted international financial help, they would have to get in line with capitalist policies that favored those with money and resources above all else. Nobel Prize winner Joseph Stiglitz – former chief economist and senior vice president at the World Bank – in *Globalization and Its Discontents* (2002) criticized the IMF and World Bank. Stiglitz argues that while these institutions were created to carry out Keynesian policies (whereby government investment and monetary policy would stimulate failing economies), they in fact had morphed into institutions that reflected the "interests and ideology of the Western financial community." Some critics argue that these institutions' policies actually increase poverty in the nations that sign up for assistance. One condition in the Structural Adjustment Programs of the IMF, for example, is that countries in financial peril must sell as much of their national assets as possible to private bidders. This means that Western corporations are able to make huge gains at deep discounts. At the same time, indebted nations are forced to increase their tax rates while decreasing the rate of taxes paid by corporations doing business within their borders. The IMF and World Bank ostensibly work to prevent financial crises around the world, and their policies-at least publicly-are intended to stabilize the world's economic system. But in the process of imposing free-market policies on nations in need of financial help, they openly fund governments hostile to human and labor rights. At least 21 nations run by dictatorships received funds from the IMF between 1960 and 2000.

The US government's complicity in supporting globalization and global financial regulations in these ways is in part due to Cold War politics. In an attempt to keep nations of the world within the US capitalist orbit and away from its Cold War enemies, policymakers were keen on providing foreign nations with markets, jobs, and capital support. The 1972 Foreign Trade and Investment Act was a law that would have restricted and regulated imports and prevented flight of industry abroad; but it failed. In 1989 economist Richard Rothstein wrote a study on the apparel industry that concluded, "Behind the lack of enthusiasm for restriction of apparel imports lies a desire to curry favor with apparel exporting nations for foreign policy reasons completely extraneous to textile and apparel trade." Such insights could easily be applied more broadly to trade in auto parts, electronics, and textiles.

In addition to shaping the global movement of capital, federal policy eased the entry of foreign products into the United States and created high levels of inflation that undermined living standards among ordinary citizens. In an attempt to reduce the rapid inflation of the 1970s and early 1980s, Federal Reserve Chairman Paul Volcker tried a policy known as monetarism. Monetarist theory taught that the government needed to hold the country's money supply in check in order to stop inflation. The more the government increased the money supply, monetarists taught, the higher prices would go. This policy was the exact opposite to that which Keynesian supporters employed to combat the Great Depression during World War II, and in the postwar years when government spending was championed as key to economic recovery and continued prosperity. So, in many ways, monetarism was more than a tweaking of the nation's economic policy: it was a political redirect away from government spending. Put simply, the scheme did not work. Interest rates and the value of the dollar hit new heights. Countries fell over one another to sell their goods in the United States in order to obtain inflated US dollars.

Along with monetarism emerged a candid political commitment to market forces that denied government's responsibilities to regulate big business or to protect labor rights. Beginning as early as the late 1930s, business groups mobilized to dismantle New Deal protections of unions and workers. By the 1980s their agenda dovetailed with what became known as the Reagan "revolution." President Reagan's administration was characterized by a commitment to rolling back wealthy people's tax rate so that these newly "freed" dollars would pour into investments and "trickle down" to everyone else. It was defined by a commitment to deregulate industry, whose leaders-Reagan and his supporters believed-were hampered by such rules as those pertaining to health and safety. It was this thinking that led to a financial deregulation bill that stopped many restrictions on savings and loan associations, sparked a rush of speculation and profiteering, and ended in a major economic collapse and the biggest federal financial bailout – $500 billion – in US history up to that time. Reagan's revolution also was committed to destroying unions whose contracts, work rules, and power supposedly violated the liberties and decision-making freedoms that those on the right of the political spectrum believed business leaders deserved.

Conservative ideology also supported beefed-up attacks on workers' right to strike. The Supreme Court upheld employers' right to hire permanent replacement workers for striking workers back in 1938, and this tactic was increasingly used in the public sector in the late 1960s and 1970s. But on August 3, 1981, the practice drew national attention, in part because President Reagan's actions were so draconian. That day, more than 12,000 members of the Professional Air Traffic Controllers Organization (PATCO) walked off the job for a shorter workweek, more pay, and better conditions. In doing so they violated a federal law prohibiting federal employees from striking, a law that had been broken repeatedly in the past. This time, however, Reagan went before a national audience and expressed his horror that federal employees would break the law in such a way. He declared that those air-traffic controllers "who failed to report to duty this morning, they are in violation of the law and if they do not report for work within 48 hours they have forfeited their jobs and will be terminated." Over 11,000 of them stayed out. Reagan fired them all, had their union leaders arrested, forbade each of them future employment with the Federal Aviation Administration, froze millions in strike funds, and put out the call to hire workers to replace them permanently. By October, the Federal Labor Relations Authority decertified PATCO. The union was single-handedly destroyed.

In the wake of Reagan's actions, hiring replacement workers became a trend outside the public sector as well. Copper-mining company Phelps Dodge led the way when it refused to accept the contract terms that other major copper producers had agreed to with labor, demanded concessions, and then permanently replaced its long-time unionized workers. Within two years the unions that had represented Phelps Dodge mineworkers for decades were decertified. Other private employers followed suit. Using permanent replacement workers became the practice at Eastern Airlines, the New York Daily News, Caterpillar, International Paper, and Greyhound Incorporated. According to the AFL-CIO, the 1980s witnessed the permanent replacement of 300,000 workers. The use of replacement workers debilitated unionized workers' primary weapon, the strike. The power to strike meant workers could come together to pressure their employers' bottom line until that employer came to the bargaining table to resolve pressing issues. Fear of being permanently replaced meant that workers thought twice before calling a strike. Fewer and fewer did. From the mid-1970s through 1981, strikes numbered around 300 per year. By the mid-1980s, however, they had fallen to about 50 and continued to decline. Workers had lost their strongest bargaining chip.

Reagan also continued a decades-long tradition of manipulating the membership of the National Labor Relations Board to undermine its role as protector of labor rights and democratic workplaces. Established in 1935 as an agency to oversee workers' rights to unionize, the NLRB morphed in the postwar period into an employer-advocacy agency. As early as Eisenhower's administration, Republicans whittled away at labor's rights; and Supreme Court rulings favored individual and property rights over collective ones. Reagan's appointments to the NLRB significantly accelerated the process of undermining collective bargaining rights and trade union power. Under North Carolina native Donald Dotson's chairmanship, the board allowed employers more easily to resist unionization; provided legal rationale for concessionary bargaining and runaway shops (when a business relocates to avoid a union drive); and put into question government's ability to apply principles of democracy in private workplaces. During Reagan's presidency, the number of unfair labor practice cases decided by the board dropped 40 percent from 1982 to 1983. Reagan's successor, George H. W. Bush, furthered the trend of what James Gross, in his award-winning history of the NLRB *Broken Promise: The Subversion of US Labor Relations Policy, 1947–1994* (2003), calls "a deliberate attempt to have the agency wither under the weight of an unprecedented and ever-growing backlog." In the Reagan–Bush era, the board was fully appointed with five members only 38 percent of the time, worsening the effects of an already large backlog of cases and complaints.

With no strong federal arm to shore-up workers' rights to form unions and fight as unionists, the federal government allowed employers to go on a union-busting spree. And they did. From the 1980s through the 2000s, management showed an increased willingness to violate the National Labor Relations Act. Turning to a cadre of union-busting law firms, corporations received legal advice on how to break their unions while staying within a hair's breadth of the law. Union-busting consultants urged employers to take anti-union initiatives, tell their employees that they are abso-lutely opposed to unions, and then scare them into not signing union cards. Some tactics included forcing employees to sit through anti-union videos. Others included employers forcing workers to have one-on-one meetings with their direct supervisors who told lies concerning dues, strikes, and the tyranny of union power. When all else failed, lawyers worked overtime to delay union elec-tions through appeals; and if elections were actually held and won, management refused to negotiate contracts. Anti-union employers had become masterful at working the system.

Union-busting tactics sometimes were supplemented with a Human Resources model of management to preempt union drives in firms where campaigns were not yet underway and to undermine them where entrenched unions were vulnerable to decertification. The late twentieth century witnessed a surge in management's cooptation of unions' most attractive features such as fringe benefits, job security, and open-door policies to listen to workers' on-the-job concerns. These union-busting and HR practices grew in the 2000s to a multi-billion dollar industry that has been widely documented by the AFL-CIO, labor rela-tions scholars, historians, and former union busters themselves.

As political forces aligned against unions, labor continued with some success to seek alliances and influence with Democratic Party politicians. Although by the 1980s labor's numbers and political power had been significantly diminished, unionists were still able to stop Congress from enacting some of the worst fanta-sies emerging from the right, including a revision of the (maximum) eight-hour day and an end to health and safety regulations. Labor worked with Democratic Party leaders to bring bills to the floor in exchange for labor's lobby in support of a broad range of issues. Orin Hatch (Representative from Utah), Chair of the Senate Labor Committee, complained, "it is next to impossible to do anything without the approval of labor union leaders in Washington." Even still, labor's political weakness was apparent in the legisla-tion it won. In June 1988, in companies in which 50 or more workers were employed, employers were required to give their workers 60-day advance notice before laying them off. Bills to increase support for childcare and a Family Medical Leave Act passed Congress: President Bush vetoed them in 1990.

Adding to the political problems of workers and their unions was the fact that the Democratic presidential administration that followed Bush's, that of Bill Clinton, did not significantly turn the tide. Clinton did support some pro-labor policies: he finally enacted the Family Medical Leave Act; did not speak against striking UPS workers in 1997; increased the minimum wage; and made pro-union appointments to the NLRB and the labor department. But while some crumbs fell to workers, the main course fed corporate profit. In 1994, with a Democratic administration and Congress in power, labor was unable to get a bill passed to stop employers from legally replacing strikers permanently. Working people also witnessed Clinton boldly reform "welfare as we know it." His reform of Aid to Families with Dependent Children played into conservative imagery of "welfare queens" or unwed mothers who had one baby after another in order to work the system and increase their monthly welfare stipends. In the mythology of the period, these women refused work and were assumed to be drug addicts. In 1996, Clinton won passage of the Personal Responsibility and Work Opportunity Reconciliation Act, which turned welfare programs over to states. If they wanted federal block grants to assist, however, state legislations would have to impose time limits on cash assistance and work responsibilities on every recipient. The shortsightedness of his assault on working people and the working poor is masterfully recorded in Barbara Ehrenreich's *Nickeled and Dimed: On (Not) Getting By in America* (2001), which dramatically documents the difficulties of living by Clinton's welfare to work policy: low-wage, degrading jobs force individuals to pay for childcare, travel to and from work, and medical expenses on their own depreciated dime.

Clinton further undermined working people by signing into law the 1999 Financial Services Modernization Act. The 1999 act abolished the 1933 Glass-Steagall Act, which had reformed banking in a number of ways, including separating commercial banking (checking, savings, and deposits) from investment banking. The idea behind Glass-Steagall was that commercial banks should not be allowed to make risky bets with money people put in their bank accounts: that kind of risk, associated with insurance, commodities, stocks, and real estate investments, should be allowed, but in different kinds of financial institutions. Glass-Steagall ordered the separation of commercial and investment banking because of what had led up to the Great Depression: massive banking houses participated in insider trading and financial manipulation that worsened the economic crisis. Not only did Clinton-era deregulation undo those precautionary regulations and provoke a flurry of mergers and monopolization in the nation's financial sector, but it also weakened working people's position as consumers in relation to creditors.

More troubling for labor unions was Clinton's support of the North American Free Trade Agreement (NAFTA) – an agreement between Mexico, the United States, and Canada to erase barriers to trade and investment. Despite their attempt, unions were unable to stop its 1994 passage and were incapable of unseating members of Congress who had voted for it. Clinton tried to assuage labor by signing the North American Agreement on Labor Cooperation (NAALC), a labor agreement within NAFTA that theoretically was to provide "a mechanism for member countries to ensure the effective enforcement of existing and future domestic labor standards and laws without interfering in the sovereign functioning of the different national labor systems." But workers in Canada, the United States, and Mexico were quick to learn that this agreement offered them little real protection. No government had to improve its standards. Each just had to meet the ones it had on the books. Mexico had some strong labor rights written into law, but evasion was not difficult because enforcement was lax. The body created to investigate violations was empowered only to hear complaints that dealt with forced labor, worker compensation, migrant rights, and equal pay. It was only *required* to respond to problems of child labor, minimum wages, and health and safety. In Mexico, this meant that workers were repeatedly denied their constitutional right to organize their own unions and bargain contracts. In 1996, for example, the International Labor Rights Fund alleged that in Mexico Sony

Corporation suspended and fired workers who tried to organize an independent union, and an investigation ensued. As it turns out, not only was Sony guilty of those practices, but it had also mishandled union elections and collaborated with police who violently suppressed unionists. The result of this investigation and findings were recommendations for seminars and workshops, punishment hardly worth Sony executives losing any sleep over. The problem for labor was that Sony's abuses were just the tip of the proverbial iceberg. NAFTA had unleashed a torrent of corporate movement to regions with cheap labor sources and weakened union movements. As Norman Caulfield in *NAFTA and Labor in North America* (2010) rightly observes, "This is especially important in the NAFTA context because denial of this right deprives workers of the ability to negotiate productivity gains." As a result, Caufield finds, "real wages have not kept up with labor productivity growth in Mexico... and in fact they have fallen significantly behind."

Clinton's general attitude to labor was to keep his distance, ignore corporate assaults against workers and their unions, and commission studies on workplace relations to determine whether the labor reform that US unions demanded was even necessary. In 1994, Secretary of Labor Reich appointed a commission on the future of worker–management relations headed by Harvard Professor John Dunlop. In the face of overwhelming evidence of employer opposition to organizing efforts and antagonism to unions, the commission found that labor relations were working just fine; that employee involvement in shopfloor decision-making was important; and that the Wagner Act should be revised so that management could establish employee-participation committees. Shored up by research conducted by labor scholars Richard Freeman and Joel Rogers, the commission concluded that US workers preferred cooperative relations with employers to adversarial unions. The idea that emerged was that if labor agreed to revise the Wagner Act provision against company unions, they might win long-needed reforms to labor law, such as passing the "card check," which would allow unions to achieve formal certification when a majority of workers sign cards. No election would be needed. In the end, labor lost its card check reform; and while business leaders technically lost their appeal for a formal revision of the Wagner Act, they were able to blithely continue on their union-busting path to "teamwork."

The AFL-CIO Leadership's Resistance to Change

In the period from 1970 through 2000, working people fought a losing battle to maintain status and power at work and in society. At least until 1995, when a new leadership swept into AFL-CIO offices, federation and international union leaders helped make this bad situation worse. With few exceptions, they acted defensively and dug their heels into familiar sectors of the economy. From the 1970s until the mid-1990s, the AFL-CIO's top leadership was helplessly tethered to traditional practices and conservative politics.

One-time plumber, George Meany, held the presidency of the AFL-CIO from the federation's merger in the mid-1950s until 1979. During his 27-year stint, the federation was plagued by internal turmoil. The American Federation of State, County, and Municipal Employees (AFSCME), the International Association of Machinists (IAM), and the Communications Workers of America (CWA) disagreed with political positions Meany took, and in 1976 they joined six other unions to formally organize a coalition and operate independently from the AFL-CIO. The United Auto Workers (UAW), also disgruntled in the 1960s with the AFL-CIO's conservative political direction, abandoned the federation in 1968 and joined forces with the Teamsters in a short-lived coalition they called the Alliance for Labor Action. Still, the cigar-chomping Meany seemed unfazed by the conflict swirling around him, and in 1970 boasted about "holding the boys together."

Meany was shortsighted when it came to women, new immigrants, and unorganized workers more generally; these groups were hardly his concern. In 1972 he asked, "Why should we

199

worry about organizing groups of people who do not appear to want to be organized?" And in response to a proposal by UAW leader Walter Reuther that the AFL-CIO organize unorganized and sporadically employed workers, Meany sarcastically stated: "Well, good luck on that one." The contrast to Lewis's 1930s leadership of the CIO could not have been starker.

In 1979, Meany died, leaving the head post vacant and the possibility open that new leadership would bring the AFL-CIO's attention to unorganized workers and to calls for more democracy at its grassroots. But federation business soon returned to the status quo. On the one hand, the college-educated and civil rights supporter Lane Kirkland took over; and unions in exile (the UAW, the Teamsters, and the Mineworkers) returned to the fold. At the end of the 1980s the AFL-CIO was more unified organizationally than it had been since World War II. On the other hand, Kirkland's politics were not much different than Meany's. He remained hostile to the left, supported Reagan and Bush's foreign policy, and avoided new organizing initiatives in the face of a failed legislative blitz to reverse permanent strike-replacement legislation. Rather than recruit new union members, the labor movement hunkered down and consolidated its numbers through a series of union mergers. Between 1955 and 1979 there were typically two or three mergers a year, but between 1985 and 1994 there were four or five. The mergers created strange, hybrid unions: industrial and building trades unions increasingly represented pubic employees and hospital workers, for example. Such conglomerations undermined hopes for unions to develop unified and coherent industry-wide strategies.

Kirkland represented a slight improvement over Meany, but was unresponsive to the shift that was occurring at the grassroots of unions and in working communities. On the one hand, their lack of foresight at the top level did not preclude workers from pushing for change from within their own unions. The AFL-CIO's national leadership has largely symbolic powers, and the labor movement it supposedly represents is decentralized, which means that much decision-making occurs within each international union. If the ranks rallied and demanded change from their international, they could succeed without getting the federation's blessing. This would be difficult and time consuming, but possible. On the other hand, federation leaders' unresponsive nature hurt innovative rank-and-file workers a great deal. Because federation leaders are the public face of the union movement – they have the ear of the president and the power to direct the federation's resources to new priorities and goals – Meany and Kirkland's unwillingness to support innovation ultimately would cost the movement public support. It also led to an internal shake-up and to Kirkland's routing.

From the mid-1970s until the mid-1990s, Meany and Kirkland played defense. If a sign of a healthy movement includes democratic processes, dynamic organizing drives, and rank-and-file participation, the labor movement was sickly and plagued with international unions committed to business models in which insular unions served their members. It also broke out in a rash of high-profile corruption cases within its member unions. National headlines blasting corruption in construction unions, painters' unions, and the Teamsters union, among others, created the myth that all unions and their leaders have ties to the mafia or plans to run off with members' health, welfare, and pension funds.

Additionally, Meany and Kirkland left a legacy of uninterest toward a new demographic and working-class politics. Labor's leaders maintained a holding pattern as the world of work and workers dramatically changed. The US economy transformed to a global mobile force; and as businesses, communities, and individuals demanded more services, the economy became more service oriented. Between 1979 and 1993 the number of the nation's jobs in the service sector increased by 38 percent while production work fell 12 percent. Service jobs were mostly non-union, low paying, and dead end. Between 1979 and 1987, more than 10 million new jobs were created that paid $13,000 a year or less, while only 1.6 million new jobs paid more than $26,800. To make matters worse, a large number of these service workers worked on a contingent basis.

The women's movement, a shift to home work, and the use of contingent labor meant that increasing numbers of non-union women worked for wages. By 1979, half of all women over the age of 16 were a part of the workforce, and by 1990, that had increased to 60 percent. Increasingly these women were mothers with children aged 6 and under. As US-born women left the home in greater numbers in search of paid labor, they helped create a new demand for cleaning and care workers that was increasingly filled by immigrant women. Uprooted by social, economic, and political forces beyond their control, immigrant women-both documented and undocumented-have become what one scholar refers to as "their nations' most profitable export." Workers gunning for these new jobs scrambled to the United States in response to World Bank and IMF policies: 6 million Filipino and Filipina workers left home for work in the United States and Europe, in part to part help pay down their nation's debt. Over 60 percent of Filipino migrants are women, primarily serving as domestic workers, many in the United States. As global forces push labor out of poor Asian, African, Latin American, and Caribbean households, transnational corporations and agencies create transnational households. Pierrette Hondagneu-Sotelo in *Domestica: Immigrant Workers Cleaning and Caring in the Shadows of Affluence* (2007) documents the experiences of Mexican and Central American women in Los Angeles who work in Anglo homes. The most exploited of these women are the most recently arrived, who do not speak English, and who are typically made to be available around the clock as nannies and housekeepers. Even the best of these jobs-intended for immigrant women whose social standing renders them invisible-come with low wages, no security, and undervalued work. Questions regarding citizenship, downward social mobility, disenfranchisement, and emotional turmoil haunt Latina and Filipina mothers living in the United States, especially those who take care of other people's families while their children live an ocean away.

Not surprisingly, neither Meany nor Kirkland rolled out the red carpet to welcome women into the federation. By 1992, the eight largest AFL-CIO affiliates, in which over 50 percent of the members were women, awarded women only a small percentage of leadership positions. By 1995, women headed only three out of twenty AFL-CIO departments. Women tried to work in the building trades, but their male members continued their long tradition of muscling women out: by 1989, nationally, women's biggest inroads came in the painters' union, but they still made up less than 7 percent of the painters. Such organizations that pushed for female-friendly labor policies as the Coalition of Labor Union Women (CLUW) and 9to5 were important manifestations of women's activism, but they operated at the margins of the larger movement where they were not as threatening to the likes of Meany or Kirkland.

Joining women in their struggle for dignity at work were immigrant men making their way across the US border from various regions of the world. While European and Canadian immigration remained constant after 1970, immigration from Asia and Latin America almost doubled, while immigration from African nations nearly tripled. Wars, repressive government policies, and failing economies explain part of the reason for a resurgence of interest in moving to the United States from Asian, African, Latin American, and Caribbean countries. But US trade policy and the US economy also played a role. US and international laws increasingly freed corporate movement and dislocated working people abroad. At the same time, US immigration policy failed to protect the rights of vulnerable newcomers; corporate interests explain the lack of protections offered to guest workers. Immigrant hotel, laundry, farm, and slaughterhouse workers found a similar coincidence: when their calls for better work conditions threatened their employers' bottom line, their employers fired them, deported them, or called in immigration agents to sift out the undocumented and deport them. The new wave of immigrants was deeply diverse. For example, by 1990 about a quarter of Latinos in the United States were from Cuba and Central and South America, joining a larger contingency of Spanish-speaking immigrants from Mexico and Puerto Rico. Guatemalan refugees had little in common politically, economically, or socially with those from Puerto Rico, yet many of these post-1970s immigrants found common ground in the low-wage, contingent, and non-unionized world of work available to them and the scarcity of their workplace rights.

Not only had the official labor movement generally ignored the changing face of the workforce, but it also had heavily relied on Democratic Party support, even as the core of the organized labor movement – white working-class men – turned against the Democratic Party. In the post-civil rights period, racism and anti-feminism were twin sentiments that fed a growing anti-liberal movement among white union workers. White union men, who previously stood at the heart of Roosevelt's New Deal coalition, beat a path to join Reagan's revolution. Despite Reagan's hostility to unions and support of US manufacturing abroad, more than half of all white members of union families voted for him in 1984. Republicans convinced white union voters that the late twentieth century's Democratic Party was one of elites who were out of touch with workers' values and that Republicans were the righteous defenders of America's traditional values, free markets, and enterprising business innovators. Conveniently writing out of the narrative class antagonism and corporate crime and scandal, Republicans won new allies at a great cost to working-class unity.

Democratic politicians saw the writing on the wall and moved the political center to the right. In the face of lost jobs and declining communities, many white unionists turned their hostility toward Democratic politicians and union leaders. So did southern white Democrats who increasingly changed their party loyalty to the lily-white Republican Party, whose numbers got a boost from shifts in the population from the rust belt to the sunshine belt across the South and the Southwest. Increasingly, Democratic Party candidates realized that in order to win they would have to play according to Republican rules. Through 1992, no Democratic presidential candidate won the White House without winning a part of the South. No surprise then that the shift among white union voters from the 1970s through the 1990s witnessed a parallel movement of the Democratic Party to the right.

Innovation and Possibilities

Given the less favorable union climate and AFL-CIO leaders' commitment to stasis, it might be surprising to find that from 1979 through the mid-1990s a surge of activity and innovation pulsated within the larger union movement. Some labor actions were more successful than others, but as a whole these interventions suggested that there might still be ways to win dignity at work. They also revealed to enterprising unionists that reaching outside of the labor movement to community activists sometimes won them allies strong enough to win against the likes of multinational corporations and the forces that sustained them.

Much of this activity was generated from rank-and-file and insurgency groups that served as incubators of innovation. Local activists within these groups took it upon themselves to develop new strategies and revive older ones to fight inactivity on the part of their fellow union brothers and sisters, complacency on the part of their international unions, and economic attacks on the part of their employers. Old tactics that were given new life included Jerry Tucker's plan to "run the plant backwards." A talented staff member of the UAW's fifth region, Tucker worked with local union leaders to fight concession demands by orchestrating in-plant actions whereby workers stuck strictly to their job description. Generally, when a machine broke, experienced workers knew how to make it work again and would fix the problem quickly, even though that was not technically their job to do any repairs. But in running the plant backwards, Tucker instructed his fellow workers to wait for management to direct a solution to fix the problem when a machine went on the fritz. Productivity at Moog Automotive in St. Louis was so negatively affected by this strategy that after six months, management accepted the union's bargaining position and gave amnesty to union workers. Such in-house insurgencies animated one-time apathetic workers and mobilized members who had been disconnected from their union locals.

Another revived strategy relied on strong community coalitions in the face of unreliable government. Sometimes these coalitions provided support to unions under attack, as in 1986 when a group of largely Mexican women teamsters in California were faced with wage cuts and reduced medical benefits. With the help of unorganized canners and community groups, they led a successful strike at Watsonville canning. A six-woman hunger strike and massive organizing kept the plant closed for six months. In the end the strikers conceded some wage cuts but won a right to return to the plant by seniority and kept their medical benefits intact.

Other times, coalitions formed to support unions in-the-making. In the 1980s, in New Haven, Connecticut, the Federation of Hospital and University Employees' Local 35 committed to unionize white-collar workers on the campus of Yale University. The organizing campaign morphed into a community-wide effort embracing students, faculty, and the broader New Haven community. Once the election was won, the coalition moved into a contract-signing mode, framing the issues involved as those of social justice and equality for African Americans and women. In September 1984, when two thirds of Yale's clerical and technical workers left their jobs, 95 percent of the maintenance and service workers supported their picket lines. Sympathetic faculty members held classes off campus, while the larger movement got strong backing from the local labor movement, New Haven's black ministerial alliance, and New Haven's Board of Aldermen. Approximately 600 supporters were arrested performing acts of non-violent civil disobedience. Such an alliance empowered Yale's clerical and technical workers to stick it out until Yale agreed to a contract giving 20 percent salary increases over three years, better pensions and job security, and a plan to undo years of discriminatory job classifications.

Sometimes these coalitions pulled labor activists out of union-only circles and into networks promoting broad social goals. For example, out of the strike of Yale workers, a community–labor alliance continued to meet to strategize ways to increase Yale's support to its surrounding community and convince its leaders to divest university monies from businesses in the apartheid nation of South Africa. Labor and community groups organized against local economic devastation in the face of plant closings.

The Naugatuck Valley Project in Western Connecticut, for example, gathered local union members, churchgoers, and community organization activists to develop employee buyouts of companies before their absentee owners closed their doors. Such alliances also furthered the goals of local unionists and community organizations through political coalitions: the Legislative Electoral Action Program (LEAP) in Connecticut; the Northeast Coalition Project in New England and the Mid Atlantic; and the Minnesota Alliance for Progressive Action.

Living-wage campaigns were another form of these broad coalitions. Living-wage supporters argued that those who work full-time, year-round should be able to support a family at least at the poverty line. Most union members agreed. Bringing together new coalitions of workers, these campaigns broadened the fight from worksite-specific campaigns to community-wide movements, waged through political mobilization, media relations, and public pressure. By the summer of 2002, 85 city living-wage ordinances had been passed and the movement spread to college campuses where students – many of whom were people of color – organized mass mobilizations that included clergy and community groups.

While much community and labor coalition work focused on local communities, workers were increasingly aware of the need to reach beyond the local to forge international relationships with fellow workers. Such outreach met with mixed results. US Oil, Chemical and Atomic Workers unionists found that traveling to the German home of their employer, BASF, and appealing to fellow unionists and others abroad to pressure BASF to settle with its locked-out workers, was a fruitful strategy. Less fruitful but still inspiring was a trip that A. E. Staley corn-syrup processing workers, locked out from their factor in Decatur, Illinois, took to the stockholders' meeting of their British employer, Tate and Lyle, based in London. In the early 1990s, South Africa and Belgium Caterpillar workers held brief sympathy strikes for workers in the United States; Liverpool's dockworkers in England effected a picket line in Oakland, California, through a call to community activists, retirees, and students on the Internet; and the United States/Guatemalan Labor Education Project successfully mobilized to bring a union contract to garment workers in a Guatemalan Phillips Van Heusen plant.

At other times more sustained relationships developed between unionists across national borders, who helped one another in their struggles against transnational employers. Some of the more interesting of these include the alliances built in the early 1990s between the Mexican independent union Authentic Labor Front Mexican (FAT) and the United Electrical Workers (UE) and later with the Teamsters. Such networks facilitated UE support of FAT organizing in Central Mexico's metal and electrical industries and in turn welcomed FAT organizers' support when UE reached out to documented and undocumented immigrant workers in Milwaukee's Aluminum Casting and Engineering Company in the early 1990s. The Communication Workers of America established an alliance with the Telecommunications Union of Mexico (STRM) and the Communications, Energy and Power workers of Canada (CEP) and set up a cross-border organizing school and mobilized its forces to fight against Sprint's attempts to keep its international facilities union free. These examples of international outreach are just a few of the creative ways labor activists responded to NAFTA and global changes in the economy.

In this period from the 1970s to the 1990s, international labor work was experimental; clear victories were not easily claimed. One exception was the innovative activism of the 1,700 workers locked out and replaced at Ravenswood Aluminum Corporation's West Virginia plants. Not only did the USWA workers target Coca-Cola and Stroh's Brewing Company, which used Ravenswood aluminum cans, but they also turned international pressure on one of the company's investors: Marc Rich, a Swiss-based billionaire investor who was also a fugitive from the United States for tax evasion and fraud. Hiring a full-time European coordinator for its campaign, the USWA succeeded in embarrassing Rich throughout the world and in working with East European unionists who in turn hampered Rich's attempts to expand into their regions, ultimately prevailing over this multinational corporation.

Figure 4.1 The University of Miami janitors' strike, 2006. Photo by Diego Mendez/SEIU.

Back in the United States, to the surprise of their employers and AFL-CIO leaders who had assumed that immigrant workers would not easily organize, immigrant workers participated in some of the most innovative campaigns for labor rights of the decade. The best example of this is the Justice for Janitors campaign launched by the Service Employees International Union (SEIU). That decades-long fight drew national attention on June 15, 1990, when 400 striking janitors took to the streets in LA's Central City district. Janitors linked arms to cross the street and were met by 50 baton-wielding police officers who pounded on them indiscriminately. Thirty-eight marching and beaten janitors went to jail. Undeterred by such a show of police force, on this day hundreds of janitors stayed on the streets, and their courage was contagious. To their side came other workers and a few politicians, including Jesse Jackson, who held a mop in hand. As a result of their action and the public pressure they brought to bear,

LA janitors won a wage increase of more than $2 an hour and full family health insurance coverage. The momentum of such a victory allowed Justice for Janitor campaigns to spread around the country. Using demonstrations, street theater, community organizing, and hunger strikes, unorganized immigrant workers successfully pushed for master contracts that covered entire regions rather than single employers and raised hopes for labor's future.

Another innovation of the period was the attention that labor unions gave to university graduate students. Certainly less exploited than immigrant janitors, grad students still shouldered all kinds of teaching, research, and grading tasks at the university without the ability to negotiate the terms of their employment. Administrators argued that they were not employees, merely students training to be professionals. Graduate employees knew better. The university depended on their labor to teach sections of classes and assist with valuable research projects on the cheap and without a voice on the job. Graduate employees at the Universities of Michigan and Wisconsin had won union recognition back in the 1960s. In the 1990s their members provided valuable assistance to campuses throughout the Midwest and the country; and international unions offered their resources to help organize the workforce, which turned over regularly from semester to semester. Through letter-writing campaigns, rallies, marches, conferences, concerts, "grade-ins," and all manner of public theater, graduate employee campaigns brought the issue of contingent labor to corners of academia often thought removed from the turmoil of labor conflict. Slogans such as "The University Works Because We Do" and creative face-to-face and door-to-door organizing campaigns to fight against state laws, administrations' anti-union tactics, and graduate students' alienation from the labor movement resulted in important victories on several campuses.

The late 1980s and 1990s were also a time when key labor battles erupted against corporate giants Hormel, Pittston Coal, A. E. Staley, Caterpillar, and Bridgestone/Firestone. In each case, unionized workers attacked lean production schemes with new tactics. Their battles resulted in clear losses or mixed outcomes at best. Still, each struggle represented a new dynamism within an otherwise declining movement, and focused the nation's attention on the future of labor in the United States.

Members of the United Food and Commercial Workers local union P-9 in Minnesota stood up against Hormel's demands for concessions and the company's use of permanent replacements in creative and militant ways. Barbara Koppel's 1991 Academy Award-winning documentary *American Dream* incorrectly depicts Hormel's workers as victims of the larger, amorphous political and economic forces around them. Rather than victims, P-9 workers transformed their union from a complacent organization into a vibrant movement that embraced 3,000 union supporters and farm, peace, and social justice activists. P-9 unionists hired consultant Ray Rogers to help organize a corporate campaign that helped publicize Hormel's ties to South African companies. They also voted to strike and called for a boycott of Hormel products.

P-9 workers were fighting the fight of their lives and were committed to a long-term battle, but their international union, the United Food and Commercial Workers (UFCW), had enough. Its president ordered strikers back to work in March 1986; when they refused, UFCW leaders put the local in trusteeship, took over the union hall, and urged fellow trade unionists to ignore the call to boycott. Workers found it impossible to continue under such circumstances and threw in the towel. The defeat was a gut-wrenching loss, but the character of the fight, the commitment of its community supporters, and the creativity of its corporate campaign suggested deep down, at the grassroots of labor, there were still visionaries, gamblers, and fighters.

In April 1989 an estimated 2,000 United Mine Workers officially struck against Pittston Coal and inspired over 35,000 others to participate in wildcat strikes. Pittston management had pulled itself out of the Bitumous Coal Operators Association and its negotiations with the UMWA. Going on its own, Pittston management unilaterally decided it would stop paying for medical benefits to its pensioners, disabled workers, and former workers' widows. It also imposed Sunday shifts, irregular work schedules, and limited payments into its retirees' benefit trust fund. Pittston workers had gone 14 months without a contract, but these terms were just too harsh. In places like southwest Virginia, where millions of dollars in healthcare and pension dollars flowed, communities rightly felt under siege. "If Pittston Coal could get rid of 1,700 people having coverage through retirement...people who had given their lives to a company, and the widows who had coverage, who would be next?" asked a local union official. "We thought it would be a snowball effect, not only in the coal industry but in others." When the company took away retirees' health cards, they ignited a firestorm. Union members and retirees and their relatives wondered: what kind of company reneges on benefits for people who suffered from health problems and injuries sustained from having worked underground their entire lives?

The Pittston strike drew national attention. Every day the company tried to move police-escorted truckloads of coal out from mines, and every day they were met by rainstorms of rocks that broke windows and balls of nails melded together that popped tires. One route from the mines was so well fortified that locals called it the Ho Chi Minh Trail. Union wives organized into a group they dubbed the Daughters of Mother Jones (after mine worker activist and icon Mother Jones) and picketed the mines during the 14-month period their husbands worked without a contract. During the strike they continued their visible role picketing. They also joined students, community groups, and striking workers in using non-violent civil disobedience in the form of sit-downs and roadblocks. Some wildcat strikers and supporters went out on their own, slashing tires, breaking windows, and destroying equipment. Recalling the strike to a *Bristol Herald Courier* reporter on September 6, 2009, the Vice President of UMWA, the dynamic Cecil Roberts, stated: "People understood that if you fill up the jailhouses and fill up the courthouses then sooner or later you'll get someone's attention. Soon we got the attention of the judges, and soon we got the attention of the governor, and soon we got the attention of the President of the United States, and he sent the Secretary of Labor down to the coalfields."

The Secretary of Labor, Elizabeth Dole, was joined at the mines by hordes of supporters, from fellow unionists such as Cesar Chavez to artists, songwriters, and civil rights leaders. Reporters also moved in to capture the strike. One reporter for the *Roanoke Times*, Greg Edwards, recalled, "The scene was very theatrical. It kind of lent itself to a lot of news coverage." This was especially true as nearly forty Daughters of Mother Jones occupied the lobby of Pittston headquarters while singing union songs, or as they gathered with their families at Camp Solidarity, a field on the bank of the Clinch River where union supporters ate and rested. Pittston management used replacement workers and the law, which was against the strikers. But in the end, miners won their health and safety benefits and Pittston paid benefits to retirees. Management, however, won the ability to run their plants seven days a week and the right to put workers on a rotating schedule. To coal officials, the strike resulted in a draw, but to members of the UMWA and its officials, it was an important victory. Roberts argued that it was the beginning of labor's resurgence. He was wrong, but his enthusiasm was contagious.

In fact such enthusiasm spread to the Central Illinois "War Zone" in and around Decatur, Illinois, where the potential creativity and power of local labor unionists and their supporters was on display in the early 1990s. Workers at A. E. Staley (Decatur), Bridgestone/Firestone (Decatur), and Caterpillar (Decatur, Aurora and Peoria) faced demands to speed up work and allow for more "flexibility" in their contracts. In the face of declining health and safety standards and the international ownership of their industries, workers at these three companies supported one another through a Friends of Labor group, picketing, organizing mass demonstrations and rallies, and pressuring local political officials. At first local 837 of the Allied Industrial Workers relied on Ray Rogers, who helped run a largely failed corporate campaign. Then local activists turned to Jerry Tucker, leader of the UAW's own rank-and-file movement. For months, union members did not strike; instead they slowed production through coordinated actions. They were so good at it that Staley management locked them out in August 1994 and would not permit them back to work. Through Tucker's leadership, union activists pressured Miller and Pepsi to drop Staley as a supplier of their corn syrup; grew a massive solidarity effort that included clergy, academics, and socialists; and sent "road warriors" around the country to build support and spread the word. They also organized massive rallies in Decatur, where the global forces of capitalism had a sharp, local bite. There police liberally used pepper spray against non-violent protestors and cleared the roads of people who lay down to block them so that Staley could not get its product out of Decatur and into the world.

In the midst of the conflict, international union leadership let them down. The southern-based and conservative United Paper-workers' International Union (UPIU) merged with the Allied Industrial Workers; UPIU leaders ruled against a Pepsi campaign; and ultimately, UPIU leaders pushed a weak agreement on Staley

Figure 4.2 Supporters from Champaign-Urbana and St. Louis, including the author, blocking the Staley plant gate at a June 4, 1994, non-violent civil disobedience action. Soon after the photograph was taken, dozens of additional protesters joined in. Photograph by Jerry Fargusson. Courtesy, Ethel Fargusson.

workers. In the same stroke of misfortune, Bridgestone/Firestone workers' union, the United Rubber Workers, was taken into the USWA, whose leaders agreed to many concessions. The strong arm of union leaders, once again, had squelched the swell of grassroots solidarity, militancy, and activism.

Jeremy Brecher, in his revised edition of *Strike!* (1997), reminds readers that by 1995 the number of large strikes – involving 1,000 or more workers – had hit a fifty-year low. When strikes did occur, as examples from the late 1980s and early 1990s suggest, losses were the norm. Plant closings, reorganization, uninterested politicians, and union-busting campaigns had taken their toll. Labor activists understood that economic and political forces were aligned against them. What angered so many was labor leaders' unwillingness to rethink the service-oriented model of unionism – leaders provided services and benefits to disengaged customers/members – to which most were committed. Hunkering down with their dwindling forces, most labor leaders resisted committing to the amount of work and level of political reorientation required to become a fighting union bent on organizing new members.

Still, there were some who refused to let the feet-dragging of the official labor movement get in the way of working people and everyday justice. Worker centers facilitated the most successful example of mobilizing workers outside the house of labor. These worker centers emerged in immigrant communities as a way to help community members navigate the legal minefield of employment. Operating as early as the 1970s, worker centers focused on pay, health, safety, immigration status, and rights at work. While work centers had no direct power in the workplace, as unions did, they provided essential help in getting immigrant and unorganized workers more generally organized.

These centers appeared where immigrant workers searched for work. The Workplace project in Suburban Long Island helped immigrants in restaurants, construction, landscaping, and housekeeping demand standard wages. The Coalition of Immokolee Workers organized a successful boycott against Taco Bell and its parent, Yum Foods, and received more pay for those who harvested tomatoes. Asian Immigrant Women Advocates works with women

215

in garment, hotel, electronics, and restaurant industries. In 1992 its members organized a campaign with pickets in eleven cities and endorsements from over 400 organizations for seamstresses in San Francisco to win back wages from Jessica McClintock.

The small-framed and straight-talking Kim Bobo and her Interfaith Worker Justice Movement (IWJ) are also partly responsible for the growth of the worker center model. Bobo founded IWJ in the mid-1990s in response to the lack of religious groups' formal attention to economic justice. Committed to supporting workers under siege, IWJ has stood with Cintas' laundry workers in their fight for union recognition and with the Immokalee Workers Coalition against Taco Bell. IWJ has made its argument for a higher minimum wage before Congress, run a summer recruiting program to train a new generation of labor activists among the clergy, and exposed what Bobo refers to as "wage theft" (employers' refusal to pay employees what they have been promised). In the instance of Case poultry workers in Morganton, North Carolina, a failed campaign by the Laborers' union was ameliorated by the efforts of Kim Bobo and the IWJ to establish a worker center as a more permanent structure to help workers.

Then there were the cases in the 1990s when immigrant workers successfully mobilized themselves, outside of labor unions and worker centers. In the summer of 1990, in response to technological changes in their factory, a group of largely Mexican workers at American Racing Equipment Wheel Factory in Los Angeles organized and led a three-day wildcat strike. Similar self-activity occurred among Mexican drywall hangers who effectively shut down housing construction in six southern California counties in late 1991. Even undocumented immigrants challenged the idea that their labor would be easily exploited and organized openly for their labor rights.

Change from the Bottom-Up

Bubbling up from all this ferment was the realization that the official labor movement needed to be revamped, awakened, and remobilized. By the mid-1990s there was no shortage of labor activists and scholars interested in rethinking the structures and functions of unions in the AFL-CIO federation. Through a rich assortment of labor resources, a heated dialogue ensued over the future of the labor movement. By 1979, Labor Notes, an organization committed to labor organizing, emerged as a leading resource for rank-and-file activists in which staff members could work to build a community of activists through their journal, books, conferences, and training schools. Discussion also carried on in the *New Labor Forum* and *Working USA*, journals that provoked debate on labor's future. By the 1990s, the Center for Working Class Studies at Youngstown State University in Ohio and the national organization, Labor and Working Class History Association, brought scholar activists into the conversation. All parties understood the importance of a newly invigorated labor upsurge. They just could not agree on how to generate momentum for it.

In 1995, inspiration moved like-minded labor unionists to lead a coup at the highest level of the AFL-CIO. Lane Kirkland and his fellow AFL-CIO executive board members were first confronted at their February meeting that year in Bal Harbor, Florida, by Staley's "road warriors" – politicized, energized activists on the road to spread the word of what was happening in Decatur and gather support for more militant leadership. Since meetings were closed to the rank and file, the road warriors stood in the hallways of the Sheridan Hotel and waited for breaks in the union executives' schedules so that they could shake hands and make their appeal public. According to C. J. Hawking and Steve Ashby's account of the strike, *Staley: The Fight for a New American Labor Movement* (2009), Decatur's activists were mostly well received. There were, however, some officials who got angry. The Illinois AFL-CIO president, for instance told the Decatur activists that they were an "embarrassment."

While this action by local activists resulted in pledges of support by high-level leaders to come to Decatur, the meeting at Bal Harbor proved significant for another reason. There, about ten of the 35 international union presidents argued that it was time for Lane Kirkland to step down as president – an office he had held

217

for 16 years. Some thought that Kirkland's second in command, Thomas Donahue, should follow in succession. Others felt the labor movement was on the cusp of bigger outreach and wanted more fundamental change. Hawking and Ashby argue that the Decatur activists' visit had the unintended consequence of providing more momentum to the internal movement for change. Given that there had only been four presidents in the 108-year history of the AFL and AFL-CIO (and that none of those elections had been contested), it was clear that the surge and energy from struggles in the 1980s and early 1990s served as a siren call for the labor movement to march forward in a new direction.

After the AFL-CIO executive's meeting in February 1995, an oppositional coalition called New Voices formed to challenge Kirkland, and when Kirkland stepped down and put Donahue forward in his place, the New Voices slate ran against him. Running SEIU's Jon Sweeney for President, UMWA's Rich Trumka for Secretary-Treasurer, and AFSCME's Linda Chavez-Thompson for executive Vice President, New Voices' slate made its appeal to union ranks around the country. Sweeney was no radical: he opposed single-payer healthcare and emerged from the SEIU where Justice for Janitors inspired millions but democratic unionism did not usually prevail. Nevertheless, his style of leadership, one in touch with larger changes in the lives of working people and struggles of local activists, helped propel Sweeney to the helm of the AFL-CIO. In the first contested election of the AFL-CIO since 1896, Sweeney and his New Voices slate emerged victorious, and rank-and-file activists throughout labor's ranks hoped that this change would prove to be more than symbolic.

In light of the breadth and depth of challenges they faced, Sweeney and his New Voices leadership mapped out an ambitious agenda, promising to make changes where possible. New Voices leaders committed AFL-CIO resources to a wide and varied agenda: putting millions of dollars into organizing new members; developing new strategies to reach out to unorganized immigrant populations; establishing a women's department at the executive level; reversing most of the AFL-CIO's Cold War policies, programs, and institutions (including shutting down the American Institute for Free Labor Development and the Asian American Free Labor Institute and ending the AFL-CIO's link with CIA-sponsored unions); reinvigorating local labor councils and developing new focused strategies to create Union Cities; pouring on political pressure in the form of an "America-needs-a-Raise" campaign to increase the minimum wage; mobilizing labor's political pressure at the grassroots; and fighting against NAFTA even when that meant turning against labor's traditional Democratic Party base.

By the century's end, New Voices leaders amassed a decidedly mixed record. Their biggest commitment was to shift some union leaders' focus from a service to an organizing model and challenging international unions to spend cash to bring union membership to millions of unorganized workers. To their credit, New Voices established an organizing institute and set up "Union Summer," an annual event that brings more than a thousand college students into organizing campaigns across the country. Shifting their focus to low-wage workers, AFL-CIO leaders put their resources behind campaigns to organize workers in hotels, construction, and healthcare jobs. They also turned their attention to President Clinton's welfare-to-work programs that were intended to move welfare recipients off of government assistance and into jobs. Sweeney also sat down with leaders of Mexico's independent labor federations and reached out to Bobo and the IWJ. By 1997 an Advisory Committee on the Future of Central Labor Councils had debated a new strategy to mobilize their individual state-level federation members into a statewide political force. They also discussed ways to turn their 600 citywide central labor councils – where local AFL-CIO affiliates met and debriefed one another about life at work – into robust local forces to promote organizing and fight anti-union politicians and business practices. At the outset about 100 central labor councils signed on to a Union City initiative, and a strategic campaign drew resources and attention to such high-profile target cities as Las Vegas. Some of the most exciting local initiatives emerged from the AFL-CIO's organizing department's project to convince union locals to organize collaboratively. The Stamford Organizing Project, for example, united thousands of low-wage workers including Haitian taxi drivers, Jamaican nursing home workers, and South American janitors behind a broad range of public demands that extended from the workplace into the community and connected economic issues to racial injustice. United with local clergy, public housing tenants, union members, and civil rights activists, the AFL-CIO connected with and helped energize a local social movement.

And yet, while the first years of New Voices' leadership gave labor's allies much to cheer, it was clear that organized labor had yet to make its reformation a revolution. While organizing new members was a clear priority, New Voices leaders were less successful supporting unionized workers under siege. One of the most important of the conflicts that continued to brew when the New Voices team took office involved Detroit's newspaper workers. In that city in the summer of 1995, six unions went on strike against the Detroit Newspaper Agency. Thousands of union members from the UAW, electrical workers, and steel workers joined striking teamsters and communications workers. When court injunctions stopped mass picketing at the Detroit Newspaper Agency's major printing plant, activists took mass pickets to distribution centers and published their own weekly paper, the *Sunday Journal*, which by 1997 reached a readership of 165,000: after a five-year battle, their effort ended in failure. Historian Jeremy Brecher, for one, faults the AFL-CIO leadership for not effectively mobilizing larger support systems for these workers under siege, leading to their ultimate failure.

This inconsistent support of labor struggles gives some scholars and activists such as Steve Early (in "Thoughts on the 'Worker–Student Alliance' – Then and Now") reasons to question AFL-CIO leaders' commitment to working people. Some of the focus of this critique is directed at Union Summer and what Early describes as the "parachuting" of college students into labor conflicts while paying less attention to rank-and-file workers already on the ground. Other critiques focus on the leadership's bureaucratic and intellectual approach to problems, citing how the AFL-CIO has generated an array of work groups, institutes, conferences, and studies from the top. Because of these factors, some believe that this crop of AFL-CIO leaders is more comfortable operating in a top-down fashion than in working to mobilize the ranks for action. Some argue that this top-down perspective was most troubling in Sweeney's commitment to industrial relations strategies where labor's "wins" are best achieved when employers also "win." Economist Howard Botwinick (in "Labor Must Shed its Win/Win Illusions: It's Time To Organize and Fight," *New Labor Forum*) cautions against Sweeney's approach and argues that labor needs to impose "serious economic and political costs on capital" to get employers to bargain in good faith. To do this, Botwinick and others agree, unions need to foster democracy and militancy at the grassroots. Workers need the right to strike. And while grassroots militancy is essential to union campaigns, the AFL-CIO leadership has not had much success convincing international unions to focus on organizing. In 1998, they released Richard Bensinger, the AFL-CIO's organizing director, from his post. Apparently, he pushed union leaders too hard in trying to get them on message. Local insurgency had made some inroads, but much had been left unchanged.

In the end, the union movement still bled members. In 1995, 16,360,000 Americans belonged to unions; by 2000 that number had fallen by 102,000. The AFL-CIO had only increased its organizing budget from 22 to 24 percent and counted few numerically significant victories. Organizing goals ran up against the AFL-CIO's commitment to get out the union vote at election time. Increased spending on issue ads and staff mobilization for elections meant that federation efforts saw the registration of more than 2 million new voters, and the federation succeeded in its drive to increase the minimum wage and to stop fast-track legislation in relation to NAFTA. The price for these small victories, however, was that new organizing campaigns screeched to a halt during campaign season. Yearly membership losses and largely symbolic electoral victories raised the questions of how sustainable the labor movement would be and for how much longer.

221

Conclusion

The period from the 1970s through the 1990s was an especially difficult one for working people. Corporations experiencing falling rates of profit scrambled to save their bottom line. In turn, plant relocations, demands that unions agree to concessions, strategies to increase workplace efficiency, dependence on out-sourcing, and the increased use of contingent labor reshaped the experience of work for millions of Americans. Government policies facilitated much of these changes. Through tax codes, IMF and World Bank policies, Cold War and free-market initiatives, and anti-union appointments to the NLRB, workers and their unions found their strike weapon and their unions decimated (and many of their jobs moved overseas). Conservatives and Republicans' attacks were one thing, but in this period even Democratic Party leadership proved more committed to creating policies to promote globalization and wealth for capitalists than to securing a future for working America.

In the face of economic, political, and ideological forces against working people and their unions, the New Voices leadership of the AFL-CIO represented the hope of new life for labor and better conditions for working people more generally. Facing problems related to living and working in a global, rather than a national, economy, at century's end, the prognosis for working people and their movement was mixed. Certainly signs of life pulsated through the country, but they had yet to revitalize, reawaken, and convince international union leaders to change their ways. The majority of working America failed to see that they shared a stake in the labor movement and that the future of democracy in the workplace (and decent living standards for all) depended on it.

Thirty-two years ago, on a tip from a cousin and a family friend, my dad left Local 3 and the electrician's trade behind and headed down to Florida to work in the restaurant business. Without the protection and benefits of a union, rebuilding the security of the life he had known up north was a struggle. After a year he bought a pizzeria, hired a small staff, worked 12 to 14-hour days, and managed to scrape by. Even though he owns his own business, my dad is fundamentally a working person who shares the same worries about the soaring costs of healthcare, utilities, taxes, and rent with his buddies back in the city. He has a democratic, everyman sensibility about himself and wants a better future for his grandchildren, co-workers, and their families. It is people like him – and those who work alongside him – whom the labor movement has failed and who desperately need labor to reawaken once again.

Epilogue
The Illusive American Dream: A Personal Journey

In the spring 2011 volume of *Labor: Studies in the Working-Class History of the Americas*, accomplished scholar and journal editor Leon Fink alerted his readers to growing despair in the discipline of labor history. On the one hand the field is a growing and dynamic one, with its own journals, conferences, and highly vetted prizes. On the other hand, its audience is on the decline and the labor movement is in turmoil. Labor historians' writing is passionate about the promise of working-class activism, solidarity, and the promise of a democratic labor movement, but there is not much to be optimistic about given today's labor leaders and their narrow concerns and efforts. Many labor scholars entered the field driven by their connection to social justice movements, and while today's working class is ever deserving of justice, most working people's daily experience is disconnected from power or to the groups and individuals who work for change and who understand the central role of class in perpetuating today's societal inequalities.

Some scholars are turning the depressing current state of the economy and class movements into fruitful lines of inquiry for

Working Hard for the American Dream: Workers and Their Unions, World War I to the Present, First Edition. Randi Storch.

future working-class scholars. In her *Labour History* article "Retooling the Class Factory: United States Labour History After Marx, Montgomery, and Postmodernism," Elizabeth Faue suggests that scholars should ask new questions about class to better uncover the personal drama and uncertainty of people's lives. For too long, according to Faue, labor historians have placed too much attention on institutions and what happens in factories and union bureaucracies. By doing so, generations of labor and working-class scholars have squeezed working people into a one-size-fits-all class model that is narrow and does not adequately describe the richness of working-class experience. Most working people do not earn their keep in factories or pay union dues. Faue calls for a look at the subjective and personal experience of class. The last ten years have been harsh ones for working-class America. In many ways, Faue's call for a turn to the personal is a fitting way to explain just how illusive the American Dream has become for working Americans.

Economic changes in the last decade have made it difficult to work for wages with dignity. The town I work in, Cortland, New York, was at one time – like many Central New York communities – a manufacturing hub. People here made wire screens, Brockway trucks, and pottery. Housing in the community shows that there was once great wealth and lots of comfortable living close to work. Not so much anymore. Yes, there are a few places still in business where people make things, but they are the exception. In the first years of the twenty-first century the last blows of the economy's reshuffling were still being felt. The town's tax deal with Rubbermaid expired so the company closed the plant and moved. Smith Corona also closed its Cortland offices where generations of community members had made their living. Politicians and members of the chamber of commerce obsess over how to make the city more "business friendly," which is code for "how many tax exemptions can we offer to lure business to Cortland and for how long can we give them tax breaks." Fewer taxes for them means higher property taxes for homeowners and less resources for the community at large. Many of the homes previously occupied by working families are awkwardly divided into dilapidated rental properties. New technologies, trade agreements, and corporate mobility rocked Cortland, just as they did communities throughout the industrial Midwest and Northeast.

Still, manufacturing in the United States did not vanish. Much of it moved to the South. There has been discussion of the loss of US manufacturing jobs to China and Mexico, for example, and in the last decade one fifth of factory jobs have disappeared (some of them have been lost to new technology). But in 2007, 13.3 million people have jobs in manufacturing. From the period of World War II through the 1960s, working people in these industries fought hard for union protection, good wages, and benefits that improved living conditions in their communities and provided economic stability to their families. But companies have relocated to the South because these states and their business communities are committed to keeping unions out and to showering prospective companies with tax deals, which ultimately deprive local communities of much needed resources. In 1961, 54 percent of the United States lived in the Midwest and Northeast, but the 2010 census indicated that in that year only 39 percent of the population lives in those regions, while the South and West have increased their numbers and political clout.

In the two decades after World War II, manufacturing work was not necessarily enjoyable work but it offered security. Today's economy is one that is more heavily based in services, but the jobs in this sector are often physically demanding and emotionally taxing. Gross Domestic Product figures for the first years of the twenty-first century indicate that whereas manufacturing is responsible for 22.9 percent, service producing industries are responsible for 66 percent. Two years later, manufacturing's number declined to 21.1 percent while services increased to 67.1 percent. There is a wide array of jobs that are service producing (from domestic service to financial consultants), but the ones that do not require higher education are not remunerative or secure. A glance at the classified section of my local newspaper makes this clear: a local newspaper would like to hire a driver for a rural shift (bring your own car), a local bank wants a part-time custodian, and the community college is hiring second-shift cash-iers (noon to 8:00 p.m.) for their dining services (parents with small children will just have to make some kind of individual arrangement because childcare is not a job benefit). The Bureau of Labor Statistics (BLS) forecasts that such low-wage jobs as these will comprise six of the top ten job growth categories between now and 2014. Others include fast food work, nursing home aides, and retail sales.

Most of my personal knowledge of service work comes out of the years spent eating, working, and waiting for my parents' shift to end at their pizzeria. The restaurant business is not for the faint hearted. You can have an excellent product, motivated staff, and the will to succeed and still fail. In addition to finding the right location to establish the business, you need deep pockets (or access to them) for monthly, weekly, and sometimes daily ups and downs of the business cycle. Most people who go into the business do not have extensive resources, and most restaurants fail within their first three years of life.

I grew up listening to my mom and dad try to make sense of why one week's numbers were less than the last week and less than the year before. "Everyone is getting ready to go back to school," my mom would say. "Who has money to eat out?" "The holiday is coming. Who has money to eat out?" Sometimes working with a staff as small as my mom and my dad, the two struggled to make the move from New York to the South a success. Because married women are entering the workforce in larger numbers, this double wage earner situation is common. In 2007, husbands and wives both worked in 57.6 percent of fami-lies, down from a 1999 peak of 60.3 percent.

Against all odds and despite the fact that their pockets were less than deep, my parents "made it" (at least for now). Success, however, looks rough from the outside. On the one hand, my father makes the "family wage" he once earned as a union elec-trician, which means that my mother is no longer required to bring home earnings to make ends meet. They own a home, sent two kids to college, and take the occasional vacation. On the other hand, my dad is 70 years old and works like a dog. Vacations are occasional in large part because he works almost every day and for much of the day and night. Time off for him means that others pick up the slack, sometimes working ten hours at a time, a favor he feels he must return. According to a survey by the Families and Work Institute, he is not alone. The typical worker in the United States clocks 1,804 hours a year, which is 135 hours more per year than his or her counterpart in Britain, 240 hours more than the average French worker, and 370 hours (or nine full-time weeks) more than the average German worker.

While interactions with customers, staff, and delivery people enliven the work, days are long and at 70 he has no clear exit strategy. A preexisting health condition meant that my parents spent too much of their weekly income on health insurance and not any on retirement, but the thought of not having insurance was too scary. Increasingly working people are taking that gamble. From 2000 to 2006 the number of Americans without health insurance increased from 8.6 million to 47 million. Corporate welfare policies and labor union contracts that cover healthcare no longer reflect the reality or practical expectations of most working people. Using emergency rooms for basic medical treatment is more common. Forget about preventative care.

For my dad, Medicare now helps a great deal, but other uncertainty persists. Every few months his landlord raises the rent or the fees on his business and he takes the hit in his paycheck. In the late 1990s, on a tip from a "friend," my parents put whatever funds they could scrape together into the stock market and called the investment "retirement." The downturn of 2002 swept it all away. He was one of many. In 2002 Nasdaq lost 31.53 percent of its value, and the Dow lost 16.76 percent of its worth.

Making a go of life while working in a small restaurant has never been easy, but the crunch of recent economic times has made it even worse since selling food implies that there will be those who have money for a meal out. In the late 1990s, it was common for people to live on their credit cards and second mortgages. It seemed like everyone my parents knew heard a story about someone getting in the real estate market with very little and flipping the property to lucrative ends. One of my parents' cooks thought that he would give it a try, but his timing was not good. He ended up buying when housing prices were at their peak and could not find renters. Nor could he find a buyer. After a few months of paying huge mortgage payments and taxes, the value of his property plummeted. When his payments exceeded the value of his property, he just stopped paying and the bank took his house away. In 2009 the US Foreclosure Market reported that in the month of February, one in every 440 homes in the country received a foreclosure filing. The highest rates were in Nevada, Arizona, and California. But even in a state such as Florida, where a 45-day voluntary foreclosure moratorium was in effect, foreclosures increased by 14 percent. The year 2005 was the first time since the Great Depression that the nation's personal savings rate fell below zero. Americans were spending more than they earned in hopes of a big payoff. Instead, many were sent into a freefall when the real estate bubble popped.

According to the *Washington Post*, in May 2010 signs indicated that consumers were saving again, about 4 percent of their paycheck. While personally responsible, saving money creates a problem for the US economy more generally since consumer spending contributes to 70 percent of the nation's Gross Domestic Product. People who willingly spend their paychecks at pizzerias, salons, and hotels, for example, help keep our service-based economy moving. Consumer spending has been rising at a rate of 2.5 percent per quarter since 2009, but that is less than half of the growth that followed the recession of the 1980s.

High rates of unemployment make it difficult for some to help turn these figures around. Take my dad's childhood friend Frank (his name is changed to protect his privacy) who trained as a cook and had an entire career as a successful chef and restaurant owner. His problem was that he retired before the 2001 recession hit, but at 60 years old found it impossible to find fitting work. He tried selling real estate, but his gruff, back-of-the-restaurant personality was not suitable. He tried driving a cab, but he could not make it financially feasible. Now he competes with college graduates for entry-level $10 an hour jobs, to no avail. He is part of a growing army of the "long-term unemployed" – people who have been without work for one year or longer. At the start of the March 2001 recession, 11.1 percent of unemployed people were in this category, but by the beginning of our most recent "Great Recession," 17.5 percent of all unemployed were long-term unemployed. In 2009 Gross Domestic Product figures indicated that the percentage of private sector services contracted by 2.1 percent while manufacturing declined by 6.4 percent. In May 2012 the country's unemployment figure stood at 8.2 percent, which means that the government is aware of 12.7 million people who want to work but cannot find a job. These unemployment rates and economic contractions mean that fewer and fewer businesses are hiring, fewer people have expendable income, and fewer people are going to spend their money in restaurants.

My parents' business is a mom-and-pop operation. Their staff is few and like family. They have Christmas and Fourth of July parties together and several of them attended my wedding. More common for today's working-class person, however, is a job at a mega-retailer like Wal-Mart, whose corporation only wants its employees to think that they are family. Wal-Mart employs 1.4 million workers, more than any other company. In the quarter that ended in January 2010, Wal-Mart announced a profit of $4.63 billion, yet they offer some of the lowest wages and poorest benefits around. And their low standards are contagious. In 2003 southern California grocery chains demanded lower wages and less health benefits for their future employees because Wal-Mart was moving into their region. Their employees went on strike and lost. Wal-Mart's downward pull emerged victorious.

A small cottage industry of literature has built up on Wal-Mart, and much of it focuses on the troubling impact of the retailer on its labor policy and environmental footprint, not to mention the negative impact shopping at Wal-Mart has on struggling downtown businesses. Wal-Mart, however, is just one among the many mega-retailers pulling down working-class Americans' quality of life. Steven Greenhouse's excellent book *The Big Squeeze: Tough Times for the American Worker* (2009) looks broadly at working life in America, and finds that corporate America's need to show ever-increasing profits leads to downright denigrating work conditions for their employees. Greenhouse's journalism revealed management manipulating their employees' time clock at Taco Bell, Wal-Mart, and Family Dollar. Corporate pressure to minimize payroll expenses pushed in-store managers to illegal activity. Greenhouse also found corporate employees locked in their workplace at night, unable to leave even in the case of medical emergency. He reports on longtime employees who when fired were given only thirty minutes to clear out, and on call centers whose managers deducted bathroom breaks from their employees' time sheets. Target, Safeway, Albertsons, and Wal-Mart subcontracted their cleaning crews to contractors who required janitors to work thirty midnight shifts a month. Investigators exposed these contractors' illegal practices. They almost never paid social security or unemployment insurance taxes, and they ignored laws calling for time and a half overtime pay, even though their employees put in 55 hours or more each week. On occasion, these contractors even abandoned badly injured workers at the hospital. Greenhouse reports on cases where subcontractors left their employees at bus stations with tickets back to Mexico.

The American Dream has brought waves of immigrants to the United States to make a better life for themselves and their children. Today the dream is alive, but the reality is difficult to achieve. In my parents' pizzeria, members of the United Nations might feel at home. Cubans, Mexicans, Columbians, Ecuadorians, and Nicaraguans are just a few of the nationalities preparing food, waiting on tables, or making dough. One guy, a Cuban who arrived in the United States along with over a hundred thousand refugees during the Mariel boatlift of 1980, started his career sweeping up and speaking no English. He is now head cook, owns his own home and car, and has a family. Most others are second-generation immigrants who work part time while taking classes at the community college. Some work long enough to save up seed money to make the move out of the pizzeria. One young Cuban woman was just accepted at a local university. One Vietnamese delivery person, an Italian pizza maker, and a Colombian cook were each successful at opening their own restaurants.

231

Figure E.1 Hyman Storch (second from the left) and his crew, 2012. Reprinted by permission of Jenelle Hamer.

But more often than not, leaving to open a new business proved personally devastating in the 2000s. In one case, a talented young Mexican man found that no matter how many hours he worked and no matter how delicious his food, the poor neighborhood in which he located his business did not bring in enough paying customers. Within one year, he was back at the pizza oven with my dad.

Since the 1970s, when 4.7 percent of the US population was made up of immigrants, the percentage of foreign-born people has been on the rise. In 2009 the immigrant population in the United States stood at 12.5 percent of the population, up from 11.1 percent in 2000. The bulk of those immigrants hail from Latin America and Asia, but the largest concentration of foreign born in the United States – 29.8 percent in 2009 – come from Mexico. By some estimates more than half of the Mexican immigrants who are in the United States do not have proper documentation.

Perhaps if the political climate were not so reactive and the bounce back from the Great Recession not so flat, less public anger would be generated over the place of Mexican immigrants and their children in the United States. But economic recovery has been slow and politics mean, so that people of Mexican descent often do arduous manual labor and service work to support their families (both in the United States and in Mexico) in a culture that promotes hostility to their presence.

Whether foreign or US born, stagnating wages challenge the individual's long-term life plans. In 2000 the BLS determined that 898,000 hourly workers earned minimum wage, but that 1.75 million hourly employees earned wages below the minimum. In 2011, 1,677,000 people worked in jobs that paid minimum wage, but 2.15 million worked in hourly jobs that paid below the minimum. An estimated 80 percent of minimum-wage workers do not earn enough money to pay for the necessities of life. Working 2,080 hours a year at the current minimum wage of $7.25 per hour brings home $15,000. For those making more than minimum wage, the picture of earnings is not significantly better. According to the Department of Labor, private sector wages grew by 1.6 percent by the third quarter of 2010, hardly a cause for celebration.

Working people have a hard time reconciling their stagnant wages and disappearing benefits in the face of corporate profit and CEO salaries. According to the November 24, 2010, issue of the *New York Times*, US businesses earned profits at an annual rate of $1.659 trillion in the third quarter. Despite the 2007 recession and slow growth of the economy since, corporate profits have grown at some of the fastest rates in history and in 2010 made up 11.2 percent of the nation's Gross Domestic Product. They are not, however, being shared equitably with the workers who help to generate them. Between 1990 and 2003, CEO salaries increased an average of 313 percent. In 2011, according to an AP study, the typical CEO made $9.6 million. In 2005 the average CEO earned 262 times the pay of the average worker. Another way of looking at it is that the average CEO made in one day what the average working person made in one year, and then the gap widened even further. By 2009, Standard and Poor's 500 chief executive officers averaged $10.5 million a year, which amounted to 344 times the pay of a typical working person. What these figures suggest is that US workers have had a harder time wrestling a larger piece of the pie from their employers. The share of profits that corporate employers pay to their workers has fallen to its lowest level since 1929. This is true even though employee productivity has risen by 15 percent from 2001 to 2007. "Draw one line on a graph charting the decline in union membership, then superimpose a second line charting the decline in middle-class income share," writes Timothy Noah in *The Great Divergence: America's Great Inequality Crisis and What We Can Do About It* (2012), "and you will find that the two lines are nearly identical." Without unions, workers have lost their ability to negotiate their fair share; communities, families, and public schools throughout the country are paying the price.

During the George W. Bush administrations, labor leaders expected to have their rights eroded further; and Bush and his appointees delivered. Much of the nation's attention was consumed by the tragedy of the September 11, 2001, attacks on the World Trade Towers and the Pentagon and the war against Iraq that ensued. With questions regarding the United States' use of torture and the effects of the 2001 economic recession fresh in people's minds, few paid attention to the Bush administration's attacks on the Department of Labor, a federal agency with the mission of protecting US workers, and to the severe cuts to such of its enforcement operations as workplace health and safety, minimum wage, fair hours, and child labor laws. The main job of the agency, penalizing employers who break federal law, was abandoned and attention placed on investigations against unions. Under Bush's watch, corporate leaders had such significant influence over policy that in the face of child labor violations at Wal-Mart, Bush-appointed officials in the federal labor department signed a secret agreement that gave Wal-Mart management 15 days' advance notice before inspectors planned a visit. Bush also appointed former industry executives to the Mine Safety and Health administration who neglected to collect fines in almost half the cases in which they had been levied. Bush's administration kept the minimum wage at a depressed rate of $5.15 per hour, which in 2007, after adjusting for inflation, was 33 percent below its 1979 level. At the same time, his tax policies focused on minimizing investors' costs, lowering taxes on dividends and capital gains, and phasing out the estate tax that affected the richest Americans. According to Greenhouse, Bush's tax cuts saved the average middle-class taxpayer $744 a year while saving $44,212 a year for the top 1 percent of taxpayers and $230,136 for the top tenth of 1 percent of households.

The NLRB continued to be used in an anti-labor, partisan fashion. Instead of its original mission of overseeing workers' right to union representation, the NRLB ruled in three important cases, collectively referred to as "Kentucky River," that employers had the right to reclassify job titles, even low-level ones, as supervisory, therefore making it illegal for those workers to have union representation. In their dissent, NLRB members Wilma Liebman and Dennis Walsh say the decision "threatens to create a new class of workers under federal labor law – workers who have neither the genuine prerogatives of management, nor the statutory rights of ordinary employees."

With such disregard for unions and working conditions, it is no surprise that labor leaders supported Barack Obama's candidacy and labor spent tens of millions of dollars organizing support for his campaign. But labor leaders' support for Obama was not simply a strike against Bush and the Republican Party. It was built on a wave of hope and promises. Once Obama was swept into office in November 2008, organized labor thought he would prioritize their fight to push through new legislation he had co-sponsored as a Senator, the Employee Free Choice Act (EFCA). EFCA addressed unions' organizing method, making it easier to bring union representation to workers through card-signing rather than secret-ballot elections, which employers increasingly illegally undermine. Small fines, imposed by the NLRB when they make the effort, have convinced employers to do whatever it takes to stop unions from coming into their workplace, no matter what the rulebooks say. EFCA included provisions to impose more severe fines on employers engaged in unfair labor practices, including triple back pay for workers wrongfully fired. But by July 2011 it was clear that EFCA was dead: Democrats did not have the political will to give it life, and President Obama never made it a priority.

Rather than remove obstacles to union organizing, Obama spent his political capital on a $787 billion stimulus bill to infuse much-needed money into the economy, which labor leaders supported because federal dollars fueled road, bridge, and other public construction projects, kept schools afloat, and helped local communities support their social services. These initiatives were good for working families, unions, and communities. But Bush's 2008 bailout of Wall Street banks and US auto companies derailed Obama's pro-worker initiatives. Anger from a wide-range of Americans who continued to see their homes foreclosed, loans refused, and credit destroyed reflected some of the ways in which they sensed that the government's focus was decidedly less on Main Street and more on Wall Street. Frustrated with what seemed like the government's disproportionate concern for stabilizing financial markets, the public was not enthusiastic when Chrysler and General Motors came to Obama for a second bailout to remain afloat. The billions given under Bush were not enough to turn the tide. Much of the public's focus on the new loan terms fell on the UAW and concessions from its members. The government required that these car companies restructure themselves to become more efficient and profitable, and they gave the UAW and its members' benefits no shelter. Even though management decisions were the ones that had led the auto companies on their downward economic spiral and workers' productivity had been one of the only bright spots in the American auto industry, the Obama administration's deal was punishing to the UAW. The federal government took ownership stakes in GM and Chrysler with the goal of making them profitable and their cars more fuel-efficient. The agreement also allowed employers to make contributions to the UAW retiree health funds in the form of stocks rather than cash. It also forced the UAW to agree to wages and benefits that would be competitive with those offered by foreign, non-unionized automakers.

The willingness of working people to divide along their class interests also hampered Obama's administration. The Tea Party is the most recent political expression of Christian white working-class Americans to act against working-class economic interest. Tea Party supporters and their candidates have aligned themselves with corporate capitalism, race-based social privileges, and the Republican Party. Silent in the Bush years, when the economy spiraled into a freefall, Tea Party activists found new interest from white working audiences in the early days of the nation's first black presidency. As the economy crumbles around them, rather than question financial markets and corporate policy, these working people act on the behalf of billionaires and corporate leaders who financially back the Tea Party movement. Tea Party advocates came out in droves to attack plans that would have provided government-supported healthcare – "Obamacare" – to the benefit of insurance and healthcare companies. In the 2010 midterm elections, 138 candidates ran for Congress with Tea Party support. Few Republicans find their way to victory without it. Tea Party mobilization against moderate Republicans has left the ideological ones in DC, resulting in Washington gridlock and a national shift of politics even farther to the right. Tea Party supporters treat the collective interests and public institutions as potentially un-American, at least suspicious and probably socialist, and instead champion private interests as natural and righteous.

In 2010, before the midterm elections, labor hoped Obama would give EFCA another shot, but instead he gambled on a plan to reform the US healthcare system. In the healthcare debate, Obama enraged labor by making a back-room deal with the for-profit hospital industry in which he reportedly agreed that a public option for health insurance would not be part of Congress's final bill. As labor activists mobilized their base in support of the public option, Obama negotiated it away and sought taxes on union workers' health benefits to help cover the nation's healthcare costs. Conservative critics of the president accuse him of being labor's lackey. Certainly labor sees things differently, and calls within unions for labor to take its support away from the Democratic Party are evidence of this.

Unions hoped that with EFCA, Obama would act in some New Deal fashion and push through a robust jobs bill, including support for green industries moving into some of the abandoned factories of America's rustbelt communities, but to no avail. Still, some good has come of the first two years of Obama's first term in office, but these measures are not sweeping enough to make much of a difference.

He passed the Fair Pay Act as a way to broaden women's ability to sue in court against wage disparities they faced when doing the same job as a man, and he extended unemployment benefits. He was also able to win the appointment of Patrick Gaspard, Executive Director of the Democratic National Committee, who came from SEIU as the Director of the Office of Political Affairs. He also successfully appointed Hilda Solis as secretary of the Department of Labor. Under Solis, the Department of Labor handed British Petroleum the biggest fine in the federal agency's history for worker safety violations in conjunction with a catastrophic oil-rig explosion and spill in the Gulf of Mexico. Solis gave a bland speech in 2011 on the 100th anniversary of the Triangle Shirtwaist Factory Fire in New York City, but other than the BP settlement, little has emerged from her desk to help labor. Other appointments were not so easy. Republicans blocked more than a dozen.

These small crumbs come at a time when the labor movement has yet to revitalize itself. In 2000, 13.6 percent of US workers were union members, which included the 9.8 percent who were private sector workers and 42 percent who were public sector workers. In 2010 the numbers were even worse. Overall union density fell to 12.4 percent of the workforce – 7.7 percent of the private sector and 40 percent of the public sector. Small union density is made particularly acute by the fact that most union members live in six states: New York, Pennsylvania, Illinois, Ohio, Michigan, and California. In the South, however, anti-unionism persists and density is low. According to Greenhouse, six states have unionization rates under 5 percent.

In the context of economic instability, membership losses, and employer attacks on new organizing campaigns, the union movement fractured further under stress. On the eve of the AFL-CIO's

50th anniversary, in July 2005, leaders of the International Brotherhood of Teamsters, the Service Employees International Unions, Unite Here, the United Farm Workers of America, and the United Food and Commercial Workers International Union took their membership and their bank accounts out of the AFL-CIO's reach and started their own labor federation, named Change to Win (CTW). CTW also welcomed the United Brotherhood of Carpenters and Joiners of America, a union that had left the AFL-CIO in 2001. In 2006 CTW also won the allegiance of the Laborers International Union of North America when it officially left the AFL-CIO.

The professed mission of the new federation was, according to their website, "To unite the 50 million workers in Change to Win affiliate industries whose jobs cannot be outsourced and who are vital to the global economy. We seek to secure the American Dream for them, and for *all* working people." The CTW federation offered a new model in union organizing and collective bargaining, with more attention to building membership, working cooperatively with employers and keeping dues low, and less attention to lobbying Washington insiders.

The federation had some early successes. Teamsters organized several thousand school bus drivers, and Unite Here organized over 6,000 hotel workers and negotiated employer neutrality for organizing drives at new hotels in six big cities. Working with the Los Angeles Alliance for a New Economy (LAANE), Teamsters organized 60,000 truck drivers at US ports. In 2007 federation members began a drive to organize the country's 440,000 drug store workers with a focus on CVS, a large anti-union employer, and the Laborers began organizing more than 50,000 residential construction workers in Phoenix, Las Vegas, and near Los Angeles.

But problems with CTW that were immediately apparent have only grown with time. Andrew Stern, the egotistical former leader of SEIU, announced at the federation's St. Louis Kickoff that a major power shift was occurring within the labor movement. Most commentators and scholars believed that Stern's split was more about his own personal ambition than a benevolent desire to help. Stern ran the CTW federation with a strong fist. Decision-making was highly centralized and those on the CTW staff that disagreed with Stern found themselves unemployed. He has placed local unions who crossed him into receivership, and has gone to war with union leaders inside the federation who questioned his leadership style. Despite CTW's argument that it needed to split from the AFL-CIO to organize on a new scale, it really has not done so. The nation's union movement organized at the same rate it did before CTW formed and has seen growth in the same areas. The CTW unions that had not been organizing effectively – the Teamsters, Laborers, and UFCW, for example – restructured their organizations since their new affiliation with CTW. At the same time, however, six AFL-CIO affiliates pitched in an additional $150 million to organizing. Couldn't this new commitment and restructuring have been done without splitting the labor movement? Additionally, Stern was initially adamant that AFL-CIO leaders paid too much attention to politics, but even on this issue he soon came around to the AFL-CIO position that political clout was essential to fix a broken NLRB. It would also be needed if EFCA, or any version of it, was ever going to pass.

So, in the end, there was little difference between the AFL-CIO and the CTW unions on matters relating to organizing and politics. There was, however, increasing fallout over Stern's willingness to make contract concessions in order to gain organizing rights. SEIU's policy of "bargaining to organize" meant that union leaders agreed to limit such union workers' rights as that to speak out on bad conditions in nursing homes. They also included low wage increases and bans on strikes. Stern grew SEIU locals to more than 100,000 workers who sometimes lived in more than one state. These mega-unions might have power and political clout, but were not models of democracy – often run by appointed people who were loyal to Stern and not accountable to the ranks. In some observers' opinions, Stern was feeding the "this is why we hate unions" flames.

In addition, Stern's reputation was under attack for his role in a conflict between two progressive unions: Unite and HERE. In 2004 Unite, which represented garment and apparel workers, and HERE, which represented hotel and casino workers, considered merging. Stern of the SEIU thought it better for them to come into his union and invited them into it. Both Unite's and HERE's presidents, Bruce Raynor and John Wilhem, refused and formed Unite Here, with a commitment to organize workers across the country. Soon tension between the two leaders mounted – Raynor complaining about how union resources were managed and Wilhelm upset over the weak and business-friendly terms of union contracts. Into the tension moved Stern, who welcomed the unions, once again, into SEIU. When Raynor agreed, moving his 150,000 members into SEIU and forming a new local, Workers United, Wilhelm accused Stern of raiding his union and organizing a hostile takeover of its hotel and casino jurisdictions. SEIU and its new affiliate Workers United began a turf war with Unite Here over workers in casinos and the hotel industry, and there was also the question of which union would be entitled to Workers United's assets and their Amalgamated Bank with $5 billion in assets. But as far as Stern was concerned, bigger was better. In an interview he gave with the *Las Vegas Sun* (May 10, 2009) he claimed that Wilhelm had made a big mistake by not having agreed to join SEIU because "he would be a powerhouse as part of SEIU, with our geographic reach and political power."

In response, in September 2009 Unite Here brought what was left of their hotel, restaurant, and clothing employees back into the AFL-CIO and started a trend. Soon there after, the Carpenters followed. CTW also lost LIUNA. The AFL-CIO, led since September 2009 by the popular and well-respected former mine union leader Rich Trumka, was thrilled to have these member unions back in the fold, but is still waiting for CTW's four remaining affiliates to come home.

Trumka's good fortune was short-lived. As the dust from the worldwide economic recession that began in December 2007 began to settle, money-starved state leaders and their constituents turned against public workers with ferocity. Despite the fact that the greedy acts of Wall Street bankers and hedge-fund managers had gone a long way toward creating the financial meltdown, the unprecedented rate of foreclosures, a tragic spike in the unemployment rate, and the general economic instability, the media fed Americans a steady diet of coverage lambasting public servants and their unions as part and parcel of what soon became known as the

"Great Recession." Attacks on public sector workers have continued unabated from the 1980s, but the Great Recession caused
them to spike. According to the census, state revenues fell by an
average of 31 percent in 2009, which represents a loss of $1.1 tril-
lion. With state governments looking at record deficits, governors
and state legislatures are desperate to find places to cut. Too often
they are turning to their schools, universities, and public services.
With a diminished commitment to the common good and civic
engagement and with an increased interest in lowering their tax
bill, the public returns those state representatives who speak loudly
of the merits of the free market to office time and again.

When my parents were growing up, they respected teachers
and were thrilled to learn that my sister would find security in the
New Jersey public school system and its teacher union. Four years
in college, and all of the steep student loans, would pay off for her,
as she would find in gainful and meaningful employment in the
field of teaching. Even though her pay would not allow her to live
a life of luxury, it would suffice, surely it would be worth it. After
all, she would be entering a profession with strong unions whose
fight for healthcare and comfortable retirement plans would
balance the difficulties of the job. As it turns out, my sister works
with students with serious disabilities: this speciality in teaching
was her heart's calling. Some of these chldren are on the low end
of the autism spectrum; some growl at her, others bite her. Like
all teachers, every year she goes through a ritual series of workplace-
induced viruses, and she has to juggle family responsibilities with
parent meetings and after-school events. No one would deny that
her job is a stressful one, but it provides a vital service to her students, their parents, her community, and the larger society.

There are thousands of other people like my sister who are
finding themselves under intense public assault. Her own governor, Chris Christie, has been one of the most vocal opponents of
teacher unions. Pitting teachers like my sister against the students
they work with each day, Governor Christie called for New Jersey's teachers to take a one-year pay freeze as well as to give 1.5
percent of their salary to cover their health benefits. As reported
on *Democracy Now!* in 2010 Christie taunted, "See, it's easy to say

it's about the kids when people are showering 4 and 5 percent raises on you every year. It's easy to say it's about the kids when you're getting 100 percent of your medical benefits paid for by the public, as is happening here in Ramsey and all over the state for the teachers' union...Now we've reached the moment where the till is empty. And we have to see, what are they going to do?" Instead of questioning the current inequities in the nation's tax codes, Christie and many other state leaders like him have decided to go after those who have committed their lives to trying to make our communities better. Christie, for example, cut $820 million in K-12 education funding for the 2010–11 school year. Cutting vital school resources with one hand, he points to the failure of low-performing schools with the other. His solution? Close down failing schools, back private efforts through tax-supported scholarships, give parents a "choice" – public or private education – and most important, end teacher tenure.

Exceeding Christie's rhetoric and actions is Scott Walker, the Governor of Wisconsin. In the face of serious budget shortfalls, Walker might have followed in a progressive Wisconsin tradition and rethought tax structures and the state's vision of economic development. Instead, he granted $117 million in corporate tax cuts during a special session of the state legislature held in January 2011 and then went on the offensive to break the backs of public sector unions in the state. Walker had campaigned on the theme of job creation but in doing so did not make so much as a peep about his plan to bust public unions. Once in office, however, he moved against public unions with gusto. He did so not in the Chris Christie sort of way by slashing wages and benefits, but with a new brand of moxie: he went after union members' right to bargain collectively. The smug Walker falsely argued that given the state's current deficit, he had no other choice but to slash the wages and benefits of public workers. Clearly public sector employees' traditional right to collective bargaining had to go in order to give him the flexibility to cut and cut and cut. For no clear reason related to the budget, the governor added a demand that unions should not be allowed to collect dues automatically. What was clear, however, was that he just wanted to destroy these unions. In mid-February 2011, Democratic legislators fled the state to try to stop a vote on Walker's "Budget Repair Bill": in response Wisconsin Republicans found a voting loophole and used parliamentary rules to ram the bill through the state legislature. On March 11, Walker signed the bill into law, which played like music to the ears of Tea Party members, Republican politicians, and anti-unionists throughout the nation. It also must have pleased the Koch brothers, Charles and David, oil and gas conservatives who have very deep pockets and a giddy generosity in their support of those like Walker who are willing to attack unions. In 2010 Walker obtained $43,000 from Koch Industries PAC, his second-largest contribution. They also gave $1 million to the Republican Governors Association, which spent $65,000 to elect Walker and $3.4 million on television ads attacking his opponent, Milwaukee Mayor Tom Barrett.

Walker's law decreased Wisconsin unions' ability to bargain for benefits, it stopped unions from the easy collection of dues, and requires workers to vote unions back into existence year after year. In a cynical move, Walker exempted from his new anti-union law state police officers and firefighters, whose salaries often top the chart of public-sector employees. The police and firefighter exemptions and corporate tax breaks exposed the insincerity of action. This was union-busting, plain and simple. Without resources, Wisconsin's unions will have a tough time lobbying to change the law, organizing members, or negotiating acceptable contracts. Governor Walker's civics lesson teaches that public servants are unworthy of having input into the conditions that define their daily jobs. Rather than negotiate with those who committed themselves to serving the public, Walker denuded them of their workplace power.

No wonder the statehouse in Madison, Wisconsin, became a lightning rod where tens of thousands of labor activists from across the the nation gathered to protest this assault. There they faced off against bus loads of Tea Party activists, whose transportation to Madison was bankrolled by corporate conservatives. Union supporters wrote letters to their local newspapers, and labor scholars took interviews with the national press and media. In February and March 2011, Wisconsin teachers called in sick and

Figure E.2   Anti-Walker, anti-union busting protest at the Wisconsin capitol, February 15, 2011. Courtesy, Emily Mills.

scrambled to the state capitol, where they found tens of thousands of other public and private sector unionists (including police and firefighters) and others opposed to Walker's tactics holding up anti-Walker/pro-democracy signs, singing labor songs, and occupying the Capitol building. Those who rallied became emotionally connected to one another and the larger labor movement (and even to those fighting for democracy as far away as Egypt) through the shocking realization that something so fundamental as the right to collective bargaining, and the equalizing of workplace power that that process represents, could be so easily removed.

Wisconsin activists' longer-term strategy involved knocking on doors statewide in a campaign to recall six Republican state senators, and ultimately Walker, from office. In the summer of 2011 they succeeded in unseating two of the three Republican state senators then up for reelection (the third squeaked by under questions of ballot-counting irregularities that benefited

Republicans by just over a thousand or so votes). With Republicans holding on to the state Senate by just one seat, Walker called in his Republican friends and greatly benefited from the Supreme Court's *Citizen's United* case to help him hold the governorship through the recall election of June 5, 2012. In 2010 the Supreme Court had ruled in *Citizen's United* that citizens' financial contributions to political candidates (corporations included) is a protected First Amendment right: donors do not even have to identify themselves. A few weeks later the courts gave the green light to a new political organization, the super PAC, which could advocate for political candidates (as long as they did not "coordinate" with political candidates) and receive (and spend) unlimited financial contributions on the campaigns of candidates of their choice. Since corporate pockets are infinitely deeper than union pockets, guess what happens? In Walker's case, the ruling allowed him to fight his recall with $30.5 million compared with only $3.9 million given to his opponent. Labor mobilization and get-out-the vote activity resulted in Democrats winning back control of the state legislature and recalling one more state senator, but Walker held on to his office, to the chagrin of workers' allies everywhere.

Even before this grassroots Democratic uprising and recall campaign, other Republican governors fancied Walker's limelight and in the face of massive protest signed their own anti-union Wisconsinesque bills into law. Pundits are now pondering the future of public sector unionism and the crippling impact its further decline would have on the union movement and the Democratic Party. After all, in this current political climate, tough talk against public sector workers and their unions is popular and savvy, and draconian measures par for the course. Even President Obama refused a visit to Wisconsin in support of the Wisconsin Democrats' recall efforts; and while campaigning for his own reelection in Minnesota and Illinois, he left those scrambling to get out the vote against Scott Walker baffled. Obama said nary a word in support of their effort until sending a Tweet the night before the election, in which he claimed he stood behind Walker's opponent. No one should have been too surprised. In 2011, speaking in Minnesota, President Obama was asked about the right of public employee unions to exist. Rather than stand with the union movement or even remind those gathered which groups are to blame for our current fiscal crisis (i.e., *not* public sector unions), Obama chided the crowd – in an exhaustingly defeatist tone – that everyone would need to make sacrifices.

Even private sector unionists are breaking ranks and attacking public sector workers. In New York State, where construction trades have experienced 20 percent unemployment during the most recent economic downturn, Gary LaBarbera, President of the Building and Construction Trades Council of Greater New York, joined forces with business and real estate representatives on the newly organized "Committee to Save New York." The group is intent on lowering taxes in the state by supporting Governor Andrew Cuomo's fight to diminish state employees' wages and benefits and weaken their unions.

The irony of the head of the city's Building Trades federation taking this stand is staggering given that most trade workers make more than those working in the public sector and their building trade benefits are secure. Lenny (his name is changed to protect his identity), a retired IBEW electrician who apprenticed with my dad and worked by his side for over a decade, considers himself lucky. IBEW members agreed to take care of their retirees in their last contract and his healthcare and retirement pension is good. For him, this is a blessing because his wife suffers from a painful chronic disease and her medical care is costly. He also doesn't have to put in 12-hour days like my dad does, in his late 60s, to pay the bills. Lenny has security in his retirement, but his union leadership is joining a vocal chorus in the country attacking everyone else's ability to have security during their working lives and in retirement. According to Steven Greenhouse, three out of four low-wage workers in the private sector do not have employer-provided health insurance, eight out of nine do not participate in a pension plan, and three quarters do not have paid sick days. Rather than work to extend security to all, some are selfishly guarding benefits for themselves while denying them to others.

Other problems for unionized workers persist. As economic troubles continue to befuddle the nation, concessions continue to beset the movement. AT&T demanded concessions in the face of making $2.6 billion in profits. Still, they laid off 12,000 workers and pushed for healthcare give-backs that amounted to almost a 10 percent cut. New York City's Mayor Michael Bloomberg faced a grim financial outlook, but instead of rethinking tax structures demanded a $400 million healthcare concession from his public sector unions, and New Jersey's Democratic governor Jon Corzine (2006–2010) followed a similar path. He threatened job layoffs to get wage freezes and ten unpaid furlough days from state workers. Other private employers are coopting union members into corporate stakeholders. Teamster officials reopened a contract at the parent company of the Yellow and Roadway freight haulers and agreed to a 10 percent cut in pay and mileage compensation in exchange for workers getting part ownership in the company. GM, Chrysler, and Ford turned over the retiree healthcare trust fund to the UAW, which means that the union has ownership stakes in the auto companies. With ownership responsibilities there are concerns that union leaders will join management in enforcing harsher working conditions, lower tier pay, and bans on strikes. In any case, these arrangements wedge unions in between workers and management and compromise labor leaders' loyalties. Kim Moody in *Workers in a Lean World: Unions in the International Economy* (1997) refers to this arrangement as "corporate bureaucratic unionism" – one that goes beyond class collaboration.

The strong hand of the courts and the declining labor movement continue to keep workers' strike weapon on reserve. In 2008 there were 15 work stoppages with 1,000 or more workers, compared to 424 in 1974. In the last two decades there have not been more than 51 such stoppages in a given year. In 2005 New York City transit workers went on strike. In response a judge imposed a fine of $2.5 million, a ban on the automatic deduction of union dues from workers' paychecks, and the brief jailing of the union's president, Roger Toussaint. When Los Angeles Teachers planned a one-day strike, New York's hard line was the template California judges worked off of to squash this protest.

The world of work is still full of danger and thousands of workers die on the job. But it was in 2010 that the issue of workplace fatality and workers' vulnerability to it shook the nation. On April 5 an explosion of methane gas killed 29 miners in Massey Coal's Upper Branch Mine. Company leaders wanted the public to believe this was simply a natural disaster – gas buildup happens, you know. But Massey's disturbing health and safety record told a different story. They had been cited thousands of times for violations, a much higher rate than the national average. Usually the government charged the offending companies small fines. On occasion federal officials ordered parts of the Massey mine closed. But on April 5 all parts of the mine were open, Massey was sloppy, and miners died. Those who lost their lives were non-union. In 2009, the most recent year statistics are available, the US Bureau of Labor Statistics reported 4,340 total deaths due to workplace injury.

Some signs of hope suggest that all is not despair as US workers leave the first decade of the 2000s behind. The most exciting activity is occurring in working-class immigrant communities. On May 1, 2006, for example, millions of immigrants and their supporters marched in cities across the country against federal legislation that would have criminalized the estimated 14 million undocumented people living in the United States. That day, companies that rely on immigrant workers were shut down. This was one of the largest displays of workers' power to emerge in the United States in many years. In 2000 the AFL-CIO finally committed itself to amnesty programs that would help undocumented workers; and when Obama took office and pushed for immigration reform legislation, AFL-CIO and CTW leaders came together to oppose a guest worker program that required visas for immigrants to temporarily work in the United States and offered no path to legal residency (a policy that SEIU, Unite Here, and employers in industries that depend on Mexican workers had supported). Together the federations proposed a national commission to determine future immigration levels. Moreover, in the summer of 2011, California legislators passed half of a package popularly called the DREAM Act, which would allow undocumented youth to qualify for in-state tuition at public colleges and universities. The second, more controversial part would allow them to qualify for government loans. Against the roar of conservatives, Illinois and Maryland legislators are pondering similar dreams.

The union victory for workers at Smithfield, the world's largest pork-processing plant in Tar Heel, North Carolina, points to other hopeful signs. In the face of company election law violations, firing and physical assault against union militants, and an in-plant jail, United Food and Commercial Workers unionists won a 16-year battle to organize workers at this slaughterhouse. The United Food and Commercial Workers Union worked with worker centers to reach immigrant and African-American employees and with a national Justice for Smithfield campaign to reach a national community of faith and consumer supporters. Even before the union won official recognition, its staff helped workers who were threatened with job loss and deportation. For African-American workers, the union was pivotal to their successful fight to win Martin Luther King Day as a paid holiday. In 2006 the courts forced Smithfield to pay $1.1 million in back pay plus interest to employees who were fired for union activity, and in 2008 a union vote of 2,041 to 1,879 meant that workers would finally win a union voice at work.

When United Electrical, Radio and Machine Workers of America Local 1110 workers occupied Chicago's Republic Windows and Doors in the face of the announcement that the company was shutting its doors, another sign of life emerged. Federal law requires that employers give 60-day notice before laying workers off, but Republic employees only got three, even though some had worked for the company for over a decade assembling vinyl windows and sliding doors. Workers also questioned the government's corporate bailout plans that had not written workers such as themselves into the payoffs. Bank of America, a lender to Republic Windows, won a huge windfall from the government in the financial bailout, but Republic workers were not seeing any of it. Believing that they were owed vacation and severance pay, Republic employees won the support of then President-elect Barack Obama. In February 2009 a California-based company became interested in the factory as well. They agreed to buy the factory and re-hire most of the Republic workers. UE's leadership and work with community and faith organizations proved victorious, but innovative union activity is not a certainty these days. In fact, Republic Windows workers decertified two conservative and corrupt unions before joining UE. Democratic unions that work creatively with community partners and push for federal policies that broadly benefit working people serve as beacons in these dark times.

An encouraging sign that labor is not the only group paying attention to growing economic inequality and the political and moral problems it creates appeared on September 17, 2011, when several hundred people marched to Zuccotti Park in Lower Manhattan and birthed the Occupy Wall Street movement. Joined in the following months by thousands of protestors, occupiers established their own makeshift tent village, including a library, sanitation department, medical services, and drummers, and inspired thousands of others around the country and then the world to spread the movement. Occupiers united behind one idea: "The one thing we all have in common is that we are the 99 percent that will no longer tolerate the greed and corruption of the 1 percent" (who own 30–40 percent of the nation's privately owned wealth). Through Twitter and Facebook, the young and tech-savvy core of the Occupy movement successfully turned the nation's attention to economic inequity and brought out union members, to name just one cluster of cheerers-on, in support. Unions provided rain ponchos, showers, flu shots, food, political advocacy, and encouragement; individual Occupy protestors, in turn, gave labor a hand picketing the Hotel Bel-Air in Los Angeles, Verizon offices in Buffalo, Boston, and Washington, DC, and Sotheby's auction house outside New York's Museum of Modern Art in New York City. It should not be surprising that labor and Occupy activists have been inspired to help one another. After all, Occupy's message and that of the labor movement overlap more than a little bit. Still, there is much that separates the two movements: Occupy's movement is leaderless (no one can coopt the movement or really speak on its behalf); it is run like the democracy its supporters would like to create (all decisions are consensus based, group facilitators rotate regularly; it is not organized around policy objectives; and it is comprised of individuals whose hearts back a well-spring of progressive movements). The labor movement has an important ally here, but does not have the luxury of Occupy's open-ended agenda: labor needs to end workplace inequities it brings into the public light and it needs to do so with working people who have been politically disarmed while pushed into battle. Still, broader coalition work such as this will hopefully encourage local union movements for democracy and innovative labor–community partnerships for progressive change.

It is the weekend, so I just got off the phone with my parents and my sister. My mom had to call an ambulance to my parents' home because my dad scratched a blood vessel and it burst and would not stop bleeding. Blood thinners for his heart conditions make this side-effect common. The problem was that he only had a few hours to elevate and put compression on the spot before he needed to head out to work. My sister is also in turmoil. She has been working for a year without a contract and Governor Christie is calling for drastic cuts to public education. *The Big Squeeze* on the US worker is all consuming, and the need for today's labor movement to reinvent itself and how it connects with the public is crystal clear. No big policy shifts in government or labor loom on the horizon in ways that will greatly improve the circumstances of the folks at my parents' pizzeria, at my sister's school, or in the working class who need them to change; but hope springs eternal and if history teaches us anything, it is that the American Dream is a strong motivator.

Bibliographical Essay

This brief essay is intended to point readers to the published work that I directly relied upon to write this book. These mostly newer histories build on a strong foundation of scholarship. Fundamental, pioneering works in labor history are documented in Maurice F. Neufeld, Daniel J. Leab, and Dorothy Swanson's *American Working Class History: A Representative Bibliography* (New York: Bowker, 1983). *Labor History* annually publishes a labor history bibliography, taking Neufeld, Leab, and Swanson's bibliography to the present. Peter Meyer Filardo's annual bibliography in *American Communist History* includes important research in labor and working-class history. *International Labor and Working Class History* (ILWCH) provides review essays and highlights scholarly controversies, and *Labor: Studies of Working Class History in the Americas* and *Labor History* publishes book reviews of the most important new works in the field. New web-based resources are also helpful in learning the field. The Labor and Working Class History Association's website (LAWCHA.org) offers an excellent teaching resource page compiled and updated by Rosemary Feurer. Thomas Dublin and Katy Kish Sklar have worked with a

Working Hard for the American Dream: Workers and Their Unions, World War I to the Present, First Edition. Randi Storch.

253

team of scholars to develop their Women and Social Movements database that introduces readers to particular historic periods, frames historical questions, and includes primary sources and bibliographies to guide students looking for answers. I would like to thank *Teaching History* for granting me permission to reprint parts of my 2004 article, entitled "Teaching Class: Labor and Working Class History in the US Survey," in the introduction of this book.

General Labor and Working-Class Histories

Priscilla Murolo, *From the Folks Who Brought you the Weekend: A Short, Illustrated History of Labor* (New York: New Press, 2001); Melvyn Dubofsky, *The State and Labor in Modern America* (Chapel Hill: University of North Carolina Press, 2004); Robert Zieger, *American Workers, American Unions, 1920–1985* (Baltimore: Johns Hopkins University Press, 1986); Nelson Lichtenstein, *State of the Union: A Century of American Labor* (Princeton: Princeton University Press, 2002); Christopher Tomlins, *The State and the Unions: Labor Relations, Law and the Organized Labor Movement in America, 1880–1960* (New York: Cambridge University Press, 1985); William Forbath, *Law and the Shaping of the American Labor Movement* (Cambridge, MA: Harvard University Press, 1991); Kim Voss, *Hard Work: Remaking the American Labor Movement* (Berkeley: University of California Press, 2004); James Green, *World of the Worker: Labor in Twentieth Century America* (New York: Hill and Wang, 1998); Reg Theriault, *How to Tell When You're Tired: A Brief Examination of Work* (New York: W. W. Norton, 1997).

Chapter 1: "Everyone Was Ready for Unionism": The Precursors, Promises, and Pitfalls of Industrial Unions in the 1930s

Industrial workers' struggle to win government support of workers' rights and workplace democracy is described in Joseph

McCartin's *Labor's Great War: The Struggle for Industrial Democracy and the Origins of Modern American Labor Relations, 1912–21* (Chapel Hill: University of North Carolina Press, 1997). Chapters 4 and 5 in Kathleen Mapes's *Sweet Tyranny: Migrant Labor, Industrial Agriculture and Imperial Politics* (Urbana: University of Illinois Press, 2009) look at the question of wartime democracy from the perspective of farmers, migrant workers, and communities in the countryside. Elizabeth McKillen's *Chicago Labor and the Quest for a Democratic Diplomacy* (Ithaca: Cornell University Press, 1995) shows the alternate vision of unionism established by the Chicago Federation of Labor in this period; and Eileen Boris, in *Home to Work: Motherhood and the Politics of Industrial Homework in the United States* (New York: Cambridge University Press, 1994) suggests the importance of women's difference when looking at the effects of war and politics. The government's campaign to suppress dissent and the movements fighting to keep them alive are well documented in Ernest Freeberg's *Democracy's Prisoner: Eugene V. Debs, the Great War, and the Right to Dissent* (Cambridge, MA: Harvard University Press, 2008). Rebecca Hill, *Men, Mobs, and Law: Anti-Lynching and Labor Defense in US Radical History* (Durham, NC: Duke University Press, 2008) takes this story into the next period. Melvyn Dubofsky's *We Shall Be All: A History of the Industrial Workers of the World* (Urbana: University of Illinois Press, 2000) discusses socialist and radical labor movements of the period, as do chapters 4 and 5 of James R. Barrett's *William Z. Foster and the Tragedy of American Radicalism* (Urbana: University of Illinois Press, 1999). Paul Avrich's *Sacco and Vanzetti: The Anarchist Background* (Princeton: Princeton University Press, 1991) and Michael Miller Topp's *Those Without a Country: The Political Culture of Italian American Syndicalists* (Minneapolis: University of Minnesota Press, 2001) tell the anarchist and syndicalist stories of the period. William Z. Foster documents his own insights in *The Great Steel Strike and Its Lessons* (New York: B. W. Huebsch, 1920). The Interchurch World Movement of North America prepared an independent "Report on the Steel Strike of 1919" (New York, 1920). David Brody's *Labor in Crisis: The Steel Strike of 1919* (Urbana: University of Illinois Press, 1987) interprets events from the perspective of the official labor movement. For the war's effect on labor unrest in Chicago's stockyards, see James R. Barrett's *Work and Community in the Jungle: Chicago's Packinghouse Workers, 1894–1922* (Urbana: University of Illinois Press, 1987).

General histories of the 1920s include Irving Bernstein's *The Lean Years: A History of the American Worker, 1920–1933* (Boston: Houghton Mifflin, 1960), a classic history of workers in the 1920s; and David Montgomery's "Thinking about Workers in the 1920s," *International Labor and Working Class History* no. 32, Fall 1987, 4–24, which succinctly points to big themes and continuity between the 1920s and the 1930s.

Gabriel Kolko's *The Triumph of Conservatism: A Re-Interpretation of American History, 1900–1916* (New York: Free Press of Glencoe, 1963) and Olivier Zunz, *Making America Corporate, 1870–1920* (Chicago: University of Chicago Press, 1992) discuss economic, political, and cultural changes from corporate capitalists' vantage point. Harry Braverman, *Labor and Monopoly Capital: The Degradation of Work in the Twentieth Century* (New York: Monthly Review Press, 1998) offers a Marxist perspective on the period's economic change with sharp insights regarding the impact of new technologies on industrial workers. See also David Montgomery, *Workers' Control in America* (New York: Cambridge University Press, 1979). New corporate business models and an increasing reliance on welfare capitalism are examined in Sanford M. Jacoby, *Employing Bureaucracy: Managers, Unions, and the Transformation of Work in American Industry, 1900–1945* (New York: Columbia University Press, 1985); Gerald Zahavi, *Workers, Managers, and Welfare Capitalism: The Shoeworkers and Tanners of Endicott Johnson, 1890–1950* (Urbana: University of Illinois Press, 1988); Alice Kessler Harris, *In Pursuit of Equity: Women, Men and the Quest for Economic Citizenship in 20th Century America* (New York: Oxford University Press, 2003); and Nikki Mandell, *The Corporation as Family: The Gendering of Corporate Welfare, 1890–1930* (Chapel Hill: University of North Carolina Press, 2002). Rosemary Feurer's *Radical Unionism in the Midwest, 1900–1950* (Urbana: University of Illinois Press, 2006) has an excellent chapter on the anti-labor networks in St. Louis.

The impact of welfare capitalism on workers' activism is examined in Beth Bates, *Pullman Porters and the Rise of Politics in Black America, 1925–1945* (Chapel Hill: University of North Carolina Press, 2001); Rick Halpern, *Down on the Killing Floor: Black and White Workers in Chicago's Packinghouses, 1904–1954* (Urbana: University of Illinois Press, 1997); Lizabeth Cohen, *Making a New Deal: Industrial Workers in Chicago, 1919–1939* (New York: Cambridge University Press, 1990); Stephen Meyer, *The Five Dollar Day: Labor Management and Social Control in the Ford Motor Company* (Albany: State University of New York Press, 1981); and David Brody, *Steelworkers in America: The Nonunion Era* (Cambridge, MA: Harvard University Press, 1960). Cindy Hahamovitch in *The Fruits of Their Labor: Atlantic Coast Farmworkers and the Making of Migrant Poverty, 1870–1945* (Chapel Hill: University of North Carolina Press, 1997) and Kathleen Mapes, *Sweet Tyranny: Migrant Labor, Industrial Agriculture, and Imperial Politics* (Urbana: University of Illinois Press, 2009) analyze the impact of corporate capitalism on agricultural workers. Frank Tobias Higbie examines the impact of capitalism on migration patterns and community in *Indispensable Outcasts: Hobo Workers and Community in the American Midwest, 1880–1930* (Urbana: University of Illinois Press, 2003).

Non-industrial workers experienced 1920s capitalism from a different vantage point: see Dorothy Cobble, *Dishing It Out: Waitresses and their Unions in the Twentieth Century* (Urbana: University of Illinois Press, 1991); Susan Porter Benson, *Counter Cultures: Saleswomen, Managers, and Customers in American Department Stores, 1890–1940* (Urbana: University of Illinois Press, 1986); and Ileen Devault, *Sons and Daughters of Labor: Class and Clerical Work in Turn of the Century Pittsburgh* (Ithaca: Cornell University Press, 1990). Susan Porter Benson, *Household Accounts: Working-Class Family Economies in the Interwar United States* (Ithaca: Cornell University Press, 2007) and Eileen Boris, *Home to Work: Motherhood and the Politics of Industrial Homework in the United States* (New York: Cambridge University Press, 1994) document ways in which new, 1920s capitalist developments and workplace organization reached into the household.

Workplace segmentation and community segregation are discussed by George Sanchez in *Becoming Mexican American: Ethnicity, Culture, and Identity in Chicano Los Angeles, 1900–1945* (New York: Oxford University Press, 1993); Zaragosa Vargas, *Proletarians of the North: A History of Mexican Industrial Workers in Detroit and the Midwest, 1917–1933* (Berkeley: University of California Press, 1993); Evelyn Nakano Glenn, *Unequal Freedom: How Race and Gender Shaped Citizenship and Labor* (Cambridge, MA: Harvard University Press, 2002); Peter Cole, *Wobblies on the Waterfront: Interracial Unionism in Progressive Era Philadelphia* (Urbana: University of Illinois Press, 2007); Halpern, *Down on the Killing Floor*; and Alice Kessler-Harris, *Out to Work: A History of Wage-Earning Women in the United States* (New York: Oxford University Press, 2003). Ava Baron's edited volume *Work Engendered: Toward a New History of American Labor* (Ithaca: Cornell University Press, 1991) contains several important chapters that deal with the 1920s and the use of gender as a way to understand the changing experience of work. The state's role in promoting unequal citizenship and labor suppression is examined in Kessler Harris, *In Pursuit of Equity*; Mae Ngai, *Impossible Subjects: Illegal Aliens and the Making of Modern America* (Princeton: Princeton University Press, 2004); David Reimers, *Unwelcome Strangers: American Identity and the Turn against Immigration* (New York: Columbia University Press, 1998); chapters 5 and 6 of Mapes, *Sweet Tyranny*; and Carl Swidorski, "The Courts, the Labor Movement and the Struggle for Freedom of Expression and Association, 1919–1940," *Labor History* 45 (2004), 61–84.

The impact of corporate capitalists and the state on workers' organization in the 1920s is examined by David Montgomery in *Workers' Control in America* (New York: Cambridge University Press, 1979); David Montgomery's *The Fall of the House of Labor: The Workplace, the State and American Labor Activism, 1865–1925* (New York: Cambridge University Press, 1989); and David Brody's *Workers in Industrial America: Essays on the Twentieth Century Struggle* (New York: Oxford University Press, 1979).

A traditional defense of AFL unionism is found in Selig Perlman, *Theory of the Labor Movement* (New York: Macmillan,

1928). Cobble, *Dishing it Out*; McKillen, *Chicago Labor and the Quest for a Democratic*; and Michael Kazin, *Barons of Labor: The San Francisco Building Trades and Union Power in the Progressive Era* (Urbana: University of Illinois Press, 1987) rethink scholars' assumptions concerning the nature of AFL unionism. Andrew Strouthous, *US Labor and Political Action, 1918–1924: A Comparison of Independent Political Action in New York, Chicago, and Seattle* (New York: St. Martin's Press, 1999) is an aptly named study that questions the political work of labor movements in this period. The importance of workers' education programs and the role of women in shaping them is explored in chapter 5 of Annelise Orleck, *Common Sense and a Little Fire: Women and Working Class Politics in the United States* (Chapel Hill: University of North Carolina Press, 1995); Daniel Katz, *All Together Different: Yiddish Socialists, Garment Workers, and the Labor Roots of Multiculturalism* (New York: New York University Press, 2011); and Liz Rohan, "'The worker must have a break, but she must have roses too': The Educational Programs of the Women's Trade Union League, 1908–26," in Anne Meis Knupfer, *The Educational Work of Women's Organizations, 1890–1960* (New York: Palgrave Macmillan, 2008), 121–140. Strike activity in the 1920s is discussed in chapter 4 of Jeremy Brecher's *Strike!* (Boston: South End Press, 1997) and Robert Shogan's *The Battle of Blair Mountain: The Story of America's Largest Labor Uprising* (New York: Westview Press, 2004).

Communist attempts to organize 1920s workers are most recently examined by Josephine Fowler, *Japanese and Chinese Immigrant Activists: Organizing in American and International Communist Movements, 1919-1933* (New Brunswick: Rutgers University Press, 2007) and in relevant chapters of Randi Storch's *Red Chicago: The Communist Party at Its Grassroots, 1928–1939* (Urbana: University of Illinois Press, 2007); Bryan Palmer's *James P. Cannon and the Origins of the American Revolutionary Left, 1890–1928* (Urbana: University of Illinois Press, 2007); Edward Johaningsmeier's *Forging American Communism* (Princeton: Princeton University Press, 1994); Barrett, *William Z. Foster and the Tragedy of American Radicalism*; Mark Solomon's *The Cry Was Unity: Communists and African Americans, 1917–1936* (Jackson: Mississippi University

Press, 1998); and Robin Kelley's *Hammer and Hoe: Alabama Communists During the Great Depression* (Chapel Hill: University of North Carolina Press, 1990).

The nature of racial, ethnic, and gender conflicts surrounding 1920s unionism can be found in Howard Kimeldorf, "'Excluded' by Choice: Dynamics of Interracial Unionism on the Philadelphia Waterfront, 1910–1930," *ILWCH* 51 (April 1997), 50-71; Eric Arnesen, "Specter of the Black Strikebreaker: Race, Employment, and Labor Activism in the Industrial Era," *Labor History* 44, 3 (August 2003), 319–335; Cole, *Wobblies on the Waterfront*; Chris Martin, "New Unionism at the Grassroots: The Amalgamated Clothing Workers in Rochester, New York, 1914–1929," *Labor History* 42 (2001), 237–253; Steve Fraser, "Dress Rehearsal for the New Deal: Shop-Floor Insurgent, Political Elites and Industrial Democracy in the Amalgamated Clothing Workers," in Michael Frisch and Daniel Walkowitz, eds., *Working-Class America: Essays in Labor Community and American Society* (Urbana: University of Illinois Press, 1983); Orleck, *Common Sense and a Little Fire*. Devault, *United Apart* examines the period before World War I, but includes important insights on emerging forms of craft unionism. Karen Pastorello, *A Power Among Them: Bessie Abromowitz Hillman and the Making of the Amalgamated Clothing Workers of America* (Urbana: University of Illinois Press, 2008) takes the story of labor feminism into a later period.

Some scholars extend their analysis from the workplace to the community. Fruitful examinations look at newly forming racial and ethnic communities in light of the war and Great Migration of African Americans from the South to the North and the immigration and settling of Mexican and Mexican-American communities in the West. These include Kevin Boyle's *Arc of Justice: A Saga of Race, Civil Rights and Murder in the Jazz Age* (New York: H. Holt, 2004); Kimberley Phillips, *AlabamaNorth: African American Migrants, Community and Working-Class Activism in Cleveland, 1915–1945* (Urbana: University of Illinois Press, 1999); James R. Barrett, *Work and Community in the Jungle: Chicago's Packinghouse Workers, 1894–1922* (Urbana: University of Illinois Press, 1987); Becky Nicolaides, *My Blue Heaven: Life and Politics in the Working Class*

Suburbs of Los Angeles, 1920–1965 (Chicago: University of Chicago Press, 2002); Gilbert Gonzalez, *Labor and Community: Mexican Citrus Worker Villages in a Southern California County, 1900–1950* (Urbana: University of Illinois Press, 1994); George Sanchez, *Becoming Mexican American: Ethnicity, Culture and Identity in Chicano Los Angeles, 1900–1945* (New York: Oxford University Press, 1995); and Joe William Trotter Jr., *Black Milwaukee: The Making of an Industrial Proletariat, 1915–1945* (Urbana: University of Illinois Press, 1985). Nancy MacLean's *Behind the Mask of Chivalry: The Making of the Second Ku Klux Klan* (New York: Oxford University Press, 1994) offers a class analysis of this modern, reactionary movement.

Black nationalism and Garveyism are addressed in Judith Stein, *The World of Marcus Garvey: Race and Class in Modern Society* (Baton Rouge: Louisiana State University Press, 1986); Mary Rolinson, *Grassroots Garveyism: The Universal Negro Improvement Association in the Rural South, 1920–1927* (Chapel Hill: University of North Carolina Press, 2007); Colin Grant, *Negro with a Hat: The Rise and Fall of Marcus Garvey* (New York: Oxford University Press, 2008); and Ula Taylor, *The Veiled Garvey: The Life and Times of Amy Jacques Garvey* (Chapel Hill: University of North Carolina Press, 2002).

Scholars have begun to reconsider the effect of consumerism on working people in 1920s America. A traditional interpretation can be found in Robert Staughton Lynd and Helen Merrell Lynd, *Middletown: A Study in Contemporary American Culture* (New York: Harcourt, Brace, 1929). Dana Frank links consumer campaigns to boycotts and union campaigns in *Purchasing Power: Consumer Organizing, Gender and the Seattle Labor Movement, 1919–1929* (New York: Cambridge University Press, 1994). Annelise Orleck's *Common Sense and a Little Fire: Women and Working Class Politics in the United States, 1900–1965* (Chapel Hill: University of North Carolina Press, 1995); Lawrence Glickman's *Buying Power: A History of Consumer Activism in America* (Chicago: University of Chicago Press, 2009); and Meg Jacobs' *Pocketbook Politics: Economic Citizenship in Twentieth Century America* (Princeton: Princeton University Press, 2005) also examine consumer activism. Patricia Benson uncovers the central role of women as consumers in working-class families in *Household Accounts*. Cohen, *Making a New Deal* and George Sanchez, *Becoming Mexican American* argue that consumerism shaped workers' ethnic and working-class identities. Zaragosa Vargas, in *Proletarians of the North*, suggests Mexican and Mexican American workers agreed to labor in difficult conditions as the price to become consumers. The AFL's identification with consumerism is discussed by Thomas Stapelford in "Defining a 'Living Wage' in America: Transformations in Union Wage Theories, 1870–1930," *Labor History* 49, 1 (February 2008), 1–22; also see Craig Phelan, *William Green: Biography of a Labor Leader* (Albany: State University of New York Press, 1989) on this labor leader's commitment to consumerist politics.

The literature on the New Deal is vast. Good overviews that focus on the working-class, labor, and union issues include Paul K. Conkin's brief history, *The New Deal* (Wheeling, IL: Harland Davidson, 1992); Alan Brinkley, *The End of Reform: New Deal Liberalism in Recession and War* (New York: Knopf, 1995); James A. Gross, *The Making of the National Labor Relations Board: 1933–1937* (Albany: State University of New York Press, 1974); Colin Gordon, *New Deals: Business, Labor and Politics in America, 1920–1935* (Cambridge: Cambridge University Press, 1994); chapter 4 in David Brody, *Workers in Industrial America: Essays on the 20th Century Struggle* (New York: Oxford University Press, 1980); Gary Gerstle in "The Protean Character of American Liberalism," *American Historical Review* 99, 4 (October 1994), 1043–1073; and Nick Salvatore and Jefferson Cowie, "The Long Exception: Rethinking the Place of the New Deal in American History," *ILWCH* 74 (Fall 2008), 3–32. Irving Bernstein, *The Turbulent Years: A History of the American Worker, 1933–1941* (Chicago: Haymarket Books, 2010); Studs Terkel, *Hard Times: An Oral History of the Great Depression* (New York: New Press, 2000); and Staughton Lynd and Alice Lynd, *Rank and File: Personal Histories of Working-Class Organizers* (Princeton: Princeton University Press, 1982) contain first-hand accounts of Depression-era lives.

Depression-era migration – forced and otherwise – is discussed in James Gregory's *The Southern Diaspora: How the Great Migrations of Black and White Southerners Transformed America* (Chapel Hill: University of North Carolina Press, 2005) and Gregory, *American Exodus: The Dust Bowl Migration and Okie Culture in California* (New York: Oxford University Press, 1989); Francisco Balderrama, *Decade of Betrayal: Mexican Repatriation in the 1930s* (Albuquerque: University of New Mexico Press, 1995); chapters 5, 6, and 7 of Mapes, *Sweet Tyranny*; and chapter 5 of Cindy Hahamavitch's *The Fruits of Their Labor: Atlantic Coast Farmworkers and the Making of Migrant Poverty, 1870–1945* (Chapel Hill: University of North Carolina Press, 1997). The Depression's impact on working-class families and women is documented in Susan Porter Benson, *Household Accounts*.

Unemployed Council and Communist Party activism are described in Frances Fox Piven and Richard A. Cloward, *Regulating the Poor: The Functions of Public Welfare* (New York: Pantheon, 1971); chapter 4 of Randi Storch, *Red Chicago*; James Lorence, *Organizing the Unemployed: Community and Union Activists in the Industrial Heartland* (Albany: State University of New York Press, 1996); Glenda Gilmore, *Defying Dixie: The Radical Roots of Civil Rights, 1919–1950* (New York: Norton, 2009); and Mark Solomon, *The Cry Was Unity: Communists and African Americans, 1917–1936* (Jackson: University Press of Mississippi, 1998).

Working-class electoral politics is discussed in Cecelia Bucki, *Bridgeport's Socialist New Deal, 1915–1936* (Urbana: University of Illinois Press, 2001) and Cohen, *Making a New Deal*. For the rise of business conservatism in this period see Kim Philips Fein, *Invisible Hands: The Making of the Conservative Movement from the New Deal to Reagan* (New York: Norton, 2009). Jennifer Guglielmo's *Living the Revolution: Italian Women's Resistance and Radicalism in New York City, 1880–1945* (Chapel Hill: University of North Carolina Press, 2012) traces the trajectory of two generations of these women from their politically active beginnings to their increasingly nationalist and racist turn.

Community activism and its influence on industrial unionism are discussed in Kimberley Phillips, *AlabamaNorth*; chapter 6 of

Annalise Orleck, *Common Sense and a Little Fire*; chapter 3 in Rosemary Feurer, *Radical Unionism in the Midwest, 1900–1950*; Staughton Lynd, ed., *"We Are All Leaders": The Alternative Unionism of the 1930s* (Urbana: University of Illinois Press, 1996); Gary Gerstle, *Working Class Americanism: The Politics of Labor in a Textile City, 1914–1960* (Princeton: Princeton University Press, 2001); Halpern, *Down on the Killing Floor*; Laurie Mercier, *Anaconda: Labor, Community, and Culture in Montana's Smelter City* (Urbana: University of Illinois Press, 2001); Lisa Fine, *Reo Joe: Work, Kin and Community in Autotown, USA* (Philadelphia: Temple University Press, 2004). Jennifer Klein's *For All These Rights: Business, Labor and the Shaping of America's Public–Private Welfare State* (Princeton: Princeton University Press, 2006) examines the shift from community-based health options to private, workplace-based options.

The struggle to build the CIO is widely documented. In addition to works already listed, excellent studies include Robert Zieger *The CIO, 1935–1955* (Chapel Hill: University of North Carolina Press, 1995); Nelson Lichtenstein, *Walter Reuther: The Most Dangerous Man in Detroit* (Urbana: University of Illinois Press, 1997); Melvyn Dubofsky and Warren Van Tine, *John L. Lewis: A Biography* (Urbana: University of Illinois Press, 1986); Ron Schatz, *The Electrical Workers: A History of Labor at General Electric and Westinghouse, 1923–1960* (Urbana: University of Illinois Press, 1983); Bruce Nelson, *Workers on the Waterfront: Seamen, Longshoremen, and Unionism in the 1930s* (Urbana: University of Illinois Press, 1990); Steven Fraser, *Labor Will Rule: Sidney Hillman and the Rise of American Labor* (Ithaca: Cornell University Press, 1993); Joshua Freeman, *In Transit: The Transport Workers Union of New York City 1933–1966* (Philadelphia: Temple University Press, 2001); Cohen, *Making a New Deal*. Horace Cayton and George N. Mitchell, *Black Workers and the New Unions* (Chapel Hill: University of North Carolina Press, 1939), includes interviews.

Depression-era strikes are covered in John Hevener, *Which Side Are You On? The Harlan County Coal Miners, 1931–1939* (Urbana: University of Illinois Press, 2002); David Selvin, *A Terrible Anger:*

The 1934 Waterfront and General Strikes in San Francisco (Detroit: Wayne State University Press, 1996); Sidney Fine, *Sit Down: The General Motors Strike of 1936–7* (Ann Arbor: University of Michigan Press, 1969); Melvyn Dubofsky, "Not So 'Turbulent Years': A New Look at the 1930s," in Charles Stephenson and Robert Asher, *Life and Labor: Dimensions of American Working Class History* (Albany: State University of New York Press, 1986); chapter 5 in Jeremy Brecher, *Strike!*; Michael Goldfield in "Worker Insurgency, Radical Organization, and New Deal Labor Legislation," *American Political Science Review* 83, 4 (December 1989), 1257–1282; and two of the three episodes discussed in Howard Zinn, Robin Kelley, and Dana Frank, *Three Strikes: Miners, Musicians, Salesgirls and the Fighting Spirit of Labor's Last Century* (Boston: Beacon Press, 2002).

Works that take a critical view of CIO unionism include Elizabeth Faue, *Community of Suffering and Struggle: Women, Men and the Labor Movement in Minneapolis, 1915–1945* (Chapel Hill: University of North Carolina Press, 1991); Lynd, ed., *"We Are All Leaders"*; Charles Williams, "The Racial Politics of Progressive Americanism: New Deal Liberalism and the Subordination of Black Workers in the UAW," *Studies in American Political Development* 19, 1 (2005), 75–97; Mercier, *Anaconda*.

The Communist Party's role in trade union organizing is discussed in Harvey Klehr, *The Heyday of American Communism: The Depression Decade* (New York: Basic Books, 1985); chapters 4 and 5 in Storch, *Red Chicago*; Fraser Ottanelli, *The Communist Party from the Depression to World War II* (New Brunswick: Rutgers University Press, 1991); Roger Keeran, *The Communist Party and the Auto Workers' Union* (Bloomington: Indiana University Press, 1980); Robin Kelley, *Hammer and Hoe: Alabama Communists During the Great Depression* (Chapel Hill: University of North Carolina Press, 1990); Harvey Levenstein, *Communism, Anti-Communism and the CIO* (Westport: Greenwood Press, 1981).

The Popular Front is analyzed in Michael Denning, *The Cultural Front: The Laboring of Culture in the Twentieth Century* (New York: Verso, 2011); Robert Cherny, "Prelude to the Popular Front: The Communist Party in California, 1931–1935," *American Communist*

History 1, 1 (June 2002), 5–42; James R. Barrett, "Rethinking the Popular Front," *Rethinking Marxism* 21, 4 (October 2009), 531–555.

Chapter 2: Big Wars, Big Labor, Big Costs

General works for this period include James Atleson, *Labor and the Wartime State: Labor Relations and Law during World War II* (Urbana: University of Illinois Press, 1998); Dorothy Cobble, *The Other Women's Movement: Workplace Justice and Social Rights in Modern America* (Princeton: Princeton University Press, 2004); and Nelson Lichtenstein, *Labor's War at Home: The CIO in World War II* (New York: Cambridge University Press, 1997).

Wartime union struggles often continued efforts begun during the Depression. Notable additions that focus on union building during the war and Cold War periods include Bruce Nelson in "Organized Labor and the Struggle for Black Equality in Mobile during World War II," *Journal of American History* (December 1993), 952–988 and Robert Korstad, *Civil Rights Unionism: Tobacco Workers and the Struggle for Democracy in the Mid-Twentieth Century South* (Chapel Hill: University of North Carolina Press, 2003).

Discussion of wartime policy and race relations can be found in Andrew Kersten, *Race, Jobs, and the War* (Urbana: University of Illinois Press, 2007); Daniel Kryder, *Divided Arsenal: Race and the American State During World War II* (New York: Cambridge University Press, 2000); Emilio Zamora, *Claiming Rights and Righting Wrongs in Texas: Mexican Workers and Job Politics During World War II* (College Station: Texas A&M University Press, 2009); Eileen Boris, "'You Wouldn't Want One of 'Em Dancing with Your Wife': Racialized Bodies on the Job in World War II," *American Quarterly* 50, 1 (March 1998), 77–108; Boris, "Black Workers, Trade Unions, and Labor Standards: The Wartime FEPC," in Henry Louis Taylor Jr. and Walter Hill, eds., *Historical Roots of the Urban Crisis: African Americans in the Industrial City, 1900–1950* (New York: Garland, 2000), 251–273; Laurie Green, "Where Would the Negro Women

Apply for Work? Gender, Race, and Labor in Wartime Memphis," *Labor: Studies in Working Class History of the Americas* 3, 3 (Fall 2006), 95–117.

Research on women and their struggles in wartime workplaces includes Ruth Milkman, *Gender at Work: The Dynamics of Job Segregation by Sex During World War II* (Urbana: University of Illinois Press, 1987); chapter 6 of Pastorello, *A Power Among Them*; Emily Yellin, *Our Mother's War: American Women at Home and at the Front During World War II* (New York: Free Press, 2004); Maureen Honey, *Creating Rosie the Riveter: Class, Gender and Propaganda During World War II* (Amherst: University of Massachusetts Press, 1984); Karen Anderson, *Wartime Women: Sex Roles, Family Relations and the Status of Women During World War II* (Westport: Greenwood Press, 1981); Nancy Gabin, *Feminism in the Labor Movement: Women and the United Auto Workers Union, 1935–1975* (Ithaca: Cornell University Press, 1990); Richard Santilán, "Rosita the Riveter: Midwest Mexican American Women During World War II, 1941–1945," *Perspectives in Mexican American Studies* 2 (January, 1989), 115–147.

The CIO's attempts at organizing the South are discussed in Barbara Griffith, *The Crisis of American Labor: Operation Dixie and the Defeat of the CIO* (Philadelphia: Temple University Press, 1988); William Jones, "Black Workers and the CIO's Turn Toward Racial Liberalism: Operation Dixie and the North Carolina Lumber Industry, 1946–53," *Labor History* 41 (2000), 279–306; Zieger, ed., *Southern Labor in Transition, 1940–1995* (Knoxville: University of Tennessee Press, 1997); and Timothy Minchin, *Fighting Against the Odds: A History of Southern Labor Since World War II* (Gainesville: University Press of Florida, 2005). For a history of unions in the South see Robert Zeiger, *Organized Labor in the Twentieth Century South* (Knoxville: University of Tennessee Press, 1991).

Local examples of domestic anti-communism and the Cold War's impact on labor are closely examined in Shelton Stromquist, ed., *Labor's Cold War: Local Politics in a Global Context* (Urbana: University of Illinois Press, 2008) and Robert Cherny, William Issel, and Kieran Taylor, eds., *American Labor and the Cold War:*

Grassroots Politics and Postwar Political Culture (New Brunswick: Rutgers University Press, 2004). The impact of anti-communist pressures on CIO unionism is described in Steven Rosswum, ed., *The CIO's Left-Led Unions* (New Brunswick: Rutgers University Press, 1992). The democratic difference of left-led unions is examined in Judith Stepan Norris and Maurice Zeitlin, *Left Out: Reds and America's Industrial Unions* (New York: Cambridge University Press, 2002) and Ellen Schrecker, *Many are the Crimes: McCarthyism in America* (Boston: Little, Brown, 1998). Steve Rosswum, *The FBI and the Catholic Church, 1935–1962* (Amherst: University of Massachusetts Press, 2009) offers an excellent analysis of the cooperation between the FBI and the Church against communists in this period. Laurie Mercier, "'A Union Without Women Is only Half Organized': Mine Mill, Women's Auxiliaries and Cold War Politics in the North American Wests," in Elizabeth Jameson and Sheila McManus, eds., *One Step over the Line: Toward a History of Women in the North American Wests* (Edmonton: University of Alberta Press), 315–340 presents a gendered examination of Cold War conflict; Jack Metzgar's *Striking Steel: Solidarity Remembered* (Philadelphia: Temple University Press, 2000) eloquently argues for the importance of the 1959 steel strike and the persistent influence and importance of industrial unionism. My interpretation of this event closely draws from his.

Joshua Freeman, *Working-Class New York: Life and Labor Since World War II* (New York: New Press, 2000) and Kevin Boyle, *The UAW and the Heyday of American Liberalism, 1945–1968* (Ithaca: Cornell University Press, 1995) describes the potential of postwar liberalism. Critiques on this vision can be found in Elizabeth Fones-Wolf, *Selling Free Enterprise: The Business Assault on Labor and Liberalism, 1945–1960* (Urbana: University of Illinois Press, 1994) and Kim Phillips-Fein, "If Business and the Country Will Be Run Right: The Business Challenge to the Liberal Consensus, 1945–64," *ILWCH* 72 (2007), 192–215. The failed racial dimension of postwar liberalism is portrayed in Thomas Sugrue, *The Origins of the Urban Crisis: Race and Inequality in Postwar Detroit* (Princeton: Princeton University Press, 2005).

Chapter 3: Civil Rights versus Labor Rights, 1960s–1970s

A good overview of political tensions in this period is presented by Nelson Lichtenstein, *The State of the Union: A Century of American Labor* (Princeton: Princeton University Press, 2002); discussion of national politics and Nixon's labor policies can be found in Jefferson Cowie, *Stayin' Alive: The 1970s and the Last Days of the Working Class* (New York: New Press, 2010); Dubofsky, *The State and Labor*; and Zieger, *American Workers, American Unions*. Economic conditions of the period are outlined in James O'Conor, *The Fiscal Crisis of the State* (New York: St. Martin's Press, 1973) and analyzed in Judith Stein, *Running Steel, Running America: Economic Policy and the Decline of Liberalism* (Chapel Hill: University of North Carolina Press, 1998).

Venus Green, *Race on the Line: Gender, Labor and Technology in the Bell System, 1880–1980* (Durham, NC: Duke University Press, 2001) documents the racial and gender dimensions of the technical deskilling of telephone work. My interpretation of the rise in public employee unionism is largely based on Joseph McCartin's articles: "Bringing the State's Workers In: Time To Rectify an Imbalanced US Labor Historiography," *Labor History* 47, 1 (February 2006), 73–94; McCartin, "'A Wagner Act for Public Employees': Labor's Deferred Dream and the Rise of Conservatism, 1970–1976," *Journal of American History* 95 1, (June 2008), 123–148; and McCartin, "'Fire the Hell out of Them': Sanitation Workers' Struggles and the Normalization of the Striker Replacement Strategy in the 1970s," *Labor: Studies in Working Class History of the Americas* 2, 3 (Fall 2005), 67–92. See also Alan Draper, "Public Sector Workers: A New Vanguard," *Working USA* 4 (2000), 8–26.

Studies that analyze the relationship between unions and civil rights activism include Laurie Green, *Battling the Plantation Mentality: Memphis and the Black Freedom Struggle* (Chapel Hill: University of North Carolina Press, 2007); Michael Honey, *Southern Labor and Black Civil Rights: Organizing Memphis Workers*

(Urbana: University of Illinois Press, 1993); Leon Fink and Brian Greenberg, *Upheaval in the Quiet Zone: A History of Hospital Workers' Union Local 1199* (Urbana: University of Illinois Press, 1989); Marshall Ganz, *Why David Sometimes Wins: Leadership, Organization and Strategy in the California Farmworker Movement* (New York: Oxford University Press, 2009); Larry Isaac and Lars Christiansen, "How the Civil Rights Movement Revitalized Labor Militancy," *American Sociological Review* 67, 5 (October 2002), 722–746; Michale Flug, "Organized Labor and the Civil Rights Movement of the 1960s: The Case of the Maryland Freedom Unions," *Labor History* 3 (1990), 322–346. Rank-and-file movements are documented in Dan La Botz, *Rank and File Rebellion: Teamsters for a Democratic Union* (New York: Verso, 1990); Glenn Perusek and Kent Worcester, eds., *Trade Union Politics: American Unions and Economic Change, 1960s–1990s* (Atlantic Highlands: Humanities Press, 1995); David Witwer, "Local Rank and File Militancy: The Battle for Teamster Reform in Philadelphia in the early 1960s," *Labor History* 41, 3 (August 2000), 263–278. Annelise Orleck documents a fascinating case of welfare activism in *Storming Caesar's Palace: How Black Mothers Fought Their Own War on Poverty* (Boston: Beacon Press, 2005). Health and safety struggles are discussed in Jefferson Cowie, *Stayin' Alive: The 1970s and the Last Days of the Working Class* (New York: New Press, 2010). Alan Draper's *Conflict of Interests: Organized Labor and the Civil Rights Movement in the South, 1954–1968* (Ithaca: ILR Press, 1994) charts the relationship between southern labor unions and the civil rights movement and Peter Levy's *The New Left and Labor in the 1960s* (Champaign: University of Illinois Press, 1994) documents the relationship between student groups and the labor movement.

Use of the Equal Employment Opportunity Act and Title VII to challenge discrimination in established unions is examined in Paul Frymer, "Acting When Elected Officials Won't: Federal Courts and Civil Rights Enforcement in US Labor Union, 1935–85," *American Political Science Review* (2003), 483–499; Nancy MacLean, *Freedom is Not Enough: The Opening of the American Workplace* (Cambridge, MA: Harvard University Press, 2006).

Broader discussions of the struggle to make unions more democratic include David Lewis Coleman, *Race Against Liberalism: Black Workers and the UAW in Detroit* (Urbana: University of Illinois Press, 2008); Cobble, *The Other Women's Movement*; Dennis A. Deslippe, *"Rights, Not Roses": Unions and the Rise of Working-Class Feminism, 1945–1980* (Urbana: University of Illinois Press, 1990); Nancy Gabin, *Feminism in the Labor Movement*; chapter 7 in Pastorello, *A Power Among Them*; Kathleen Barry, *Femininity in Flight: A History of Flight Attendants* (Durham, NC: Duke University Press, 2007). Joshua Freeman, *Working Class New York: Life and Labor Since World War II* (New York: New Press, 2001) describes the Ocean Hill controversy that erupted between teachers and African-American community members as well as the racist attitudes of some New York City unionists. In *Whose Detroit: Politics, Labor and Race in a Modern American City* (Ithaca: Cornell University Press, 2001), Heather Thompson looks at the contest over race and policies in this period from multiple perspectives. A negative perspective on the ability of unions to diversify can be found in Herbert Hill, "The AFL-CIO and the Black Worker: 25 Years After the Merger," *Journal of Intergroup Relations* 10 (1982), 5–79. A broad look at civil rights struggles in the North can be found in Thomas Sugrue, *Sweet Land of Liberty: The Forgotten Struggle for Civil Rights in the North* (New York: Random House, 2008). Excellent work on southern labor struggles can be found in Timothy Minchin, *Hiring the Black Worker: The Racial Integration of the Southern Textile Industry, 1960–1980* (Chapel Hill: University of North Carolina Press, 1999); and Robert Zieger, *Southern Labor In Transition*.

Chapter 4: Working More for Less and Other Troubles for Workers in the Late Twentieth Century

A general work for this period is Jefferson Cowie, *Stayin' Alive*. Studies that document declining manufacturing industries and the impact that de-industrialization has on communities include

David Bensman and Roberta Lynch, *Rusted Dreams: Hard Times in a Steel Community* (New York: McGraw Hill, 1987); Sherry Linkon and John Russo, *Steeltown USA: Work and Memory in Youngstown* (Lawrence: University Press of Kansas, 2000); Ruth Milkman, *Farewell to the Factory: Auto Workers in the Late Twentieth Century* (Berkeley: University of California Press, 1997); Jefferson Cowie, *Capital Moves: RCA's Seventy Year Quest for Cheap Labor* (Ithaca: Cornell University Press, 1999). Emma Rothschild, *Paradise Lost: The Decline of the Auto-Industrial Age* (New York: Random House, 1973) focuses on the auto industry.

Numerous scholars discuss changing corporate practices in this period. Some of the most helpful to me include Dana Frank, *Buy American: The Untold Story of American Nationalism* (Boston: Beacon Press, 1999); Kim Moody, *Workers in a Lean World: Unions in the International Economy* (New York: Verso, 1997); Daniel Sidorick, *Condensed Capitalism: Campbell Soup and the Pursuit of Cheap Production in the Twentieth Century* (Ithaca: Cornell University Press, 2009); Barry Bluestone and Bennett Harrison, *The Great U-turn: Corporate Restructuring and the Polarizing of America* (New York: Basic Books, 1988); Sanford Jacoby, *Modern Manors: Welfare Capitalism Since the New Deal* (Princeton: Princeton University Press, 1997); and William Greider, *One World Ready or Not: The Manic Logic of Global Capitalism* (New York: Touchstone, 1997).

Writers who focus on the role of technology in the workplace are Barbara Garson, *The Electronic Sweatshop: How Computers are Transforming the Office of the Future into the Factory of the Past* (New York: Simon and Schuster, 1988); Charles Sabel and Michael Piore, *The Second Industrial Divide: Possibilities for Prosperity* (New York: Basic Books, 1986); Harley Shaiken, *Work Transformed: Automation and Labor in the Computer Age* (New York: Holt, Rinehart and Winston, 1985); David Noble, *America By Design: Science, Technology and the Rise of Corporate Capitalism* (New York: Knopf, 1977); Daniel Cornfield, *Workers, Managers, and Technological Change: Emerging Patterns of Labor Relations* (New York: Plenum Press, 1987); and Shoshana Zuboff, *In the Age of the Smart Machine: The Future of Work and Power* (New York: Basic Books, 1988).

Mike Parker and Jane Slaughter's edited collection, *Work Smart: A Union Guide to Participation Programs and Reengineering/ With Union Strategy Guide* (Detroit: Labor Notes Books, 1997) and Tom Juravich, *Chaos on the Shop Floor: A Worker's View of Quality, Productivity and Management* (Philadelphia: Temple University Press, 1998) offer activists' and workers' perspectives on workplace restructuring.

Works critical of government policy include Judith Stein, *Running Steel, Running America*; Susan Tolchin, *Dismantling America: The Rush to Deregulate* (Boston: Houghton Mifflin, 1983); Richard Rothstein, *Keeping Jobs in Fashion: Alternatives to the Euthanasia of the US Apparel Industry* (Washington, DC: Economic Policy Institute, 1989); and Joseph Stiglitz, *Globalization and Its Discontents* (New York: Norton, 2002). In his award-winning history of the NLRB, *Broken Promise: The Subversion of US Labor Relations Policy, 1947–1994* (Philadelphia: Temple University Press, 2003), James Gross reveals the ways in which the NLRB has been transformed into an obstacle to union activism. Taylor Dark, *The Unions and the Democrats: An Enduring Alliance* (Ithaca: Cornell University Press, 1999) argues that labor's support of the Democratic Party was not useless. Norman Caulfield, *NAFTA and Labor in North America* (Urbana: University of Illinois Press, 2010) uses NAFTA to explain labor's diminished political and economic role. Nick Salvatore and Jefferson Cowie in "The Long Exception: Rethinking the Place of the New Deal in American History" *ILWCH* 74 (Fall 2008), 3–32 argue that working-class political conservatism in this period represents political continuity with US ideology of the late nineteenth century. Barbara Ehrenreich's *Nickeled and Dimed: On (Not) Getting By in America* (New York: Metropolitan Books, 2001) exposes the ill-thought welfare to work policy of the Clinton administration.

Global pressures on a changing workforce are discussed in Eileen Boris and Cynthia R. Daniels, *Homework: Historical and Contemporary Perspectives on Paid Labor at Home* (Urbana: University of Illinois Press, 1989); Pierrette Hondagneu-Sotelo, *Domestica: Immigrant Workers Cleaning and Caring in the Shadows of Affluence* (Berkeley: University of California Press, 2007); Rhacel Salazar

Parrenas, *Servants of Globalization: Women, Migration and Domestic Work* (Stanford: Stanford University Press, 2001); Berch Berberoglu, *Labor and Capital in the Age of Globalization: The Labor Process and the Changing Nature of Work in the Global Economy* (Lanham: Rowman and Littlefield, 2002); Carmen Teresa Whalen, *From Puerto Rico to Philadelphia: Puerto Rican Workers and Postwar Economies* (Philadelphia: Temple University Press, 2001); and Cindy Hahamovitch's award-winning book, *No Man's Land: Jamaican Guestworkers in America and the Global History of Deportable Labor* (Princeton: Princeton University Press, 2011).

The New Voices agenda is set out in Jo-Ann Mort's edited collection, *Not Your Father's Movement: Inside the AFL-CIO* (New York: Verso, 1998) and John Sweeney with David Krusnet, *America Needs a Raise* (Boston: Houghton Mifflin, 1996). See also Richard B. Freeman and James L. Medoff, *What Do Unions Do?* (New York: Basic Books, 1984). Kate Bronfenbrenner, "The Role of Union Strategies in NLRB Certification Elections," *Industrial and Labor Relations Review* 50 (January 1997), 195–212 emphasizes the importance of direct grassroots and person-to-person organizing tactics. Critiques of the AFL-CIO and their affiliates abound. Some helpful collections include Andrew Martin, "Why Does the New Labor Movement Look So Much Like the Old One? The 1990s Revitalization Project in Historical Context," *Journal of Labor Research* 27 (2006), 163–186; Ruth Milkman and Kim Voss, eds., *Rebuilding Labor: Organizing and Organizers in the New Union Movement* (Ithaca: Cornel University Press, 2004); Jane Latour's powerful work, *Sisters in the Brotherhoods: Working Women Working for Equality* (New York: Palgrave Macmillan, 2009); Bruce Nissen, ed., *Which Direction for Organized Labor* (Detroit: Wayne State University Press, 1999); Steve Early, "Thoughts on the 'Worker–Student Alliance' – Then and Now," *Labor History* 44 (2003): 5. Ray Tillman and Michael Cummings, eds., *The Transformation of US Unions: Voices, Visions, and Strategies from the Grassroots* (Boulder: Lynne Rienner, 1999) includes insightful essays critical of the New Voices leaders and engages with rank-and-file reform movements. Kate Bronfenbrenner et al., *Organizing to Win: New Research on Union Strategies* (Ithaca: ILR Press, 1998) is the most important research on and call for effective union organizing campaigns. Marie Gottschalk's, *The Shadow Welfare State: Labor, Business and the Politics of Health Care in the United States* (Ithaca: ILR Press, 2000) provides an excellent analysis of labor's role in encouraging the privatization of healthcare and problems such a position creates. Works that reflect on the past and project hope into the future include Rick Fantasia, *Cultures of Solidarity: Consciousness, Action and Contemporary American Workers* (Berkeley: University of California Press, 1988); Dan Clawson, *The Next Upsurge: Labor and the New Social Movements* (Ithaca: ILR Press, 2003); Kim Moody, *US Labor in Trouble and Transition: The Failure of Reform from Above, the Promise of Revival from Below* (New York: Verso, 2007); and Howard Botwinick, "Labor Must Shed its Win/Win Illusions: It's Time To Organize and Fight," *New Labor Forum* 2 (Spring 1998), 92–103.

Industrial strikes during this period are discussed and analyzed in Peter Rachleff, *Hard-Pressed in the Heartland: The Hormel Strike and the Future of the Labor Movement* (Boston: South End Press, 1993); Steven K. Ashby and C. J. Hawking, *Staley: The Fight for a New American Labor Movement* (Urbana: University of Illinois Press, 2009). Mike Davis and Michael Sprinkler, eds., *Reshaping the US Left: Popular Struggles in the 1980s* (New York: Verso, 1988) includes informative chapters on P-9, Watsonville, and GM's Van Nuys plant. Chapters 8 and 9 in Jeremy Brecher's *Strike!* analyze the variety of the period's labor struggles. Tom Juravich and Kate Bronfenbrenner, *Ravenswood: The Steelworkers' Victory and the Revival of American Labor* (Ithaca, NY: ILR Press, 1999) offer an engaging narrative of that fight.

Scholarship that focuses on the important role of immigrant workers in new labor activism is numerous. Leon Fink uncovers the struggle between Guatemalan refugees, Mexican workers, community supporters, and the Laborers' union and Case poultry in *The Maya of Morganton: Work and Community in the Nuevo South* (Chapel Hill: University of North Carolina Press, 2003). Ruth Milkman, *LA Story: Immigrant Workers and the Future of the US Labor Movement* (New York: Russell Sage Foundation, 2006) and Milkman, *Organizing Immigrants: The Challenge for Unions in Con-*

temporary California (Ithaca: ILR Press, 2000) include insightful analysis of various immigrant-led campaigns. The third section of Xiaolan Bao, *Holding Up More than Half the Sky: Chinese Women Garment Workers in New York City, 1948–92* (Urbana: University of Illinois Press, 2001) describes the 1982 garment worker strike. Cindy Hahamovitch's *No Man's Land* puts guest worker programs in their historical context and clarifies the enormous odds stacked against these workers ever gaining enforceable workplace protections.

Innovative approaches to working-class and union activism are discussed in Janice Fine, *Worker Centers: Organizing Communities at the Edge of the Dream* (Ithaca: Cornell University Press, 2006); Robert Pollin and Stephanie Luce, *Living Wage: Building a Fair Economy* (New York: New Press, 1998); Andrew Herod, *Labor Geographies: Workers and the Landscapes of Capitalism* (New York: Guilford Press, 2001); and in several contributions in M. Paloma Pavel, ed., *Breakthrough Communities: Sustainability and Justice in the Next American Metropolis* (Cambridge, MA: MIT Press, 2009). Unionism and working-class activism in higher education are discussed in Robert H. Metchick and Parbudyal Singh, "Yeshiva and Faculty Unionization in Higher Education," *Labor Studies Journal* 28, 4 (Winter 2004), 45–65; Gregory Saltzman, "Union Organizing and the Law: Part-time Faculty and Graduate Teaching Assistants," *The NEA 2000 Almanac of Higher Education*, 43–55; Kitty Krupat, "Rethinking the Sweatshop: A Conversation About United Students Against Sweatshops (USAS) with Charles Eaton, Marion Trab-Werner and Evelyn Zepeda," *ILWCH* 61 (Spring 2002), 112–127; Daniel Tope, Marc Dixon, and Nella Van Dyke, "'The University Works Because We Do': On the Determinants of Campus Labor Organizing in the 1990s," *Sociological Perspectives* 51 (2008), 375–396; and Robin D. G. Kelley, "The Proletariat Goes to College," *Social Text* 49 (Winter 1996), 37–42.

More contemporary scholarship that informs the epilogue includes Elizabeth Faue, "Retooling the Class Factory: United States Labour History After Marx, Montgomery, and Postmodernism," *Labour History* 82 (May 2002), 109–119; Kim Bobo, *Wage*

Theft in America: Why Millions of Working Americans Are Not Getting Paid – And What We Can Do About it (New York: New Press, 2009); Steven Greenhouse, *The Big Squeeze: Tough Times for the American Worker* (New York: Random House, 2009); Nelson Lichtenstein, *The Retail Revolution: How Wal-Mart Created a Brave New World of Business* (New York: Metropolitan Books, 2009); and Timothy Noah, *The Great Divergence: America's Growing Inequality Crisis and What We Can Do About It* (New York: Bloomsbury, 2012). *New Labor Forum* is an excellent progressive source for contemporary labor discussion and debate.

Index

Page references in *italic* indicate an illustration.

Working Hard for the American Dream: Workers and Their Unions, World War I to the Present, First Edition. Randi Storch.
© 2013 John Wiley & Sons, Ltd. Published 2013 by John Wiley & Sons, Ltd.